By the hard work of others, we are led
to the most beautiful things that have been dragged
out of darkness and into the light.
Everyone is invited to experience the light
of every age and every people.
So, let us walk hand in hand with those from every age.
Let us turn from this brief and transient time
and offer our minds and hearts to the past,
which is long and eternal.

—Seneca, *On the Shortness of Life*

THE CLASSICS CAVE
Sugar Land

THE CLASSICS CAVE
the earliest light for a brighter life
www.theclassicscave.com

ARE YOU looking for the best books ever? Or new ways to read and benefit from them? To practice what you've read? To learn and grow a little? Let the Cave be your guide!

THE CLASSICS CAVE (the Cave) is an educational* organization centered on the classics of Greek and Roman antiquity, with an emphasis on the best of ancient Greek literature.

OUR MISSION is to shine the light of the past into the present for a brighter life today.

OUR GOAL is practice—the application of ancient wisdom and ways to our contemporary lives.

WE publish books, develop and provide online content, organize and do outreach, and produce and distribute a variety of print and other media intended to entertain and educate, inspire, encourage, and cultivate.

VISIT THE CAVE online (www.theclassicscave.com) to support our mission and to access a growing catalog of engaging books and other beneficial content designed for individuals, educators, groups, and all others interested in benefiting from ancient literature.

SUPPORT THE CAVE by telling others about our work and by leaving a positive review online. You may also wish to buy a book or join The BAGL Club or the AAGS (to adopt an ancient Greek). Or sponsor the BAGL. Or partner with us by giving a donation. Thanks!

With GRATITUDE, we thank our readers, members, sponsors, donors, and all participants in Cave content—you who make the work and outreach of the Cave possible. Without you, the Cave would not exist!

*For the Cave, **education** is that happy transition from ignorance to knowledge; from foolishness to wisdom; and from mediocrity or vice to excellence or virtue, culminating in good habits and character.

In Praise & Recognition of the Ancient Greeks

"Of all peoples the Greeks have best dreamed the dream of life."
—Johann Wolfgang von Goethe, *Maxims and Reflections*

"The only literature, to which I would allow a place in the ordinary curriculum, are those of the Greeks and Romans . . . While, in studying the great writers of antiquity, we are not only learning to understand the ancient mind, but laying in a stock of wise thought and observation . . . the treasure which they accumulated of what may be called the wisdom of life. . . . All that is left to us of the ancient historians, orators, philosophers, and even dramatists, are replete with remarks and maxims of singular good sense and penetration, applicable to both political and to private life."
—John Stuart Mill, *Address at the University of St. Andrews*

"All the branches of [Greek] learning . . . contain also liberal instruction that is better adapted to the use of truth, and some most excellent precepts of morality."
—Augustine of Hippo, *On Christian Doctrine*

"Philosophy . . . is the clear image of truth, a divine gift to the Greeks."—Clement of Alexandria, *Stromata*

"In Greek philosophy we watch problems come to light that have by no means lost their relevance for us, we find answers suggested that are not without value. . . . Greek philosophy remains one of the glories of the European achievement."
—Frederick Copleston, *A History of Philosophy*

"To know himself a man must know the capabilities and performances of the human spirit. The value of the humanities—of *Altertumswissenschaft*, the science of antiquity—is that it affords for this purpose an unsurpassed source of light and stimulus. Whoever seeks help for knowing himself from knowing the capabilities and performances of the human spirit, will nowhere find a more fruitful object of study than the achievements of Greece in literature and the arts."

—Matthew Arnold, *The Higher Schools & Universities in Germany*

"To whatever heights you ascend in literature the Greeks are always there. Literature is one of the greatest forces in the world and always has been and always will be so. It comes to us with open hand, offering us knowledge, spiritual inspiration, the vast world created by human imagination, laughter and tears, happiness, sympathy, enjoyment, forgetfulness. Over a large part of this spacious kingdom of the mind rule Greece and Rome."

—Senator Henry Cabot Lodge, from *Value of the Classics*

"That is why the Greeks maintain a hold on education. With a clearness of thought and expression, . . . they offer us many things—unsurpassed achievements in art and literature, the example of a rich, complete life, the spectacle of reason incarnate, reason in religion, politics, philosophy, history, letters, life. They knew less than we, but they had more of the spirit which begets knowledge."

—Richard W. Livingstone, *A Defense of Classical Education*

"Our whole civilization is rooted in the history of these peoples [Greece and Rome], and without knowledge of them cannot be properly understood. The small city communities of Greece created intellectual life in Europe. In their literature we find models of thought and expression, and meet the subtle and powerful personalities who originated for Europe all forms of poetry, history and philosophy, and even physical science itself, no less than the ideal of freedom and the conception of a self-governing democracy; while the student is introduced to the great problems of thought and life at their springs, before he follows them through the wider but more confused currents of the modern world."

—British dignitaries, *excerpt from a signed public letter*

HAPPINESS

HAPPINESS

What the Ancient Greeks Thought and Said about Happiness

in their own words

Homer, Hesiod, Sappho, Solon, Simonides, Theognis, Pythagoras, Pindar, Bacchylides, Aeschylus, Sophocles, Euripides, Aristophanes, Herodotus, Thucydides, Socrates, Antisthenes, Xenophon, Plato, Isocrates, Aristippus of Cyrene, Diogenes of Sinope, Pyrrho of Elis, Demosthenes, Aristotle, Epicurus, Zeno of Citium, Crates of Thebes, Epictetus, Plutarch, Diogenes Laertius, Lucian of Samosata, Sextus Empiricus, Plotinus, Julian (the Roman emperor), and Others

selected, introduced, and edited by
Tim J. Young

CAVE BONFIRE SERIES
*what the ancient Greeks thought
and said about a topic*

THE CLASSICS CAVE
Sugar Land

Happiness:
What the Ancient Greeks Thought and Said about Happiness

ISBN 978-1-943915-01-9

Published in the United States by
The Classics Cave
P.O. Box 19038
Sugar Land, TX 77496
contact@theclassicscave.com
www.theclassicscave.com

The Classics Cave (the Cave) is an educational organization centered on the classics of Greek and Roman antiquity, with an emphasis on the best of ancient Greek literature. Our mission is to shine the light of the past into the present for a brighter life today. Our goal is practice—the application of ancient wisdom and ways to our contemporary lives. We publish books, develop and provide online content, organize and do outreach, and produce and distribute a variety of print and other media intended to entertain and educate, inspire, encourage, and cultivate.

    Visit the Cave online (www.theclassicscave.com) to support our mission and to access a growing catalog of engaging books and other beneficial content designed for individuals, educators, groups, and all others interested in benefiting from ancient literature.

CONTENTS

CONCLUSION
What the Ancient Greeks Thought and Said about Happiness

PART 3
Points of Wisdom & Ways of Practice

OTHER MATTERS OF INTEREST
Related to Happiness

INTRODUCTION

"My brother Gallio, it is the wish of all to live happily. But we're in the dark when it comes to figuring out what makes for a happy life. . . . Let us, therefore, determine the goal and the way. And let us find an experienced guide who has explored the region toward which we are advancing."

—Seneca, On the Happy Life

I S IT POSSIBLE to search for something if you don't exactly know what it is you're searching for? *Think about it.* And if you found this something, how would you know it was the thing you were searching for if you didn't already know it in the first place?

This was Meno's question.

Meno, a well-to-do young man from Thessaly, was a budding philosopher studying with the Greek sophist Gorgias. He raised the question while chatting with Socrates some 2,500 years ago in Athens' marketplace, the *agora*.

Picture them. There they are sitting in the shade of an olive tree. Next to them is an old man in a dilapidated stall hawking small amphorae of cheap wine. Meno and Socrates both know that to get a better vintage you have to go a few rows over to the retailers that sell imported Pramnian wine from Lesbos or apple-perfumed wine from Thasos. Opposite them, a young mother is peddling oblong loaves of bread and tall ceramic jars of olive oil sealed with stretched goatskin and twine. Beyond her, countless men, women, and children mill around the *agora*. Some are Athenian citizens; some are not. Quite a few aren't even Greek. Then there's Meno's entourage, the crowd of slaves that attends and serves him everywhere he goes.

Socrates glances at one of the slaves with curiosity before declaring, "That's just a debater's argument, Meno—to ask how you can look for something if you don't even know what you're looking for. Did you get that from Gorgias?"

Gorgias was famous for arguing that "nothing is." This in contrast to Parmenides, who argued that everything simply *is*.[1]

"Well?" Meno insists.

Even though Meno and Socrates were seeking to understand the nature of *aretē*, a Greek word with a long and varied history of definitions, including "excellence" and "virtue,"[2] we might ask the same question about happiness. How can we search for happiness or what it means to be happy if we don't exactly know what it is to begin with?

Socrates smiles. "We can," he responds, "because we already know the reality of all things in our souls."

Our souls, he contends, are immortal and have already experienced all things as they are in themselves. Learning or searching for something, therefore, is actually only recollecting or remembering something we already know, something we've already experienced.

It's an interesting idea. Anyway, don't we feel that way? We sense we already know what something is, but we struggle to define it with precision—things such as *aretē*, or friendship and justice, or goodness, truth, and beauty, or, yes, even happiness.

Whatever we may think about Meno's question or Socrates' response, it may be useful to have a better understanding of what some people believe about happiness today before we venture into the land of ancient Greek sentiments. Let's begin by doing what Meno and Socrates couldn't do since they didn't have the option. Let's open a dictionary.

The Dictionary Definition of Happiness

When we crack open a red desk copy of *Webster's New College Dictionary* and page over to "happy," the adjectival form of the noun "happiness," we find, "Happy: Enjoying, displaying, or characterized by pleasure or joy."

Okay. Makes some sense, we may think. Pleasure is a very tangible thing. And so, it's straightforward. On second thought, though, maybe it's not. Anyhow, what, exactly, is joy?

We look it up. "Joy: Great pleasure or happiness. DELIGHT" —the dictionary's caps.

There's pleasure again. But now we've got delight.

"Delight: Great pleasure or gratification. JOY."

What? we shrug together. The dictionary is sending us back to joy. But there's also pleasure again, not to mention gratification.

We've now seen pleasure included in definitions for happy, joy, and delight. And even though we thought pleasure was a fairly straightforward thing, there may be something more to it. So, there we go.

"Pleasure: An enjoyable sensation or emotion." Then, at the definition's end, we see "DELIGHT." And we sigh.

One, we can't help but notice the "joy" part of en*joy*able. And the all-caps delight? We've already been there.

We go back to joy, imagining we may have missed something. But we haven't. There's pleasure—*and* delight *and* happiness.

Hold on a second.

We now realize something we should have noticed before in this *Choose Your Own Adventure*-like dictionary journey to discover what happiness or being happy means. *Webster's* has played us for a fool, running us round like a dog wanting a treat tied to its own tail. And so, we end up back where we began—at the word happy or happiness. No matter which word we go with first, we end up returning to happiness. Happiness is apparently defined by . . . *happiness.* Yes, the definition involves other words, but it's a circular definition. And the definitions for other words—joy, delight, pleasure—aren't really any better.

Apparently, the words happy or happiness are meaningless. On second thought, though, we might simply allow that happy (or happiness) is part of a sense complex tied up with pleasure, joy, and delight, assuming we know what *these* mean. Whatever the case, we haven't really arrived anywhere precise.

Fortunately, there's another way to understand happy or happiness. If we grasp the origins of the word, then perhaps we'll have a better understanding of what it means. It's the etymological way.

This seems to be the second approach of *Webster's*. Definition two for the word happy: "Marked by good luck: FORTUNATE." The etymology of the word ultimately derives from the Old Norse word *happ*, meaning "chance, good luck, fortune."

Still, however much it denotes something significant about the earliest understanding of happiness, the etymological definition merely gives us the *means by which* or the *how* of happiness (luck or fortune) rather than *what* happiness is or *why* anyone would want to be happy.

So then, what do we have? *Webster's* circular definition of "happy" has left us shrugging our shoulders, and the etymology has only given a partial clue to what being happy means.

Happily, we're in good company. Many recent philosophers, psychologists, and others have judged it hard to know *exactly* and *precisely* what happiness is, not to mention how one gets it or why one would want it.

With this in mind, let's glance at a few examples of recent thinking about happiness.

Contemporary Ideas about Happiness

We may begin with a very Greek question.[3] Is happiness one thing, as the Greek thinker Aristotle and others held, or is it many things?

In *A Brief History of Happiness*, University of California professor of philosophy Nicholas White suggests that happiness does not have one meaning.[4] Rather, happiness indicates multiple and even conflicting aims a person may have. "A good account of happiness," he claims, "has to begin with an awareness of the fact of the plurality of aims and conflicts" we humans have. Consequently, whatever happiness is, it is not one thing but many.

Martin Seligman, the godfather of Positive Psychology—a movement in modern psychology that investigates what goes right with human living and flourishing, and how to promote it, rather than what goes wrong—has a similar view to Nicholas White in terms of the manyness of happiness. In *Flourish: A Visionary New Understanding of Happiness and Well-Being*, Seligman asserts that happiness or well-being is not one thing but, in the case of his own theory, five major things: positive emotion, engagement, meaning, accomplishment, and positive relationships.[5] As for the term itself, he admits, "I actually detest the word happiness, which is so over-used that it has become meaningless." He suggests that we "dis-solve the monism of 'happiness' into more workable terms."

Dr. Seligman has a point. But let's not despair! Part of what we're trying to do is understand what people mean by happiness, even if the meaning remains somewhat unclear.

Parenthetically, banishing the word or substituting other terms probably won't help much with the meaning problem. I recall a col-league recently declaring, "I don't believe in happiness; I believe in purpose." She then referenced Oprah to make her case (at which my left brow raised ever so slightly). When I began to probe her understanding of purpose, it was equally ambiguous. So, we may as well stick with happiness—even if we define it with words such as purpose.

According to the *Stanford Encyclopedia of Philosophy*'s article, "Hap-piness," there are two basic notions of happiness. One is "'happiness' as a value term, roughly synonymous with well-being or flourishing." The other "uses the word as a purely descriptive psychological term, akin to 'depression' or 'tranquility.'" As for the first notion, there are three basic theories of well-being or flourishing, which is to say, hap-piness. They are 1.) Objective list theory (listing items that constitute or add up to happiness); 2.) Hedonism (seeking the presence of pleas-ure and the absence of pain, or a balance of pleasure over pain—often called utilitarianism); and 3.) Various desire theories (hoping to sat-isfy present and long-term, or overall, life desires).

To my mind, the neat distinctions posited between these theo-ries, however useful and valid they are in themselves, vanish upon extended reflection. The simple reason is that satisfaction of desire usually involves some measure of pleasure, that is, some positive feeling or sense of well-being, and both satisfaction and pleasure involve a list of things in or by which one finds satisfaction and delight. Viewed in this synthetic way, happiness is as much about a *what*—a list of things—as it is about the satisfaction-pleasure that arises from having, knowing, or experiencing the list, the *whats*.

Speaking of lists, let's turn for a moment to the social psychologist Hadley Cantril. In *The Pattern of Human Concerns*, his landmark world survey from half a century ago, he catalogs what makes people satisfied or happy.[6] Topping the list is an "improved or decent standard of living," followed by the same for one's children in second place. Next is health. Fourth is a "good job, congenial work," which implies a concern for a decent standard of living, and that one's work should be enjoyable or meaningful to some extent. The fifth, sixth, and eighth items on the list describe what people would like to own: a house, land, and, if possible, a business or the means by which they are employed. Seventh is a "happy family life," and ninth is the "health of [the] family." The tenth concern is for "happy old age," which interestingly echoes Odysseus' concern for happiness in Homer's *Odyssey*. These ten give us a decent picture of what people still desire and find happiness in today.

Of course, if an extraterrestrial alien (documented or not) dropped down from another planet to Mother Earth and stood in line at an average supermarket, he-she-it might draw a radically different conclusion regarding what constitutes human concerns and happiness. Picture all those magazine covers you read while patiently waiting in line for your turn to check out. Consider what they promote. Food. Fashion. Gossip. Ways to diet. Super double-t *hott* people. Who's zooming whom. Money. Sex—and, *ahem,* certain how-to recommendations. And on and on. Eventually our alien's bug-like eyes would glaze over with green alien goo as he-she-it would come to understand that happiness is being or having a list of things that are intended to satisfy desire and bring tremendous pleasure—all things that are, quite frankly, no longer useful to creatures such as the alien is because his-her-its species lives in a non-zero-sum world and procreates in a manner that is, well, out of this world.

Leaving the supermarket behind and our bit of amateur anthropology and ufology, the World Database of Happiness, directed by

Ruut Veenhoven from Erasmus University Rotterdam, defines happiness according to the second "purely descriptive psychological term" notion of happiness mentioned by the *Stanford Encyclopedia of Philosophy*. The database states, "Overall happiness is the degree to which an individual judges the overall quality of his/her own life-as-a-whole favorably." Happiness, then, is a subjective phenomenon, what many call subjective well-being. Yet more. The definition tells us that there is no one optimal state of happiness but varying degrees. It also suggests that happiness is not merely something felt but that one is aware of it. The "overall" refers to various criteria of appreciation, including one's "sensory system, cognition and affect."[7] Finally, "favorably" implies positive satisfaction or liking.

The *World Happiness Report*, edited by Jeffrey D. Sachs of Columbia University and others, similarly measures world happiness in terms of "an individual's overall evaluation of life" or what may be called "evaluative happiness." As the report explains it, "Evaluative happiness measures very different dimensions of life." Things like "higher income, better health of mind and body, a high degree of trust in one's community . . . all contribute to high life satisfaction; poverty, ill health, and deep divisions in the community all contribute to low life satisfaction." The report also specifies the measurement of "the ups and downs of daily emotions" or what is termed "affective happiness," which "captures the day-to-day joys of friendship, time with family, sex, or the downsides of long work commutes and sessions with one's boss."[8]

Let's bring this all-too brief and certainly not all-inclusive discussion of recent ideas about happiness to a close with Positive Psychology's happiness formula, which is $H = S + C + I$. But what does it signify?

Let's begin with the H first, which, of course, stands for *happiness*. According to the formula, H is our long-term, ongoing sense of well-being as opposed to short-term bursts of happiness or unhappiness due to a variety of momentary ups and downs. (There's that emphasis on life-as-a-whole again versus transient happiness.)

What are the other variables on the other side? We'll start with the last first. The I is actually the most significant variable in the equation. It's the variable of growth, of growing happier. The *I* stands for *intentional* or voluntary activity, which must be rationally determined, purposefully chosen and willed, and resolutely accomplished. According to Professor Sonja Lyubomirsky in *The How of Happiness*, examples include expressing gratitude, developing friendships, learning to meditate, changing the way one habitually thinks, exercising the body, being kind, savoring the small things of life, learning to give, and the list goes on.[9] The great news is that according to positive psychologists, intentional activity accounts for roughly 40% of our sense of happiness and personal well-being.

Many of us, however, turn to the *C* of the formula for happiness when, sadly, the *C* accounts for only about 10% of our sense of overall well-being. The *C* stands for the *circumstances* or *conditions* of our lives. It mostly answers the *what* question. We may, for instance, ask the questions, Where am I in life? Where do I live—in sunny Hawaii or cold Alaska? How am I connected to others—am I married or single? What's my job—is it significant to others or not? What's in my bank account—am I rich or poor? How do I look—am I attractive to others or not? While changing some of these can lead to a shift in our level of happiness, according to positive psychologists, more often than not the difference is weak and short-term as opposed to the stronger and more long-term change by means of intentional activity.

The *S* represents our *set point*, the remainder of our sense of happiness. We may see this as our basic nature. It's what we return to time and again despite feeling, thinking, and acting differently on occasion. The *S* is our genetic disposition, our hereditary hand of cards; it's what we were born with, what was "set" by our parents long ago, the genetic luck we were dealt nine months before we were born. And to that extent, there's really very little we can do about it after the fact.

Martin Seligman compares our set point for happiness to a thermostat. We might extend his analogy by saying that our natural ability to create happiness is like the heater the thermostat controls. Whatever the outside temperature is (the circumstances of life), no matter how cold and uncomfortable, the heater works to heat a room (our experience of happiness and well-being) to the thermostat's set point (our inherited sense of well-being). In some cases, this is enough, as when a thermostat is set at a comfortably warm 70° (presuming we like it that warm). In other cases, however, the thermostat is set at a much lower and uncomfortable temperature. In that case, we must further employ the heater—our natural ability to create happiness by means of intentional behavior (the *I* of the happiness formula)—to become warm (or happy) by sealing drafty windows, wearing warm clothing, lighting a fire, snuggling with a loved one, and the like.

It's at this point that someone may object that we've left out a significant modern view of happiness, the one coming from the standpoint of what many have recently termed "virtue ethics," though its lineage is ancient. It's true. And so, we must take a few moments to look at it.

Most of the other views seem to posit happiness as something subjective, meaning that happiness is left to the mercy of each individual. It's something we can study, sure, but only in a manner that relies on the participants of a study and the accuracy of their own judgments and self-reporting. If a man observes that *intentionally* drinking diet soda and playing cards all day and every day makes him happy, all that can be done is to acknowledge the self-reported fact and move on to someone else. And so on with any other feeling, thought, or activity.

The problem with this line of thinking is that it may leave a person adrift in the cosmos without any sense of overall meaning *as a human being*. Accordingly, this last view of happiness, virtue ethics, zeroes in on the question of what it means to be human, acknowledging that there actually *is* such a meaning.

The meaning itself is usually expressed in what we may term the goal or purpose of life (the Greek term is *telos*), a purpose that is externally provided by nature itself, the community, or God (the intelligence or rational force behind nature), rather than countless human beings randomly pursuing just as many goals. As such, we do not subjectively create or choose meaning or purpose; rather, we discover it as an objective reality. To live well, then, or to be happy, is the means by which we fulfill this purpose. This "living well" or "happiness" is called "virtue" or "excellence" by this last approach to happiness. Happiness is living well; happiness is virtue (the Greek is *aretē*). As Aristotle puts it, "Happiness is an activity of the soul that accords with perfect virtue."[10]

The bottom line: whatever happiness is, whether one thing or many, and whatever the component single or multiple aspects are, happiness is a complex phenomenon. And so, we must ask many questions: Is it something subjective or objective? Does it amount to a list of things? Is it pleasure or the satisfaction of desire? Is it cognitive or affective, neither or both? Where is happiness expressed neurologically? And what about morality? Is happiness related to one's behavior? To one's character? Is happiness living well?—a wellness and excellence that applies somehow to every human being? And what about religion? Does happiness have something to do with one's relation to God (as one religious tradition, for example, declares it—that to be happy is "to know, love and serve God")? Or is there some other factor we haven't considered?

Perhaps happiness is theoretically unknowable in any final sense. Like love is. Or the meaning of life may be. Or God. We can know *that* it is, but not exactly *what* it is.

Or perhaps we're just thinking about it too hard or too much. It's what we may call *the problem of the nose*. Look at someone's face. Notice how it all fits together as one harmonious whole—at first glance, anyway. Then look at it again and closer and you may notice something odd—this strange protrusion of triangular, rounded or pointed flesh rising up from the rest of the face. And the protrusion is punctuated with two even stranger holes that lead to who-knows-where. A moment before all was well. You knew what you were looking at and, without thinking about it, the face seemed to fit together harmoniously. Not now! Now it just seems bizarre! (And we secretly wonder if we're being influenced by that alien we met a moment ago in the supermarket.)

I submit that we are in the position once again to get a first glance at the face of happiness. Forgetting its complexity for a moment, let's turn to the ancient Greeks who offer us the opportunity to take a fresh look.

The Organization of *Happiness*

Whatever we may conclude today, the ancient Greeks had their own ideas about the nature of happiness. Beginning with the epic poetry of Homer some 2,700 years ago, many Greeks recorded these ideas—in works of poetry, drama, comedy, history, rhetoric, philosophy, and the like. To name just a few, there were the poets Hesiod, Theognis of Megara, and Pindar; the playwrights Aeschylus, Sophocles, and Euripides; the historians Herodotus, Thucydides, and Xenophon; and the philosophers Socrates, Plato, and Aristotle, not to mention many others up to Plotinus, who wrote a thousand years after Homer.

Given the wealth of testimony relative to our subject, the straightforward goal of *Happiness* is to present what the Greeks felt, thought, and said about happiness in their own words. Although there are drawbacks to such a presentation, the strength is that the Greeks are able to speak directly to us. What did Odysseus say about happiness? Or the poet Sappho of Lesbos? Or the Athenian law reformer Solon? Or the statesman Pericles of Athens? Or the philosophers Diogenes of Sinope, Pyrrho of Elis, and Zeno of Citium?

Prior to the advent of philosophy, there was no truly systematic thinking among the Greeks about what happiness is. To be sure, it is possible to tease out a system from a particular author or tradition.[11] Typically, however, we find that the notion of happiness is simply given expression by a character in a poem or play, or in an episode of one of the early histories. A hero, for instance, states the nature of happiness. A farmer prays for it and thereby gives its essential parts. A poet declares the happiness of a victor in the Olympic games based on certain grounds. A ruler asserts his happiness because of what he has. Later on, beginning largely with the investigations of Socrates, the Greeks began to systematically consider what makes for a happy life and how one might be happy.

This shift over time in the Greek approach to happiness explains the basic organization of this book. Mirroring the shift, *Happiness* is divided into two parts. Part 1, "The What, How, Where & Who of Happiness," offers a variety of vantage points on happiness, including happiness as a goal; happiness formulas; happiness as the satisfaction of desire; the *how* of happiness; the problem with happiness; as well as happy times and places; and, finally, happy gods and happy people. Part 2, "Thinking about Happiness—The Philosophers," offers more systematic Greek thinking about happiness in the form of lively dialogues and expository writing.

I should note that *Happiness* is not a comprehensive presentation of Greek beliefs about happiness. Instead, it is the most significant of what the Greeks thought and said. This means that some of what the Greeks had to say is left out. To give an example, it would have been preferable to include something extended from Pythagorean thinking. The problem is that little remains from Pythagoras himself. As for later Pythagoreans, we do have several short treatises on happiness and the good life. Unfortunately, though, they have a decidedly un-Pythagorean feel, infused as they are with later philosophical speculation, and so with what is already represented in *Happiness*.[12] Consequently, quips are included here and there from the Pythagoreans Archytas, Hippodamus the Thurian, and others, but nothing extensive.

I should also mention another issue, that of terminology. We've already seen from *Webster's* that joy, delight, and pleasure—not to mention other terms—can stand in as synonyms for happiness. A similar problem arises when selecting for ancient Greek passages having to do with happiness. Is happiness the same as pleasure? Or delight or joy? Or good luck? Or, as many Greeks believed, are the terms *good life* and happiness equivalent? As we'll see, one author's understanding of happiness will cause us to go in one direction— say toward glory, success, and wealth—whereas other authors will turn us in other directions—say toward pleasure or virtue or knowledge of absolute realities.[13]

One last point before we launch. Read *Happiness* in whatever order you wish. If you read it from beginning to end, you will have a strong sense of how Greek feeling, thinking, and speaking about happiness changed over time, from roughly 700 BC to the end of the third century AD. On the other hand, if you wish to read it more meditatively, contemplating ancient Greek reflections on the good life, now from this author and now from another, you may wish to skip around. Either plan will work. (For a few other features of the book, see the "Note" below.)

LET'S GO!

However you read, you'll likely pick up a new way of looking at happiness. It's this new way, this new understanding, that is at the heart of *Happiness* and many other books in the Cave *Bonfire* Series. Yes, the quest is to learn about history, about what the Greeks thought and said. But more, the goal is the discovery of the earliest light the Greeks have to offer us for a brighter life today. So, in learning something new, we will be learning something old, something that has been tested over time and found valuable.

You may notice that, as the light comes on, some of what the Greeks have to say about happiness is familiar to you. This makes perfect sense. After all, the Greeks are the foundation for western thinking about what it means to live well or happily.

Anyway, let's go. There's much to hear and learn, and just as much to practice.

Note ▪ You'll notice a few common features relative to each chapter in *Happiness*. First, each one begins with a brief introduction that will serve to orient you to the contents of the chapter, or, if the chapter presents a single thinker, writer, or speaker, to the central facts—or, at least, anecdotes—about that person's life, works, and ideas. Next, the material coming after the subtitle IN THEIR OWN WORDS presents the thoughts and words of the Greeks from the many works that have come down to us. Interspersed in *italics* are short commentaries that introduce or explain the content or purpose of the selections and passages that follow.

As for the different voices we'll encounter, the following is how each will be mentioned in *Happiness*. Typically, the author of a text is given in *italics* before offering his or her own words. For example: *Sappho of Lesbos* Riches mixed together with success bring the highest happiness. (Note: there are no quotation marks since we know these are the poet Sappho's own words.) That said, if the author is presenting someone else's thoughts or words, as with Socrates in Plato's dialogues, or the chorus in Sophocles' plays, or a politician in Thucydides' history, then the speaker is noted in parentheses. To give an example: *Plato (Socrates is speaking)* "The most important thing is not merely to live, but to live well. . . . He who lives well is blessed and happy." Lastly, if a whole chapter is devoted to an author, as is sometimes the case in Part 2, or if the author is obvious from the surrounding text, then mention of the author is absent.

NOTES

[1] To discover what Parmenides had to say—that "What is *is*"—read his view in the Philosophy Feature in Volume 1 of *The Best of Ancient Greek Literature* (BAGL) (The Classics Cave, 2025), 70-90.

[2] To learn more about the ancient Greek conception of *aretē*, read The Classics Cave's *Aretē: Excellence or Virtue—What the Ancient Greeks Thought and Said about Aretē*.

[3] Early Greek philosophers wanted to know whether reality is one thing or many.

[4] Nicholas White, *A Brief History of Happiness* (Malden: Blackwell Publishing, 2006), 1-5.

[5] Martin Seligman, *Flourish: A Visionary New Understanding of Happiness and Well-Being* (New York: Atria Books, 2012), 9-20.

[6] Hadley Cantril, *The Pattern of Human Concerns* (New Brunswick: Rutgers University Press, 1965).

[7] This, by the way, is something being actively explored by neurologists—how different affective and cognitive systems in the brain contribute to happiness. See, for example, Morten L. Kringelbach and Kent C. Berridge, "Towards a functional neuroanatomy of pleasure and happiness," *Trends in Cognitive Sciences* 13, No. 11. (2009): 479-487.

[8] John Helliwell, Richard Layard, and Jeffrey Sachs, eds. "World Happiness Report" (Columbia University Earth Institute, 2012).

[9] Sonja Lyubomirsky, *The How of Happiness* (New York: Penguin Press, 2008).

[10] Aristotle, *Nicomachean Ethics* 1.13.1 (1102a). To learn more about the ancient Greek conception of *aretē*, read the Cave's *Aretē: Excellence or Virtue—What the Ancient Greeks Thought and Said about Aretē*.

[11] See, for example, Tim J. Young, *A Hero's Wish: What Homer Believed about Happiness and the Good Life* (Sugar Land: EuZōn Media, 2015).

[12] See, for example, the ethical fragments we have from Archytas (which scholars do not consider genuine), Hippodamus the Thurian, or Euryphamus in *The Pythagorean Sourcebook and Library*, trans. Kenneth Sylvan Guthrie (Yonkers: The Platonist Press, 1919).

[13] For Greek terms related to happiness and being happy (for example, *eudaimonia, eudaimōn, olbos, olbios, eutuchēs, makar, makarios*), see the Glossary.

PART 1

The What, How, Where & Who of Happiness

1

THE HAPPINESS GOAL
WE ACT FOR HAPPINESS

"All men desire their own happiness." —Charles Darwin, *The Descent of Man*

IMAGINE THE GODS Apollo and Athena perched high up in an oak tree. According to Homer, they've taken on the "likeness of vultures" in order to amuse themselves with the drama that's playing out on the battlefield below, where the Greeks are fighting the Trojans. There, warriors are lined up, one against another, struggling bravely, their bronze helmets, shields, and greaves gleaming in the bright light of the morning sun. Spears fly with other missiles—stones and arrows—punching into flesh. One man falls, while another glory-boasts over his bloodied corpse that will soon serve as carrion for hungry dogs and birds.

Why are all the men fighting? Homer's *Iliad* indicates the goal is anger-fueled revenge. As Menelaus puts it, Paris must "pay the penalty" for what he's done—for taking Helen from him. But what else? Glancing through the *Iliad*, we see that men—both leaders and followers, heroes and not—are motivated by desire, fear, anger, freedom, excellence, friendship, wealth, power, shame, honor, and glory. But is there some one goal that unifies these many ends?

Writing centuries after Homer, the Greek philosopher Aristotle considered the *why* of human activity in his introductory work on ethics. Why do we humans get angry? Seek revenge? Long for wealth and honor? Form friendships and city-states? Why do we humans do anything at all?

Aristotle observed that when we act, we do so with a variety of goals in mind. (The Greek for goal, end, or purpose is *telos*.) But there are different kinds. Some goals are means to achieve other goals. Others are final in themselves. Yet even these often point to some other objective. We drag ourselves out of bed to work for money to buy a car to go out with people to get married to have children to . . . what? Is there some ultimate goal—some overarching, unifying objective, end, or good—toward which we act? For Aristotle, the answer was clear. We act for happiness.

Aristotle wasn't the only Greek that believed this. Rather, it is a common assumption that shows up again and again in Greek literature, history, and philosophy. This doesn't mean, of course, that every Greek poet, philosopher, politician, orator, or otherwise agreed about the nature of happiness, or that they all employed the same terms to describe it. Nevertheless, they all felt and thought it was true. Basic fact: we humans act for happiness.

With this in mind, let's listen to the Greeks talk, whether explicitly or implicitly, about happiness as the goal of life.

IN THEIR OWN WORDS

Aristotle It is evident that all men shoot to live well and to be happy.[1]

Aristotle Happiness is the goal of human life.[2]

Aristotle What is the highest good that action can achieve? As for its name, nearly everyone is agreed. Both the crowd of men and the few who are educated and refined call it happiness, and they assume that "living well" and "doing well" is the same thing as "being happy." But they argue about what happiness is. The account given by the many is not the same as that given by the wise.[3]

Julian (the Roman emperor) The aim and end of the Cynic philosophy, as with every philosophy, is to be happy.[4]

Johannes Stobaeus The Stoics say that being happy is the goal of every human action.[5]

Plotinus If we suppose that being happy is the supreme end to which all nature aspires, then we must assume that all animals are able to reach this goal.[6]

Archytas What goods are naturally desired for themselves and not for anything else? Evidently they include happiness since happiness is the end for which we seek everything else, while we seek happiness only for itself and not for anything else.[7]

Epictetus God made every human being to be happy, to be steady and calm.[8]

Hippodamus the Thurian In point of fact, happiness is the perfection of life.[9]

Plato (Socrates is speaking) "The most important thing is not merely to live, but to live well."[10]

Plato (Socrates is speaking) "He who lives well is blessed and happy."[11]

Epicurus Let no one put off studying philosophy when he is young, nor become weary of it when he is old, for no age is too early or too late for the health of the soul. To suggest that the time for studying philosophy has not yet come or that it is long gone is like saying that it is too early or too late for happiness. . . . We must practice those things that produce happiness since if happiness is present, we possess everything, and if it is not, we do everything to acquire it.[12]

Plato (the Mantinean wise woman Diotima is speaking to Socrates) "Our yearning for good things and to be happy is the expression of desire."[13]

A few of the Homeric Hymns end with a prayer for happiness. For instance, the singer of the Hymn to Athena implores, Grant me good fortune and happiness. *The two hymning Heracles and Hephaestus request,* Grant me both excellence and happy prosperity.[14]

Homeric Hymn to Aphrodite (Anchises, the father of Aeneas, is praying to the goddess Aphrodite after promising her an altar and sacrifices) "Be kind and grant that . . . I might live long and well, seeing the light of the sun. And may I reach the threshold of old age a happy man among the people."[15]

Homer (the blind seer Tiresias is speaking, describing what will happen to the hero Odysseus after he returns home to Ithaca, when Odysseus is old) "And death will come to you away from the sea, a gentle death that will lay you low when you have grown old. And your people will exist in happy prosperity around you."[16]

Pindar Let Chromius of Aetna know that the gods have allotted him marvelous happiness—for if one wins splendid glory along with many possessions, there is no other high place on which a mortal man may stand.[17]

Plato (Socrates is reporting the hedonist Philebus' view) "Philebus declares that the good for every living thing is enjoyment, pleasure, and delight, along with everything that agrees with these. "[18]

Diogenes Laertius Aristippus and the Cyrenaics held that there is a difference between "the goal" and "happiness." The goal is a particular pleasure, whereas happiness as a whole is made up of all the particular pleasures.[19]

Diogenes Laertius (reporting the view of Theodorus, "the atheist," who was a Cyrenaic philosopher) Theodorus understood joy to be the goal of life and pain or grief to be the greatest evil.[20]

Epictetus People want things that produce happiness, but they search for them in the wrong place.[21]

Diogenes of Sinope Why, then, do you live if you do not care to live in a noble manner?[22]

Julian (the Roman emperor) Every living thing naturally yearns and stretches out for happiness.[23]

▪   ▪   ▪

Aristotle was right. Humans do act for happiness. At least that's the goal stated time and again in ancient Greek literature.

Still, we are left with an enormous question. If happiness is the goal, then what is happiness? In the next few chapters, we'll explore how the Greeks answered this question.

NOTES

[1] Aristotle, *Politics* 7.1331b.

[2] Aristotle, *Nicomachean Ethics* 10.6.1 (1176a).

[3] Ibid., 1.4.2-3 (1095a).

[4] Julian (the Roman emperor), *Oration* 6.193 ("To the Uneducated Cynics"). Though Julian was Roman, he was educated in Athens (among other places) and wrote in Greek. Therefore, we may include him among the Greeks since he is culturally Greek.

[5] Johannes Stobaeus, *Anthology* 2.6.

[6] Plotinus, *Enneads* 1.4.1.

[7] Archytas, in *The Pythagorean Sourcebook and Library*, 186 (modified).

[8] Epictetus, *Discourses* 3.24.2-3.

[9] Hippodamus the Thurian, in *The Pythagorean Sourcebook and Library*, 215 (modified). As the "perfection," it completes life. As such, happiness is the goal.

[10] Plato, *Crito* 48b.

[11] Plato, *Republic* 1.354a.

[12] Diogenes Laertius, *Lives and Opinions of Eminent Philosophers* 10.122 (from here on, *Lives*).

[13] Plato, *Symposium* 205d.

[14] *Homeric Hymn 11 to Athena* 5; *Hymn 15 to Heracles* 9; *Hymn 20 to Hephaestus* 8.

[15] *Homeric Hymn 5 to Aphrodite* 102-106.

[16] Homer, *Odyssey* 11.134-137.

[17] Pindar, *Nemean* 9.45-47.

[18] Plato, *Philebus* 11d. These—enjoyment, pleasure, delight—*are* the good or goal of life for Philebus. They *are* happiness.

[19] Diogenes Laertius, *Lives* 2.87.

[20] Ibid., 2.98.

[21] Epictetus, *Discourses* 3.23.34-35.

[22] Diogenes Laertius, *Lives* 6.65. For Diogenes and other Cynics, to live in a noble manner is to live in a happy manner.

[23] Julian (the Roman emperor), *Letter to Themistius the Philosopher* 256b-c.

2

HAPPINESS FORMULAS
HAPPY THE MAN WHO

"Instant happiness"—the assertion appearing above a foil-wrapped
burrito on a $25.00 Chipotle gift card (happiness = a burrito)

GO TO THE papyrology room of the Sackler Library at Oxford
University and you'll find a remarkably small, sack-brown
scrap of papyrus that is mostly unintelligible but for a few divine
nicknames and a reference to a big heart or mind. Discovered late in
the nineteenth century deep in the sands of Egypt not much more
than ten miles from the Nile, the second century AD fragment is part
of a song belonging to the sixth century BC Greek poet Stesichorus.

The song, whatever it was about, was popular—so much so that
later Greeks and Romans reproduced it for nearly a thousand years.
Then, at some point in the second century AD, a scholar brought a
copy of the song to Oxyrhynchus, a large provincial capital in the
Roman province of Egypt some one hundred miles south of modern Cairo. Or possibly it was a merchant who carried it along with
other songs for trade. Or perhaps a boy copied it there in school as
an exercise to satisfy the demands of his pedagogue. Whatever the
case, the copy ended up preserved in the city's dump.

However it got there, the papyrus copy of the song we now possess is regrettably only a fragment of the original whole. And it is tiny,
measuring one inch in length by three quarters of an inch in width.
Nevertheless, its sloppily written script—favoring, by the way, the
schoolboy theory—announces something very large relative to its
small size. After obliquely referring to Ares, Athena, and another
god—possibly Artemis or "horse-driving" Poseidon—the mostly all-
caps fragment tantalizingly declares, "HAPPY THE MAN WHO . . . ," before ending in an angled and slightly jagged tear that, with a little imagination, looks like a man in silhouette shouting.

Cupping our hands together, we may call back through time to Stesichorus himself, begging, "Happy the many who *what?*" After all, if only we had the remaining part of that line, we would have a very old happiness formula. For whatever reason, though, it's gone.

It's possible the *what* was so life altering that the Oxyrhynchan boy or girl or man or woman who threw the copy away tore off the important part, the post-ellipses *what*, and stuffed it into a fold of his or her tunic before tossing the rest in the city dump.

Happy the man who . . . *what?!*

But *sigh*—we'll likely never know.

Not all is lost, though. Fortunately, we have many early Greek statements summarizing the nature of happiness. So even if we've lost Stesichorus' formula, we'll let the others suffice.

What follows is a variety of happiness formulas organized into broad categories (formulas that zero in on avoidance, for instance, or on being god-favored, or experiencing pleasure, or possessing wealth and success).

As you'll see, the formulas take on many forms. Some follow the Stesichorus pattern: "Happy the man who . . ." Others assume a different structure. Regardless, each statement conveys the essence of happiness: H = X, Y, or Z.

IN THEIR OWN WORDS

The first category to note is negative in nature, that is, what a person must go without or avoid to be happy. Let's call it the avoidance formula, *one that many ancient Greeks felt and expressed.*

Alcman Happy the man who cheerfully finishes his life without weeping.[1]

Theognis of Megara Ah! Blessed, fortunate, and happy is he who goes down to the dark house of Hades without knowing trouble.[2]

Bacchylides There is one path to happiness for mortal men: the ability to hold on to a spirit free from grief and sorrow throughout life.[3]

Sophocles (the chorus is speaking) "Happy are they who have not tasted misfortune during their lives!"[4]

Euripides (the chorus leader is speaking) "Farewell! Happy is the mortal man who can manage life with gladness and without suffering misfortune."[5]

Euripides (Hecuba is speaking) "Happiest is the man who, day after day, doesn't hit upon misfortune."[6]

Plutarch (Plutarch is citing an unnamed author, possibly Epicurus) "Happiness and blessedness do not consist in a stockpile of property and money, great deeds, or the possession of exalted positions or powers. Instead, happiness is found in freedom from sorrow, calmness, and an ordered state of mind."[7]

Most early Greeks kept in mind the gods when thinking about the nature of happiness. Whatever it was, they presumed that happiness must be something sanctioned by the gods, whether directly or indirectly. And so, the god-favored formula. *Related to this is the fact that if the gods weren't pleased by human happiness in general or with a specific individual's happiness, then that happiness would likely vanish. Why? Because the gods could be very jealous. Moreover, if possible, many ancient Greeks wished to receive the special protection of the gods both in this life and in the life to come. This divine protection was accomplished with the rites of initiation, giving rise to the* initiation formula, *a kind of happiness only available to the initiated.*

Hesiod Divinely favored (or happy) and happy in wealth is the man who knows all these things and does his work, blameless before the immortals, distinguishing the birds of omen and shunning transgressions.[8]

Xenophon (the Spartan general Clearchus is speaking to the Persian satrap Tissaphernes) "Considering, then, that such misunderstandings are best settled by a discussion, I have come here because I wish to show you that it is a mistake to mistrust us. First and foremost, our oaths sworn before the gods stand in the way of our being enemies of each other. For my part, I would never call the man happy who has knowingly disregarded such oaths. The reason is simple. I know of no swiftness of foot that could save a man in a battle with the gods—or of some place of refuge where that man could flee, or of some darkness into which he could escape, or how he could withdraw into some stronghold. Again, the reason is simple. Everything everywhere is under the control of the gods. The gods rule all."[9]

Homeric Hymn to Demeter (revealing the rites of Demeter, the Eleusinian Mysteries, and the blessings of the gods) Of all men on earth, happy is the one who has looked upon these mysteries. But the man who remains uninitiated in the sacred rites, the one who has no portion of them, he has no share in these same good things when he perishes and goes down to the gloomy darkness. . . . And of all men on earth, very happy is the one whom the gods readily hold dear, for very soon do they send the god Ploutos to his great house as that man's guest—Ploutos, the god who gives wealth to mortal men.[10]

Pindar Happy is the man who beholds the mysteries at Eleusis before going beneath the earth. He knows the end of life and its god-given beginning.[11]

Some, however, seemed to doubt the initiation formula. *One, as reported by Diogenes Laertius, was the Cynic philosopher Diogenes of Sinope.*

Diogenes Laertius The Athenians urged Diogenes to be initiated into the mysteries. They told him that in the netherworld, initiates enjoy special privileges. "It would be laughable," he said, "if the Spartan king Agesilaus and the Theban general Epaminondas continue on in the mud while some worthless jokes who have been initiated will be in the Islands of the Blessed."[12]

Knowing that the gods must somehow be with us is knowing something very significant about happiness. Still, it doesn't offer much in terms of specifics. The question remains: What specific things—whether concrete or abstract, single or many—make for happiness?

Before looking at particular things, let's note with the relativist formula that, at least for a few ancient Greeks, the nature of happy-making things is quite relative—relative to different humans and, in a few of the following cases, different animals.

Homer (Odysseus is speaking) "Different men delight in different things."[13]

Archilochus of Paros There is no single kind of human nature, but different things warm different people's hearts.[14]

Heraclitus of Ephesus Pigs delight more in mud than in clean water.[15]

Heraclitus of Ephesus If human happiness consisted in the pleasures of the body, we would declare cattle happy whenever they discovered a field of bitter vetch to eat.[16]

Moving on to specifics, there's Epicurus' basic needs formula, stating that happiness is the satisfaction of certain basic needs or wants (lackings).

Epicurus The flesh cries out, "No hunger! No thirst! No freezing cold!" Whoever confidently has what it takes to satisfy these desires may rival even Zeus for happiness.[17]

Still, most Greeks wanted more. Most wanted success and wealth—all those things that lead to a luxurious life admired by others. Consequently, the wealth and success formula.

Sappho of Lesbos Riches mixed together with success bring the highest happiness.[18]

Theognis of Megara Success and good looks fall to few human beings. Happy is the man who has a portion of both. Everyone honors him.[19]

Bacchylides Happy the man to whom a god has given a portion of fine things. He lives a wealthy life with happy fortune.[20]

Homeric Hymn to Earth, the Mother of All (the singer views Earth as the provider of all happy-making goods) I will sing of well-founded Earth, the mother of all and oldest of all beings.

She feeds everything that exists upon the earth—all things that move through the land and the sea, and all that fly. All these are nourished by your happy prosperity!

Through you, queen, men are blessed with good children and abundant harvests. It's up to you to give mortal men what it takes to live, and to take it away.

Happy is the man you readily honor in your spirit! He has an abundance of everything. His fields are laden with life-bearing grain, his flocks and herds flourish, and his house is filled with good things. Such men rule well in cities full of beautiful women. Great wealth and much happiness follow after them. Their sons exult in thriving success and good cheer, and their daughters play and skip merrily over the soft flowers of the field, clad in flower-laden bands.

This is how it is for those you honor, holy goddess—the divine one who gives without grudge.

Rejoice, mother of the gods, wife of starry Sky! And for my song, readily give to me delightful wealth as my companion.[21]

Xenophon (the Persian ruler Cyrus the Great is speaking) Cyrus said, "Let me tell you, Croesus, I don't think those who have and guard the most are the happiest men. If that were so, then the happiest men would be those who have guard duty on the city walls! After all, they are the ones who guard everything in the city. Instead, the happiest man is the one who can justly acquire the most goods and use them for noble ends."[22]

In addition to wealth and success, the Greeks discovered happiness in what we may generically label the many activities and other goods formula, something akin to "objective list theory" (see Introduction 15).

Hipponax of Ephesus Blessed is the man who hunts.[23]

Anonymous You women are happy in the delightful dance![24]

Theognis of Megara Happy the man who goes home and engages in love exercises, sleeping with a beautiful boy all day long.[25]

Solon of Athens (also attributed to Theognis of Megara) Happy is the man who has dear boys, horses with hooves that are not cracked, hunting dogs, and friends that live in other lands.[26]

Theognis of Megara My dear heart is always warmed whenever I listen to the aulos sounding its charming voice. I'm happy drinking well and singing along with the aulos. And I'm happy holding the pleasant-sounding lyre in my hands.[27]

Strabo Although it has been said that human beings act most like the gods when they're doing good to others, one might better say that this is true when they are happy. And such happiness entails rejoicing, celebrating holy days, studying philosophy, and engaging in music.[28]

Socrates didn't accept the claim that having and enjoying many things was the same as happiness. In fact, Diogenes Laertius tells us that when Socrates was strolling through the marketplace full of things for sale in Athens, he would exclaim, "How many things I can do without!"[29] It's what we may call the simplicity formula, *a happiness formula others also adhered to.*

Xenophon (Socrates is speaking) "My dear Antiphon, you appear to imagine that happiness is living luxuriously with extravagance. As for me, I hold that standing in need of nothing is divine."[30]

Diogenes of Sinope (addressing Monimus) I said to my host Lacydes, "But let the drinking cups from which we drink be of clay, small, and cheap. And may our drink be spring water, and our food a loaf of wheat bread, and the seasoning be salt or cardamom. I learned to eat and drink these things from Antisthenes, . . . things one is quite able to find on the path leading to happiness." . . .

Diogenes goes on to describe the nature of the path leading to happiness and how he quickly arrived.

"And coming to the place where happiness exists, I said, 'Because of you, Happiness, and the greater good, I persisted in drinking water and eating cardamom and sleeping on the ground.' Responding to me, Happiness said, 'But rather than a hardship, I will make these things sweeter to you than the goods of wealth that human beings honor before me. But they do not understand that they are nourishing a tyrant for themselves.' And from that point on, when I listened to Happiness talking about this, I no longer ate or drank these things as a matter of practice, but as a pleasure."[31]

Regardless of the many goods a person possessed, the poet Ariphron recognized that without health, happy-making things were worthless. Hence, the health enthusiast *formula.*

Ariphron Health! Of all the blessed gods, mortal men honor you most. May I abide with you for what remains of my life! And may you readily live with me! For if there is any joy in wealth or children, or delight in godlike royal rule over men, or in the yearnings by which we hunt with the hidden snares of Aphrodite, or if there is any other pleasure or relief from toil that has been made manifest by the gods to human beings, it thrives and shines the light of life with you, blessed Health, and with the soft voices of the Graces. Apart from you no man is happy.[32]

With the pleasure formula, *some Greeks simply identified happiness with pleasure. For Plato, however, it had to be the right pleasure. Others insisted happiness was neither a matter of "excessive pleasure" nor of "a pleasure that requires external things." We'll begin with these last ones first, ones who doubted that pleasure actually made for happiness.*

Teles the Cynic I do not see how someone will live a happy life if he really must measure it by an excess of pleasure.[33]

Teles the Cynic If the happy life must be measured by the yardstick of excessive pleasure, then no one, says Crates, will be judged happy. Rather, if anyone wishes to weigh every stage in the whole of life, he will discover that there is a far greater quantity of pain and suffering.[34]

Crates of Thebes Take care of your soul—but your body only so far as what is necessary, and externals not even that much. I say this because happiness is not a pleasure that requires external things.[35]

The Contest of Homer and Hesiod. Hesiod asks, "What is it that humans call happiness?" *Homer responds,* "Dying after living a life with the least possible pain and the most possible pleasure."[36]

Diogenes Laertius (stating the Cyrenaic philosopher Aristippus' position) Happiness as a whole is made up of particular pleasures.[37]

Epicurus There are two kinds of happiness. There's the happiness of the god, the highest kind, which cannot be increased. The other kind may increase or decrease in terms of pleasures.[38]

Plato (the Athenian is speaking) "Pleasure and pain are two streams released by nature to flow. Whoever draws the right amount from them, at the right place and time, is happy."[39]

Many Greeks believed that happiness was more of an abstract possession — a quality, state of being, condition, or habit. Hence, the good, healthy, or beneficial quality, condition, or habit formula.

Diogenes Laertius (reporting the view of Thales of Miletus) When asked, "Who is happy?" Thales answered, "The man who has a healthy body, an inventive mind, and a well-disciplined constitution."[40]

Theognis of Megara Judgment, Cyrnus, is the best thing the gods give to mortal men. Judgment understands the proper measure of everything. Blessed is the man who holds it in his mind.[41]

Julian (the Roman emperor) We must say that happiness resides in our minds, in the best and noblest part of us.[42]

Pythagoras The most important thing in human life is persuading the soul to be good or evil. Happy are those men who acquire a good soul.[43]

Plato (Socrates is speaking) "Happiest is the man who has no evil in his soul."[44]

Plato (Socrates is speaking) "He who lives well is blessed and happy. It's the opposite for the man who does not."[45]

Plato (the Athenian is speaking) "I would never agree that a wealthy man is truly happy if he is not also a good man."[46]

Aristotle Happiness is an activity of the soul that accords with perfect virtue.[47]

Crates of Thebes We Cynics say that the good and excellent man, and no other man, is called happy.[48]

Zeno of Citium Happiness consists in virtue, which is the state of the soul that tends to make the whole of life harmonious.[49]

Plutarch Happiness is a kind of doing well. And doing well is found in a man when he alone is fulfilled.[50]

Marcus Aurelius Happiness is a good and noble *daemon* or a good and noble *hēgemonikon*.[51]

Lastly, there was what we might call the only at the end *formula. That is, a person's happiness—or not—can only be determined and declared at the end, when he or she dies.*

Aeschylus (the Achaean leader Agamemnon is speaking) "A man should

only be pronounced happy when he has finished his life with welcome prosperity and well-being."[52]

*Herodotus (the Athenian wise man Solon is speaking to the Lydian ruler
Croesus)* "Whoever goes through life with the most, and dies in an
agreeable manner, is the one who deserves the name of 'happy'—
in my view, anyway."[53]

*Diogenes Laertius (relaying an anecdote about the early Cynic Antisthe-
nes)* When someone asked him what the greatest happiness was
among human beings, Antisthenes said, "To die happy."[54]

.   .   .

We've seen that the ancient Greeks equated happiness with many
happy-making things, from the absence of pain and the presence of
pleasure to a variety of goods given by the gods or won by human
effort.

There's another formula, however, that we must take a look at.
In some ways, it is a formula that is so broad and so vague that it is
meaningless. But in other ways, it sheds much light on the *what* or
content of happiness. We'll explore what it is and what it does for
us next.

Notes

[1] Alcman, fragment 1, The Louvre partheneion 37-39.
[2] Theognis of Megara 1013-1016.
[3] Bacchylides, *Processionals*, fragment 11 and 12.
[4] Sophocles, *Antigone* 583.
[5] Euripides, *Electra* 1357-1359.
[6] Euripides, *Hecuba* 627-628.
[7] Plutarch, *How the Young Man Should Study Poetry* 37a.
[8] Hesiod, *Works and Days* 826-828. "These things" refers to "how work fits together with the course of the year and with the favorable days of the month."
See The Classics Cave's *The Best of Hesiod's Theogony & Works and Days*, Introduction, 54. The translation "divinely favored" for *eudaimōn*—which is often
simply given as "happy" and thus the "or happy" in parenthesis—is inspired

by Cornelius de Heer's arguments in *MAKAP–EYΔAIMΩN–OΛBIOΣ–EYTYXHΣ: A Study of the Semantic Field Denoting Happiness in Ancient Greek to the End of the 5th Century B.C.* Amsterdam: Adolf M. Hakkert, 1969.

9 Xenophon, *Anabasis* 2.5.6-7. To state the implied god-favored formula positively, "Happy those who keep the oaths they have sworn before the gods."

10 *Homeric Hymn 2 to Demeter* 480-482, 486-489.

11 Pindar, fragment 137, in Clement of Alexandria, *Miscellanies* 3.3.17. Another reading of the end: "He knows the completion of life and its god-given origin."

12 Diogenes Laertius, *Lives* 6.39. To learn more about the Islands of the Blessed, turn to Chapter 6, "Happy Times & Happy Places."

13 Homer, *Odyssey* 14.228.

14 Archilochus, fragment 25. "Warm" here essentially means "satisfy" or "make happy."

15 Heraclitus, fragment 51, in Clement, *Miscellanies* 1.2.2.

16 Heraclitus, fragment 53, in Albert the Great, *On Vegetables* 6.401.

17 Epicurus, *Vatican Sayings* 33.

18 Sappho of Lesbos, fragment 148, in Scholiast on Pindar.

19 Theognis of Megara 933-935.

20 Bacchylides, *Victory Ode* 5.50-53.

21 *Homeric Hymn 30 to Earth, Mother of All* 1-16. "Sky," often translated as "Heaven," is Ouranos (the Greek version) or Uranus (the Latin version).

22 Xenophon, *The Education of Cyrus (Cyropaedia)* 8.2.23.

23 Hipponax of Ephesus, fragment 43, in Choeroboscus on Hephaestion.

24 Anonymous testimony 59 regarding Sappho of Lesbos, *Palatine Anthology.*

25 Theognis of Megara 1335-1336.

26 Solon, fragment 23, in Plato's *Lysis* 212e. The identical fragment is also given as Theognis of Megara 1253-1254. Theognis goes on to say that the man who does not love these "has no good cheer in his spirit" (1255-56). There is discussion among scholars about whether the text should read "dear boys," with a pederastic connotation, or "dear sons," signifying something altogether different. See Douglas E. Gerber, *Greek Elegiac Poetry* (Cambridge: Harvard University Press, 1999), 145, where he suggests, ". . . A pederastic sense seems more probable."

27 Theognis of Megara 531-534.

28 Strabo, *Geography* 10.3.9.

29 Diogenes Laertius, *Lives* 2.25.

30 Xenophon, *Memorabilia* 1.6.10.

31 (Pseudo) Diogenes of Sinope, *Letter* 37 to Monimus.

32 Ariphron, *Paean to Health,* in Athenaeus, *Scholars at Dinner* 15.701f-702b.

33 Teles the Cynic, *Discourse* 5, 51H ("On Pleasure not Being the Goal of Life").

34 Ibid., 49H. "Crates," here, is the Cynic Crates of Thebes.

35 (Pseudo) Crates of Thebes, *Letter* 3 to His Students.

[36] *The Contest of Homer and Hesiod* (the *Certamen*), 1.11 or 321 in other editions. Homer's response, "Dying after living a life with the least possible pain," could have also been included under the "avoidance formula."

[37] Diogenes Laertius, *Lives* 2.87.

[38] Ibid., 10.121.

[39] Plato, *Laws* 1.636d-e.

[40] Diogenes Laertius, *Lives* 1.37.

[41] Theognis of Megara 1171-1173.

[42] Julian (the Roman emperor), *Oration* 6.194 ("To the Uneducated Cynic").

[43] Diogenes Laertius, *Lives* 8.32.

[44] Plato, *Gorgias* 478d.

[45] Plato, *Republic* 1.354a.

[46] Plato, *Laws* 5.743a.

[47] Aristotle, *Nicomachean Ethics* 1.8.1 (1098b). "Virtue" (*aretē*) may also be read as "excellence."

[48] (Pseudo) Crates of Thebes, *Letter* 36 to Dinomachus. The "good and excellent man" is the *spoudaios* man.

[49] Diogenes Laertius, *Lives* 7.89.

[50] Plutarch, *On Fate* 7.

[51] Marcus Aurelius, *Meditations* 7.17. *Daemon*, here, means something like a guardian angel in the sense of a guide. But in this case, it is one's innermost self or spirit or even conscience. This understanding of *daemon* likely goes back to Socrates, who spoke of the *daemon* that led him, forbidding him to do one thing or another. That said, the phenomenon is present from the earliest Greek literature. The *hēgemonikon* is the "leading part of the soul," which is the same as reason.

[52] Aeschylus, *Agamemnon* 928-929.

[53] Herodotus, *Histories* 1.32.

[54] Diogenes Laertius, *Lives* 6.5.

HAPPINESS IS THE SATISFACTION OF DESIRE
GETTING WHAT YOU WANT

"Continual success in obtaining those things which a man from time to time desires, that is to say, continual prospering, is that [which] men call felicity; I mean felicity of this life. For there is no such thing as perpetual tranquility of mind, while we live here, because life itself is but motion and can never be without desire." — Thomas Hobbes, *Leviathan*

IN HIS ACCOUNT of the birth of the gods, the *Theogony*, the ancient Greek poet Hesiod reports that Desire (Eros) was born among the very first gods. So it was that, alongside Chaos and Earth, there was Desire, "the most beautiful of the immortal gods, the one who . . . conquers the mind in the chest of every god and every human being, and the wise counsels therein."[1] By this revelation, we may understand that Desire stands at the beginning of everything—before, behind, beneath, *within* everything. Desire is a great force, impelling each thing toward what it wants, and so each thing to *be* what it is, *do* what it does, and *attain* what it has.[2]

Along with every other organism on earth, simple or complex, plant or animal, human beings are creatures of desire—creatures *that* desire. The goal of this desire? It is satisfaction somewhere along a spectrum that spans from mere survival on the one side to thriving on the other. Therefore, we humans struggle to do what it takes to satisfy our many desires.

If the seventeenth century political philosopher Thomas Hobbes is right (see the epigram above), then happiness itself is the satisfaction of desire—the very desire that is behind everything we do. That is, as he puts it, "felicity"[3] *equals* "continual prosperity" or "continual success in obtaining those things which a man from time to time desires." Perhaps this happiness is not happiness in any final sense. Hobbes seems to have concluded it is not, apparently reserving such a "perpetual tranquility of mind" (or happiness) for the afterlife—at the very least, he excluded it from *this* present life. Nevertheless, it is a species of happiness, giving rise to the most fundamental happiness formula there can be—that *happiness is the satisfaction of desire*, or H = SD.

But isn't this formula all too vague? It's a good point. So before letting the Greeks speak for themselves, we would do well to state plainly why understanding happiness as the satisfaction of desire is useful to uncovering what the ancient Greeks thought and said about happiness. It is useful because the formula (H = SD) points us in the direction of the *what* or content of happiness. If we know what gives someone satisfaction, then, presumably, we also know what makes him or her happy, what gives rise to that positive sense of well-being or happiness. This is true because the content or objects of desire are ultimately the same as those things that make someone happy.

What follows is divided into two parts. The first cites those Greeks who seem to indicate, directly or more indirectly, that happiness is the satisfaction of desire (H = SD), or that the satisfaction of desire is the best of all things. The second presents things desired or what makes someone happy.

In Their Own Words

Happiness Is the Satisfaction of Desire

Even if there is not always the verbatim statement that "happiness is the satisfaction of desire" among the ancient Greeks, there is the general sense that the formula is true, that you will be happy if your desires are satisfied. In one form or another, we see it from Homer on.

The following selections present happiness as the satisfaction of desire (H = SD). We'll get to the what of happiness, or to the list of objects that give rise to satisfaction-pleasure-happiness, in a moment.

Homer (the hero Odysseus is praying for his son, Telemachus) "Lord Zeus, may Telemachus be happy among men, and may everything happen as he desires in his heart."[4]

Homer (the old man Nestor is speaking in gratitude to the warrior Achilles) "I gladly receive this gift into my hands, and my heart rejoices that you are always kind and remember me and do not forget the honor by which it is fitting that I am honored among the Achaeans. May the gods give you happiness suitable to your desires."[5]

Homer (the suitors are speaking to Odysseus, disguised as a wretched wanderer) "Stranger, may Zeus and the other immortal gods grant you whatever you most desire and what is dear to your spirit since you have stopped this insatiate man's begging in the land. . . . Rejoice, father stranger! May happiness eventually be yours, though now you are carrying the heavy weight of wretchedness."[6]

Homer (Aegyptius is describing the man who must have, he believes, called the Ithacans together in assembly) "Who, then, has called us together? . . . A noble and brave man he seems to me, a blessed man, favored by the gods. May Zeus accomplish some good for him, whatever he desires in his heart."[7]

Homer (Odysseus is speaking to Nausicaa, the princess of Scheria) "May the gods grant you just as much as you desire in your heart—a man for a husband, and a house. And may noble unity of mind and feeling accompany these. For nothing is greater and nothing better than when a man and woman dwell in their household with the same thoughts, feelings, and mind—a huge pain to their enemies and joy to their friends. Their glory is well known. "[8]

Sappho of Lesbos Some declare that a band of horsemen or footmen is the most beautiful thing upon the dark earth. Others declare it is a fleet of ships. Me? I say it is whatever a person desires.[9]

Bacchylides Wine launches a young man's thoughts to the heights. At once he's tearing down a city's walls!—and he hopes to rule over all men!—and his house gleams with gold and flashes ivory!—and over a dazzling sea wheat-bearing ships deliver mountains of wealth from Egypt! A drinker ponders things like these in his heart. . . . What greater profit is there for a man than for him to gratify his desires with fine things? . . . Still, no man has ever been completely happy.[10]

Aristotle (the inscription found on the temple of Apollo at Delos) Justice is best. Yet to be healthy is better. But nothing is sweeter for a man than to get what he wants.[11]

Dionysus Chalcus (the Bronze) From beginning to end, what is better than that which a man longs for most?[12]

Pindar (wishing well to Hieron I, the absolute ruler of Syracuse) May the whole of time direct happiness and rich possessions to him. . . . Just so, may the god come to support Hieron in the years to come and give him what he desires at the right time.[13]

Sophocles (the Phrygian woman Tecmessa is speaking about her husband, the Achaean hero Telamonian Ajax) "Death was happiness for him since he got what he desired—the death he wanted."[14]

Plato (the businessman Callicles is speaking to Socrates) "How can a man be happy if he is any man's slave? . . . The man who wants to live happily should let his desires be as strong as possible and not check them. Furthermore, he should be able to fulfill them when they are strongest thanks to his manly courage and intelligence—he should always be able to satisfy each desire as it comes. Ah, but this, I imagine, is not possible for the many. . . . And since they are unable to furnish for themselves the pleasures that would satisfy their desires, the many praise moderation and justice. . . . But truly, Socrates, luxurious living, immoderation, and license are excellence and happiness."[15]

Diogenes Laertius (reporting the philosopher Menedemus' response to the idea that H = SD) Menedemus heard someone say that the greatest good for a man would be to get what he longs for. *Diogenes Laertius goes on to say,* Hearing this, Menedemus said, "It is a much greater good to long for what is proper."[16]

Much later, the Stoic philosopher Epictetus presented H = SD in Stoic fashion. "The happy man must have all that he wishes to have." Of great significance, however, is what the happy man desires.

Epictetus It is never possible for happiness and yearning for what is not present to come together. For the happy man must have all that he wishes to have. The happy man must resemble a full man, complete. He must not be thirsty or hungry.[17]

Finally, we end with the educator Isocrates, whose very statement—that happiness is not actually getting and doing what you want—demonstrates the prevalence of the sentiment that it is.

Isocrates Happiness is not merely the ability to do whatever you want. . . . Freedom is not the same as licentiousness.[18]

The What of Happiness—Things Desired

As mentioned, if happiness is the satisfaction of desire, then we can figure out the "what" of happiness—the list of things that afford happiness—by determining the things ancient Greeks desired. The following selections reveal these things and thus the objects that satisfied ancient Greeks, making them happy. Included are prayers, best lists, wishes, statements of divine benefits, and general expressions of what happiness is. Observe, in what follows, how some desiderata are concrete and some are abstract. In terms of duration, some are short-term, things desired right now, and some are ongoing, that is, long-term and even life-long.

Homer (the Trojan hero Hector is praying for his son, Astyanax) "Zeus and the other gods, grant that this child, my boy, may be as I am. Make him outstanding among all the Trojan men, preeminent in forceful strength and noble bravery, and may he powerfully rule Ilium. And when someday he returns home from battle carrying the gory spoils of the enemy man he has slaughtered—the dead man's shield and armor—may some man say, 'He's even better than his father was!' And let his mother rejoice and delight in her heart!"[19]

Homer (Odysseus is praying for the happiness of his Phaeacian hosts)
"May the gods grant you and the nobility a happy and prosperous life, and may each man hand on to his children the wealth in his house and the honors and rights granted by the people."[20]

Homer (Odysseus is speaking to the suitor Antinous) "I too once dwelled in a house among men attached to me. I was a happy man in a wealthy house. And often I gave to wanderers—whoever they were and with whatever need they came to my house. And I had countless slaves and everything and more for living well, those things for which men are called wealthy."[21]

Hesiod (the poet is describing the blessings of the goddess Hekate) For even now, whenever some human being dwelling somewhere upon the earth offers beautiful, first-rate sacrifices and seeks to appease the gods according to custom, he calls upon Hekate. And when the goddess gladly receives that man's prayers into her house, honor follows him quite easily, and she gives him happiness as his companion. . . .

If Hekate wishes, she stands by a man and greatly benefits him. He is preeminent among the people in the assembly—if she wills it. And when men arm themselves to go into man-destroying battle, the goddess stands there by them—if she wills it—and gladly reaches out to give victory and glory to them as their companions. And in judgment she takes her seat by the side of highly regarded kings. And again, she is good luck when men contend for prizes in an athletic competition. The goddess stands there beside the competing men and benefits them. The one who wins by means of strength and courage, that man easily and joyfully hauls off a prize, and he gives glory to his parents as their companion. And she is good luck for horsemen or those who fight from a chariot—if she wills it. And for those men who work the rough and stormy gray sea, the ones who pray to Hekate and the loud-sounding Earthshaker, the glorious goddess easily gives a haul of many fish to be their companion. And she easily takes it away as soon as it appears—if her spirit is willing. And together with Hermes, she is good luck for increasing livestock wherever they stand: the droves of cattle, the large goat herds, and the flocks of woolly sheep—if her spirit is willing. She's able to increase the few to many, and the many, she's able to reduce to a few.[22]

Semonides of Amorgos The man who gets a bee-like wife is happy since blame doesn't touch her. Thanks to this woman, his wealth grows, and whatever it takes for him to live prospers. Loving and loved, she grows old with her husband, giving birth to beautiful children and distinguished offspring. She stands out among all women and divine grace surrounds her. She's not delighted by sitting around with women when they talk about those things belonging to Aphrodite. These are the best and wisest kind of women with which Zeus gratifies men.[23]

Drinking song To be healthy is best for mortal men. The second is to be beautiful in form. The third is to have honest wealth. And the fourth is to be young with your friends.[24]

Bacchylides The best thing for mortal men is to have a good fate fixed by the god.[25]

Timotheus (offering a prayer to Apollo) Come to this holy city, far-shooting Pythian, and bring happiness with you. May the people be unharmed, and may you give them peace that thrives with good order.[26]

Herodotus (reporting the greatest happiness among the Massagetae, a non-Greek central Asian people who lived in the area of present-day Turkmenistan, Uzbekistan, and southern Kazakhstan; implied is a contrast to the Greek conception of happiness or what a Greek would desire) Even though the Massagetae do not determine the end of a man's life ahead of time, when a man grows old, his whole family comes together in order to sacrifice him along with sheep and goats, and they feast on a stew made of all the meat. That is held to be the happiest death. But when a man dies of disease, they do not eat him. Instead, they bury him beneath the earth and lament the fact that he did not live on to be killed.[27]

Aristophanes (the war weary farmer Trygaeus is speaking) "Now is the time to sing as Datis did when he was working himself at midday. "I'm pleased! I'm delighted! I'm happy!" Greek men—now is the time when, delivered from troublesome affairs and from fighting, we should rescue Peace, which is dear to all!"[28]

Plato (writing to the family and friends of Dion, the absolute ruler of Syracuse) When I came to Sicily I was not at all impressed by what they call "the happy life," full as it is with Italian and Syracusan feasts. A man's life is spent stuffing himself with food twice a day, and never sleeping alone at night, and all the pursuits that go along with this kind of life.[29]

Plato (the sophist Hippias is speaking to Socrates about the "most beautiful" or "best" or "happiest" life) "I say, then, that for all men everywhere and at all times it is best to be wealthy, healthy, and honored by Greek men. And when one has finally come to old age, it is best to be honored with funeral rites by one's children in a way that befits a great man—after doing the same for his own parents, of course."[30]

Aristotle Most people associate happiness with obvious things that can be seen and felt, such as pleasure or wealth or honor. . . . But quite often the same man declares happiness one thing and then another—health when he's sick and wealth when he's poor.[31]

■   ■   ■

We've accomplished two objectives in this chapter. One, we listened to many Greeks expressing the notion that happiness is the satisfaction of desire. Satisfaction is beautiful, good, the best, happy-making. Two, using the formula H = SD, we've noticed some of what the ancient Greeks desired and, therefore, some of the *what* of happiness.

In the next chapter, we'll explore another significant dimension of happiness. If this chapter featured the *what* of happiness (things desired), the next will highlight the *how* of happiness—the means by which a person comes to be and remains happy.

NOTES

[1] Hesiod, *Theogony* 120-122. *Eros* (Desire) is often given as "Love."

[2] In Aristophanes' *Birds* 700-703, desire is that which "joins everything together," including the gods. As the chorus leader puts it: "At first, there was no race of immortals (gods) before Desire (Eros) joined everything together. Then, as one thing mixed with another, Sky (Ouranos) was born, and Ocean (Ōkeanos) and Earth (Gē or Gaia), and the whole imperishable race of blessed gods." Other words for desire are longing and yearning, as well as need (insofar as need is lacking) and want (in the sense of lacking and therefore desiring).

[3] "Felicity" comes from the Latin *felix*, which means, among other things, "lucky, happy, fortunate."

[4] Homer, *Odyssey* 17.354-355. Here, happiness equals, or is at very least closely associated with, the satisfaction of desire.

[5] Homer, *Iliad* 23.647-650. Here, Nestor correlates happiness with the—implied—satisfaction of desires.

[6] Homer, *Odyssey* 18.112-115, 122-123. The "insatiate beggar" is Iros. Again, with the suitors' prayer, we see the strong correlation of the satisfaction of desire with happiness.

[7] Homer, *Odyssey* 2.28, 33-34. The idea seems to be that a noble and brave man *is* a happy man—blessed, favored by the gods (*onēmenos*). It follows that such a man should be satisfied relative to "whatever he desires in his heart." Therefore, Aegyptius prays that it may be so. By the way, *onēmenos* (from *oninēmi*) is not a word that Homer typically uses for happiness.

[8] Homer, *Odyssey* 6.180-185. The Greek here for "desire in your heart" is the same as that used by Odysseus in praying for Telemachus, and that used by Aegyptius in praying for the unknown "noble and brave man." With this prayer, we have what the scholar Martin L. West calls a "blank check" prayer—a prayer, West says, that originates in, or at least finds parallels in, the literature of the ancient Near East (see M.L. West, *The East Face of Helicon*, 274-275; he cites Babylonian and Hebrew "blank check" prayers). Still, given the above connections of happiness and the "blank check" prayer (see Odysseus' and Aegyptius' prayers), and since Odysseus goes on to pray that Nausicaa would get what would satisfy her desires (a husband, house, unity of mind with her husband, and so on), we can assume he is praying for happiness.

[9] Sappho of Lesbos, fragment 16. As the "most beautiful thing" (*kalliston*), it is the "fairest" or "most noble" thing (both "fair" and "noble" are meanings of

kalos), which is to say it is the best thing. So, to get what you desire is the best thing. Assuming "the best thing" is the happiest thing—a common assumption among the ancient Greeks, who judged happiness the "highest good"—then the happiest thing is to get "whatever a person desires."

[10] Bacchylides, *For Alexander, Son of Amyntas*, fragment 20B. The strong implication is that complete happiness equals the gratification of one's desires with fine things.

[11] Aristotle, *Nicomachean Ethics* 1.8.14 (1.1099). The same lines are repeated in Theognis 255-256 and Sophocles, *Creusa* 356. "Sweeter" here is, of course, synonymous with "happier" or "more fortunate"—that is, there is no happier thing for a man than to get what he wants.

[12] Dionysus Chalcus, cited in Athenaeus, *Scholars at Dinner* 15.702b-c. "Better" is the comparative form of *kalos*. In this case, "better" is synonymous with "happier."

[13] Pindar, *Pythian* 1.46, 56-57.

[14] Sophocles, *Ajax* 967-968. The statement is not merely that death is happiness but that getting what you want is happiness. In this case, Telamonian Ajax desired death, which "was happiness for him since he got what he desired."

[15] Plato, *Gorgias* 491e-492c. Callicles' declaration is the strong declaration that the satisfaction of any and every desire is happiness. It is a contention that Socrates will go on to mock by suggesting that "the man who has an itch" and is "freely able to scratch the itch now and throughout his life" is the happy man. Though Socrates is joking, Callicles agrees. "Yes," he says, "I say that the man who is able to scratch lives his life pleasantly." Socrates adds, "And if pleasantly, then happily—he lives a happy life?" Callicles says, "By all means, yes." For the conversation, see Chapter 9, "Plato & Socrates."

[16] Diogenes Laertius, *Lives* 2.136. This correction by Menedemus is representative of much of ancient Greek philosophy.

[17] Epictetus, *Discourses* 3.24.17. To restate the point, happiness does not belong with or equal yearning, longing, or desire. If desire is present, happiness is absent. Why? Because desire is lacking. But the happy man does not lack anything. Indeed, "the happy man must have all that he wishes to have." What, according to the Stoic, does a Stoic—or "the happy man"—wish to have? Only that which is "up to him"—that is, that which is presently in his power to think or do. What is up to him? How he judges events. How he responds. Whether he acts in accord with nature, reason, and virtue. If what is up to him is in his power, it is done or possessed. If it is not, then it is not done or possessed—but it is, therefore, not something he desires. It follows, then, that happiness only appears with the satisfaction of desire—which is to say that "the happy man . . . *has* all he wishes to have." Of course, this begs the question whether such a "happy man" or true Stoic can exist or ever has—something the Stoics themselves debated.

[18] Isocrates, *Panathenaicus* 12.131—where doing what you want presumably leads to getting what you desire. "Freedom is not the same as licentiousness"

is actually prior to "happiness is not merely the ability to do whatever you want." But since there seems to be an equivalence between the two, the switch doesn't change the meaning. For more, see Chapter 8, "Isocrates."

[19] Homer, *Iliad* 4.475-481.

[20] Homer, *Odyssey* 7.148-150.

[21] Homer, *Odyssey* 17.419-423.

[22] Hesiod, *Theogony* 416-420, 429-447. The "Earthshaker" is Poseidon.

[23] Semonides of Amorgos, fragment 7.83-93.

[24] *Drinking song* 890.

[25] Bacchylides, *Victory Ode* 14.1-2.

[26] Timotheus, fragment 791.237-240, Berlin papyrus.

[27] Herodotus, *Histories* 1.216.

[28] Aristophanes, *Peace* 289-294. "Working himself" is masturbating. That which is desired here, that which pleases, delights, and makes happy, is peace.

[29] Plato, *Letter* 7.326b-c.

[30] Plato, *Hippias Major* 291d. "Best" is *kalliston*, the superlative of *kalos* (beautiful, fair, good). As the superlative of "good," it is "best" and thus "happiest."

[31] Aristotle, *Nicomachean Ethics* 1.4.3 (1095a).

4

THE HOW OF HAPPINESS
THE MEANS BY WHICH

"My brother Gallio, . . . let us determine the goal and the way *to happiness*.
And let us find an experienced guide who has explored the region toward
which we are advancing." —Seneca, *On the Happy Life*

THERE ARE THREE big questions to ask, explore, and, if possible,
answer when it comes to the nature and experience of happiness. The first has to do with the *what* of happiness, the subject of
the past two chapters. Another, the focus of this chapter, queries
the *how* of happiness, that is, the means by which a person comes
to be and remains happy. The final question investigates the *why* of
happiness. If happiness is *this* particular *what*, and *this* specific *how*
is the means by which of happiness, then *why* is that the case?

As for the latter question, it is hard, though possible, to tease out
the *why* of happiness from much of the earliest Greek literature, not
to mention much of the later, more philosophically oriented Greek
writings. Take Homer, for instance. It is possible to see why happiness is really the same thing as glory in the *Iliad* and the *Odyssey*. It
is so because glory establishes a hero's reputation, which allows
him to live well in terms of all good things up and down the "pyramid of desire." These goods in turn permit the satisfaction of desire.[1] Or take the late eighth century BC poet Hesiod. The *why* of
happiness in his *Works and Days* has everything to do with the nature of the gods, their jealous eye and constant observation of men,
and how they have configured the seasons and days for men to
work and become happy in wealth and prosperity. If a human
doesn't labor and interact with others in the manner given by the
gods, and if a human doesn't watch out for the variety of divine
powers, then beware, warns Hesiod, that human won't do well for
very long. Lastly, the *why* of Plato's (or Socrates') happiness arises

from human nature given by the creator. Why must humans strive for virtue or excellence (*aretē*)? Because that's the only way to fulfill or bring to completion our God-given human nature—a completion, Plato argues, that amounts to happiness.

We'll explore the *why* of happiness with some of the philosophers in Part 2. For now, let's look at the *how* of happiness.

Most ancient Greeks viewed the gods as the ultimate source of all happiness—whether it was the gods acting directly or by means of Fate and fortune. For them, the gods give happiness as a gift. We see something similar in the biblical book of Job. When Job first loses his happiness, that is, everything good in his life, he attributes all to God:

> I came from my mother's womb naked, and naked I will leave this world. The Lord God gave to me and so has the Lord God taken everything away. Even so, blessed be the name of the Lord God!"[2]

For other Greeks, happiness was attained by other, more self-originating means such the use of reason or wisdom, or the cultivation of courage and other excellences or virtues.

IN THEIR OWN WORDS

Happiness Delivered by the Gods

The following selections indicate the ancient Greek belief that happiness (or the opposite) is delivered by the gods, Fate, and other divine powers.

Homer In reply, white-armed Nausicaa said, "Stranger, since you do not seem to be a base or senseless man, and since Olympian Zeus himself dispenses fortune and happiness to men, to both the good and the bad as he wills, whether he be a brave man or a coward, noble or base—so I believe that surely he has given misfortune to you."[3]

Hesiod Property should not be stolen. God-given property is much better. For if a man seizes a pile of wealth and happiness with the strength of his hands, or he plunders it with his tongue—the sort of things that are frequently done when the love of gain deceives the mind of human beings and when shameless effrontery follows self-respecting shame—then do the gods easily leave that man in the dark, obscure, and they diminish his household, and wealth and happiness are his for a very brief time.[4]

Hesiod When Hekate gladly receives a man's prayer into her house, honor follows him quite easily, and she gives him happiness.[5]

Homeric Hymn to Demeter (Demeter is speaking) "I am Demeter, the honored one, who brings the greatest benefit both to immortal gods and mortal men, and who causes the most joy."[6]

Homeric Hymn to Demeter Of all men on earth, happy is the one whom the gods readily hold dear, for very soon do they send the god Ploutos to his great house as that man's guest—Ploutos, the god who gives wealth to mortal men.[7]

Homeric Hymn to Apollo (the leader of the Cretans is speaking) "Stranger, though you are not like mortal men in shape and size, but instead you are like the immortal gods, I greet you warmly. And may the gods grant you happiness!"[8]

Homeric Hymn to Dionysus Dionysus pitied the steersman of the ship, holding him back and making him altogether happy.[9]

Homeric Hymn to Earth, Mother of All I will sing of well-founded Earth, the mother of all and oldest of all beings. She feeds everything that exists upon the earth—all things that move through the land and the sea, and all that fly. All these are nourished by your happy prosperity! Through you, queen, men are blessed with good children and abundant harvests. It's up to you to give mortal men what it takes to live, and to take it away. Happy is the man you readily honor in your spirit. He has an abundance of everything. His fields are laden with life-bearing grain, his flocks and herds flourish, and his house is filled with good things. Such men rule well in cities full of beautiful women. Great wealth and much happiness follow after them. . . . This is how it is for those you honor, holy goddess.[10]

Orphic Hymn to Eleusinian Demeter Deo, divine mother of all, divine power of many names, revered Demeter, nursing mother, giver of happy prosperity, divine giver of riches, nourisher of ears of grain, giver of all. . . . Charming and lovely one, you nourish every mortal, you who were first to yoke the ox for plowing and to produce a desirable and abundant means of life for mortal men.[11]

Anacreon Hermes, son of Maia, give Tellias the life he desires, . . . enjoying a share of good fortune for the rest of his life.[12]

Ibycus Divine powers give much happiness in wealth to those whom they wish to have it.[13]

Bacchylides Mortal men are not free to choose the happiness of wealth. Nor are they free to turn down relentless war or civil strife, the destroyer of all. Instead, Destiny, the giver of all, shifts a cloud first over this land and then over another.[14]

Theognis of Megara No human being is noble or happy in wealth or lowly or poor in wealth without the gods.[15]

Pindar Let Chromius of Aetna know that the gods have allotted him marvelous happiness—for if one wins splendid glory along with many possessions, then there is no other high place on which a mortal man may stand.[16]

Diogenes Laertius (Diogenes Laertius is relating a story about the Cynic Diogenes of Sinope, who seems to deny that happiness comes about by means of the gods) Observing someone purify himself, Diogenes said, "Unhappy man! Don't you know that you cannot get rid of sins by means of purification rites any more than you can get rid of grammar errors?" Diogenes would generally chide men for the way they prayed, declaring that they asked for the seemingly good rather than the truly good.[17]

Happiness Delivered by Humans—Who We Are, What We Do

The next selections show that, apart from the gods and other divine powers, the ancient Greeks believed the "how" of happiness had to do more with how we humans are. Think education, training, practice, mind, heart, reason, judgment, knowledge, wisdom, virtue, disposition, character, boldness, action.

Plutarch The writer of the encomium to Alcibiades for his victory in the chariot race at Olympia—whether the author was Euripides or some other man—says that the first requirement for happiness is birth in a glorious city, one with a good reputation. But in my opinion, Sosius, this is not required for true happiness, which mostly depends on character and disposition. Indeed, it is no disadvantage to belong to an obscure and lowly city any more than it is to be born of a small and misshapen mother.[18]

Hesiod Self-respecting shame doesn't take care of the needy man—shame, which can greatly harm and benefit a man. Rather, for the needy man, self-respecting shame brings poverty and unhappiness, whereas boldness brings wealth and happiness.[19]

Thucydides (Pericles is speaking to the Athenians) "Judging happiness to be the fruit of freedom, and freedom to be the fruit of good courage, do not put off the dangers of war."[20]

Xenophon Socrates judged that education and training would make men not only happy for themselves, with the ability to manage their own households well, but it would also help them make other men happy, and to even make their cities happy.[21]

Aeschylus (the chorus is speaking) "I have a fitting word of counsel. Arrogance is truly the child of impiety, but happiness, which is dear to everyone and much prayed for, comes from a healthy mind and heart."[22]

Pythagoras Do nothing beyond what you know. In this manner your life will become happy.[23]

Sophocles (the chorus is speaking) "Wisdom rises as the first part of happiness."[24]

Epictetus For making a good voyage, a steersman and wind are necessary. And for happiness, reason and art.[25]

Gorgias of Leontini Reason is a powerful ruler! By means of the smallest and most invisible body, reason—and discourse, which follows from reason—achieves the most divine works. Reason and discourse can stop fear. And relieve one of anxiety. And produce joy. . . . The power of reason and discourse has the same relation to the soul's constitution as the power of medicines does to the body's natural constitution. For just as different drugs expel different humors from the body, and some put an end to disease, . . . so can the power of reason and discourse cause distress and fear, as well as delight and courage.[26]

Diogenes Laertius Plato held that the goal of life is to become godlike, and that virtue is sufficient in itself for happiness.[27]

Plato (the Athenian is speaking) "Apart from true reason and discourse, no man would ever become wise. And if a man has not acquired wisdom—wisdom, the greatest part of virtue as a whole—he can never become perfectly good, which would eventually make him happy."[28]

Demosthenes Intelligence, sound judgment, and much forethought lead all men to happiness.[29]

Xenophon (Socrates is relating the story of Heracles' encounter with Virtue and Vice personified) Socrates said, "As Prodicus tells it, Vice here interrupted and said, 'Have you considered, Heracles, how long and hard this road to enjoyment is that this woman Virtue is mapping for you? I will lead you along a short and easy road to happiness.'"

Virtue strongly disagrees and declares, "'But I associate with the gods and with good men, and no fine action, whether the deed of a god or of a man, is done without me. . . . So, Heracles, child of good parents, if you toil hard along the path that I, Virtue, have mapped, you can acquire the most blessed happiness.'"[30]

Aristotle Happiness is an activity of the soul that accords with perfect virtue.[31]

Diogenes Laertius Antisthenes the Cynic held that virtue is sufficient for happiness.[32]

Diogenes of Sinope I came, Father, to Athens, and learning that Socrates' associate was teaching about happiness, I went to him. And he happened to be speaking about the paths that lead to happiness. He declared that there are two and not many paths—and that one is a shortcut and the other is long. . . .

When I heard this, I kept quiet. But when we went to him again the next day, I called on him to show us the paths. Quite readily, he stood from his chair and led us into the city, straight through it to the acropolis. And when we had drawn near, he showed us two paths leading upward. The one is short, steep, and troublesome; the other is long, smooth, and easy.

When he brought us down, he said, "Such are the paths leading up to the acropolis. And such are the paths leading to happiness. Choose the path as you wish, and I will guide you."[33]

Diogenes Laertius (giving the position of the early Stoics) The virtues are goods that have both the nature of ends and means. Inasmuch as they produce happiness, they are means to good things. On the other hand, inasmuch as they are the fulfillment of happiness, being a portion of happiness itself, they are ends. . . . Similarly, vices have the nature of both ends and means. Whenever they produce unhappiness, they are means. But whenever they serve to make unhappiness complete, being a portion of unhappiness itself, they are ends.[34]

Crates of Thebes Long is the path that leads to happiness through words alone. But the path that leads to happiness through the practice of daily deeds is short.[35]

Julian (the Roman emperor) Is it not laughable when a man tries to find happiness somewhere outside himself, and thinks that wealth and birth and the influence of friends, and, generally speaking, everything of that sort is of the utmost importance? . . . We must say that happiness resides in our minds, in the best and noblest part of us.[36]

· · ·

The good news about the *how* of happiness is that the means seem plentiful—from the gods and Fate giving happiness to the abundant provision of beneficial education, reason, wisdom and judgment, the virtues, good character, practice, action, and like things.

Still, there are many problems. One, if the gods have the power to give happiness, they have the power to take it away. Job was right on this point, as was the poet behind the *Homeric Hymn to Earth, Mother of All*, who declares that "It's up to you [Earth] to give mortal men what it takes to live, and to take it away."[37] Two, the human *how* is challenging. For instance, attaining happiness by means of one virtue or another is hard work. As the poet Hesiod puts it, "The immortal gods have put sweat in front of virtue."[38] Finally, happiness itself—the *when* or *whether* of happiness—seems problematic. In Chapter 3 we heard the poet Bacchylides end his reflection on wine's effects by optimistically asking, "What greater profit is there for a man than for him to gratify his desire with fine things?" Perhaps. But then there is what he says next: "Still, no man has ever been completely happy." With this caveat in mind, we transition into the next chapter that is—fair warning—full of similar pessimism.

NOTES

[1] For the extended argument, see Tim J. Young, *A Hero's Wish: What Homer Believed about Happiness and the Good Life*.
[2] Job 1.21.

3 Homer, *Odyssey* 6.186-190.

4 Hesiod, *Works and Days* 320-326.

5 Hesiod, *Theogony* 418-420.

6 *Homeric Hymn 2 to Demeter* 268-269.

7 Ibid., 486-489.

8 *Homeric Hymn 3 to Apollo* 464-466.

9 *Homeric Hymn 7 to Dionysus* 53-54.

10 *Homeric Hymn 30 to Earth, Mother of All* 1-12, 16.

11 *Orphic Hymn 40 to Eleusinian Demeter* 1-3, 7-10.

12 Anacreon fragment 105D, Palatine Anthology 6.346. This fragment also points to the "happiness equals the satisfaction of desire" formula.

13 Ibycus, fragment 282A.

14 Bacchylides, fragment 24 in Stobaeus, *Extracts* 1.5.3.

15 Theognis of Megara 165-166.

16 Pindar, *Nemean* 9.45-47.

17 Diogenes Laertius, *Lives* 6.42-43.

18 Plutarch, *Demosthenes* 1.1.

19 Hesiod, *Works and Days* 317-319.

20 Thucydides, *History of the Peloponnesian War* 2.43.4.

21 Xenophon, *Memorabilia* 4.1.2.

22 Aeschylus, *Eumenides* 532-537.

23 Pythagoras, "The Golden Verses of Pythagoras," *The Pythagorean Sourcebook and Library*, 164.

24 Sophocles, *Antigone* 1348-1349.

25 Fragments of Epictetus 166.

26 Gorgias, *Encomium of Helen* 8, 14.

27 Diogenes Laertius, *Lives* 3.78. For Plato, becoming godlike or assimilating to god (God) is the same as happiness; therefore, virtue is the means to both.

28 Plato, *Epinomis* 977d.

29 Demosthenes, *Against Aristogeiton 1* 25.33.

30 Xenophon, *Memorabilia* 28.1.29, 32-33.

31 Aristotle, *Nicomachean Ethics* 1.13.1 (1102a). See also 10.7.1 (1177a).

32 Diogenes Laertius, *Lives* 6.11.

33 (Pseudo) Diogenes of Sinope, *Letter* 30 to Hicetas. The Cynic letters we possess—of Diogenes of Sinope and Crates of Thebes, among others—are not considered genuine by scholars. That said, they are clearly Cynic insofar as they remain faithful to Cynic goals and themes.

34 Diogenes Laertius, *Lives* 7.97.

35 (Pseudo) Crates of Thebes, *Letter* 21 to Metrocles the Cynic.

36 Julian (the Roman emperor), *Oration* 6.194 ("To the Uneducated Cynics").

37 See also Herodotus, *Histories* 1.32, where Solon explains that "the god often promises happiness to many only to take it away."

38 Hesiod, *Works and Days* 289.

THE PROBLEM WITH HAPPINESS
How No One Is Truly Happy

"Wherever he be, a man need only cast a look around to revive a sense of human misery. . . . It should never be forgotten that misfortune, be it great or small, is the element in which we live." —Arthur Schopenhauer, *Counsels and Maxims*

HAPPINESS IS ONE of those things that always seems out of reach. It's over *there*—there in the future; or it's there in some other object or experience; or someone else has it; or as soon as we grasp it here and are aware of it now, it vanishes, and so, presently, happiness is in the past.

Happiness is like the out-of-reach water and fruit that Tantalus intensely longs for deep in the caverns of Hades, or the stone that Sisyphus desperately wants to roll up and over a hill but is never able to. Here's how the hero Odysseus relates their stories in the *Odyssey*, when, to the Phaeacians, he describes his own voyage to the very limits of the earth and an open pit that leads down into the Underworld, the realm of the dead, "where there is no joy":

I also saw Tantalus suffer pains horrible to endure. He stood in a pool of water that came right up to his chin. Even so, he was thirsty given that he couldn't take a drink. For whenever that old man stooped down, eagerly desiring to drink, the water would vanish, all swallowed up, and the dark earth would appear beneath his feet. Some god would dry it up. And more! Various trees, high and leafy, would dangle their fruit just above his head—pear, pomegranate, and apple trees with their beautiful fruit, and sweet fig and flourishing olive trees. But whenever that old man straightened up and reached his hand out to take one, the wind would hurl it up to the shadowy clouds.

I also saw Sisyphus suffer pains horrible to endure while lifting a monstrous stone with both of his hands. Pressing on with hands and feet alike, he pushed the stone upward to the summit of a hill. Ah! But whenever he was about to roll it over the top, the stone's fantastic weight would turn it back. Then the cruel stone would once again come rolling down into the plain. Yet again he struggled intensely to push it up the hill—and sweat flowed down from the limbs of his body, and a cloud of dust rose up around his head.[1]

It's hard to think of Tantalus as anything but miserable. He doesn't have what he desires, and he's tortured by the fact. Moreover, the whole cosmos in the form of one god, or the gods, is against him. But perhaps matters stand differently with Sisyphus.

The mid-twentieth century French absurdist philosopher Albert Camus thought so. He was optimistic relative to Sisyphus' ongoing and apparently meaningless struggle to push the stone up and over the top of the hill. In his essay, *The Myth of Sisyphus*, he says, "The struggle itself toward the heights is enough to fill a man's heart. One must imagine Sisyphus as happy."[2]

Of course, if Camus were sitting across the table from us smoking another one of those *Gauloises* cigarettes he smoked, one after another, we may wish to probe him about the exact nature of such a happiness. The ancient Greeks themselves—some, anyway—would likely balk at his conception of a happiness that rises phoenix-like from the ashes of meaningless toil and ultimate absurdity. Others, such as the Cynic philosophers, with their "love of toil" (*philoponia*) would likely applaud the idea—but for different reasons.

Still, the general Greek view, as we saw with Aristotle, was that we humans act or work hard to achieve certain goals, including happiness. The problem with happiness, however, as some judged it, and as we learn from Odysseus' trip to Hades, is that some people never experience it, or it never fully comes, or it comes only to go.

IN THEIR OWN WORDS

We begin with the notion that human life, including happiness, is a very iffy or chance-filled affair. While we might be happy today, tomorrow is an entirely different story. So, as Simonides of Ceos puts it, "Don't ever predict how long a person will be happy." Human life is ultimately insecure.

Hermolochus A man's whole life wanders thanks to chance, unpredictable and insecure, even though hope cheers his heart. As for what is destined to happen, no mortal man accurately knows what the future will bring. It is the god who guides mortal men amid dangers, and oftentimes a fearful breeze blows against the happiness of good luck.[3]

Simonides of Ceos You are a man—so don't ever say what will happen tomorrow. Or when you see a happy man, don't ever predict how long he'll be happy. The long-winged housefly doesn't even buzz off so fast.[4]

Besides insecurity, there is the apparent fact that happiness is always incomplete. We humans are only happy sometimes and in some ways.

Pindar Each one of us passes through life with his own allotted nature. We're all different. And no man can succeed in achieving complete happiness. I cannot identify anyone to whom Fate has offered this goal as his lasting possession.[5]

Theognis of Megara One is miserable one way; another in another way. No one human being whom the sun looks down upon is truly happy.[6]

Bacchylides No mortal man is happy all the time.[7]

Bacchylides No man has ever been completely happy.[8]

Diogenes Laertius Those of the school of Hegesias denied the possibility of complete happiness. This is so because the body is infected with much suffering. And since the soul shares in the sufferings of the body, it is therefore troubled when the body is troubled. And luck prevents many things that we hope for. From all this it follows that complete happiness is non-existent.[9]

Sophocles (an unknown character is speaking) "If you include all human beings, you will not find one mortal who is happy in all things."[10]

Sophocles (the chorus is speaking) "Never has Zeus, the son of Kronos and the one who governs the course of all things, given to mortals a life free from pain. But grief and joy come to every man in turn, like the circling paths of the Bear."[11]

Homer (Achilles is speaking to Priam) At first, Achilles observes, "Ah, wretched man, you have endured so much evil." *Later, he recognizes that* "you too, old man, . . . were once happy." *Achilles explains Priam's fall from happiness to wretchedness this way:* "On the floor of Zeus' house there are two jars from which he gives gifts. The one is filled with evil and the other with good. To whomever Zeus, who delights in thunder, mixes and gives out both, that man will meet now with good and now with evil fortune. But for the man who only receives baneful gifts—ah, that man will suffer abusive treatment."[12]

Herodotus (Solon is speaking to the Lydian ruler Croesus) "It is impossible for a man to get all these things *(wealth, health, good looks, children, power, the absence of ruin, the ability to satisfy desire)* at the same time, just as no kingdom's land is self-sufficient in what it produces. Each realm's land has one thing but lacks another. Whichever has the most is the best. Similarly, no human body is self-sufficient. Each person has one thing but lacks another. And so, king, whoever goes through life with the most, and dies in an agreeable manner, is the one who deserves the name of 'happy'—in my view, anyway. First, it is necessary to see how everything will turn out in the end since the god often promises happiness to many only to take it away."[13]

Some ancient Greeks denied the possibility of happiness.

Solon No mortal man is blessed—not one. Rather, all mortals whom the sun looks down upon live a wretched life full of toil.[14]

Euripides (a messenger is speaking to Medea) "No mortal man is happy.

One may be wealthy, and because of that we may say he is luckier than another man. But he is not happy."[15]

Finally, there is the ancient Greek sentiment, found among some, that things are so bad in human life that it is better not to be born. Such a position is called "antinatalism" today.[16]

Theognis of Megara Not to be born and not to look upon the bright light of the sun—this is the best of all for mortal men upon the earth. But to lie dead beneath a huge pile of dirt and to pass through the gates of Hades—this is the best when a man is already born.[17]

Bacchylides (Heracles is speaking to Meleager) "It is best for mortal men never to be born, never to look upon the light of the sun. But since nothing good comes from crying about it, a man should talk about what he intends to accomplish."[18]

Sophocles (the chorus is speaking) "Whoever longs for a greater portion of life instead of the measure he presently has is—it is very clear to me—in a difficult position. I say this because long-lasting days store up many things that are nearer to pain and grief, whereas delight vanishes whenever someone lives longer than is necessary. Regardless, in the end there is death, the killer that brings the same end to everyone when the fate of Hades appears—and this without a marriage song or the sound of a lyre or the movement of a dance.

"Given all these considerations, it is best not to be born. But once a man is born, the next best thing is to return to wherever it is he has come from as quickly as possible. After all, what painful blow is distant even when a man is young, his heart light, and his mind without thought or care? What trouble is absent? There's bloodshed. And factions. Strife, battles, and jealousy. Old age is allotted last of all—abhorred old age, when a man is all alone without power and friends so that he experiences every misfortune."[19]

Herodotus (Herodotus is describing non-Greek Trausi customs) When a child is born, his relatives sit around and lament all the misfortune he must endure now that he is born, and they recount the many ways that human beings suffer. But the dead they hide away in the earth, competing in games and enjoying themselves. They say that the dead one has escaped all the misery of life and has achieved a state of complete happiness.[20]

*   *   *

Let's collectively gasp. Or find some other way to express astonishment at such an in-your-face pessimism. Or let's assume that much of the above was said while the poet or wise man was sick or in a bad mood.

The problem? What they said is true—at least in part.

Still, it's not the whole story. For that, we have to listen to those Greeks who believed in the possibility of ongoing happiness.

That's what we'll do in the next two chapters. We'll first tour happy times and happy places in Chapter 6. We'll then meet up with happy gods and happy people in Chapter 7. All that before moving on in Part 2 to the Greek philosophers, who taught that happiness is something we can all aim for and achieve—in part, at least—with the right understanding and effort.

NOTES

[1] Homer, *Odyssey* 11.582-600. "Where there is no joy" (*aterpēs*: unpleasing, joyless) (11.94) is the description of Hades given by the blind seer Tiresias. Upon seeing Odysseus, he asks, "What now, you unhappy man? Why have you left the light of the sun in order to come here to see the dead in this place where there is no joy." Hades—or the condition of being dead—is not a very happy place.

[2] Albert Camus, *The Myth of Sisyphus*, trans. Justin O'Brien (New York: Vintage International, 1991), 123. Note that though "absurdist" is more accurate, Camus is sometimes labeled an existentialist.

[3] Hermolochus, fragment 846, in Stobaeus, *Extracts* 4.34.66.

[4] Simonides of Ceos, fragment 521, in Stobaeus, *Extracts* 4.41.9.

[5] Pindar, *Nemean* 7.55-58.

[6] Theognis of Megara 167-168.

[7] Bacchylides, fragment 54, in Stobaeus, *Anthology*.

[8] Ibid., *For Alexander, Son of Amyntas*, fragment 20B.

[9] Diogenes Laertius, *Lives* 2.94.

[10] Sophocles, *Phaedra* fragment 681. Since the *Phaedra* only survives in fragmentary form, we do not know who is speaking, whether the chorus or another character.

[11] Sophocles, *The Women of Trachis* 126-131. "Kronos" often appears as "Cronus" in English translations.

[12] Homer, *Iliad* 24.518, 527-531, 543. Though we did not, we could have included this selection in Chapter 4, "The How of Happiness."

[13] Herodotus, *Histories* 1.32.

[14] Solon, fragment 14, in Stobaeus, *Anthology* 4.34.23.

[15] Euripides, *Medea* 1228-1230.

[16] In response to such antinatalists and to the poet Theognis of Megara and others like him (see the next point), the Greek philosopher Epicurus says, "Much worse is the man who says that it is a good thing not to be born. Yet when born, he says, it is best 'to pass quickly through the gates of Hades.'" For Epicurus, "the wise man neither spurns living nor does he fear not living." See Diogenes Laertius, *Lives* 10.126-127. The important point, Epicurus says, is to live wisely and, therefore, to live well. We at the Cave agree. As a whole, life is a good thing. To live well, as Plato and others put it, is happiness. For more of Epicurus' view, see Chapter 15, "Epicurus & Epicureanism."

[17] Theognis of Megara 425-428.

[18] Bacchylides, *Victory Ode* 5.160-164.

[19] Sophocles, *Oedipus at Colonus* 1211-1238.

[20] Herodotus, *Histories* 5.4. Though the Trausi were not Greek (they mostly lived in present-day Bulgaria, though some were in north-eastern Greece), their sentiments were—given the witness of Theognis, Bacchylides, and Sophocles, anyway—nevertheless similar to at least some ancient Greeks.

HAPPY TIMES & HAPPY PLACES
THE IDEAL OF HAPPINESS

"O happy age, O truly golden century that nourished humanity with fruits produced spontaneously, without effort or care, and . . . without superfluity!"
—Coluccio Salutati, *Letter to Leonardo Bruni*

THE POET HESIOD, known for his *Theogony* (*Birth of the Gods*) and his *Works and Days*, was a pessimist.[1]

To understand why, let's journey on a brief voyage of imagination to the year 700 BC, nearly three millennia ago. Landing in that year by some miracle of time travel, we venture down from Mount Helicon, home of the Heliconian Muses, to Ascra, a small farming village in Boeotia, located in central Greece, northwest of Athens. It's where Hesiod lived during what he called the Iron Age.[2]

When we arrive in Ascra, the villagers stare us down like the strangers we are. They notice our soft hands, odd clothes and shoes, and when we attempt to speak, our non-Greek accents. Even so, they are exceedingly kind, knowing full well how Zeus *Xenios*, the god of strangers, demands foreigners be treated.

After getting to know the inhabitants, we form a focus group with Hesiod and some of the other men and women who dwell in the village and farm its surrounding fields. A "focus group?" they will have asked with a good measure of skepticism showing on their weathered faces. But after spreading a mid-summer style feast before them, replete with Bibline wine, barley cakes, goat cheese, and roasted meat, the group warms up to answering a few questions. So, here goes.

Number one. Please raise your hand if you enjoyed the feast. All hands go up.

Two. Raise your hand if farming is going well for you this year—your fields are blooming with grain and your sheep are growing heavy with wool. Most hands go up since it has, in fact, been a good year.

Three. Now for a more general question, we say. How many of you are pleased to be living right now during the Iron Age?

The participants of the focus group look at one another, silently motioning with their eyebrows, *Now?*

After a few moments, one whispers, "Are you kidding?"

Finally, a hand goes up halfway, gesturing to get our attention. When called on, she curses her luck, saying, "I'd rather live in the halls of Hades than in the Iron Age!"

Another calls out, "She means she'd rather be dead!"

Hearing this exchange, Hesiod stands. "If you don't mind," he says, "I'd like to deliver a few lines I've been working on about the iron race of men."

Given his excellence as a poet, one graced in recent years by the Heliconian Muses, everyone readily agrees. And so, he recites:

> If only I were no longer obliged to be part of the fifth kind of men but had died before or been born afterward. For presently the race of men is truly one made of iron. Oppressed by wearisome work and suffering, men will not rest day or night. And the gods will give them anxious thoughts that are hard to endure. Yet for these people, too, the good will be mixed with the bad—the noble with the ignoble, the fortunate with the unfortunate.[3]

After everyone expresses their approval of Hesiod's lines, we decide to ask an impromptu question. How many of you feel as Hesiod feels? All hands go up.

Then, turning to Hesiod, we ask him to speak about the period of time he'd rather live in and about the humans who lived during that time.

The poet smiles as he begins to tell us about what he calls the "golden race of men," those who lived during the Golden Age under the direction of the Titan god Kronos. "They lived like the gods," he explains, "with carefree spirits, far away from toil and suffering. Wretched old age never overtook them. . . . They delighted in abundant feasts, apart from every evil."[4]

Everyone applauds. This is what they want, too. And so, we get some idea about the happiness ancient Greeks pined for—that of the Golden Age and its easy, carefree, ever-youthful life of abundance.

Along with the Golden Age, we'll visit other happy times and happy places in this chapter, including the Age of Kronos, the Heroic Age, the Islands of the Blessed, Mount Olympus, the Elysian fields, and more. In doing so, we'll form an idea about the ancient Greek ideal of happiness consisting of distant times and faraway places.

IN THEIR OWN WORDS

Many ancient Greeks—including Hesiod, as we've seen—believed the Golden Age was a happy time. The Golden Age was a time when the god Kronos (or Cronus) ruled. Who was Kronos? According to Hesiod, he was the son of Ouranos (Sky), who was the husband-son of Gaia (Earth). Otherwise, he was the husband-brother of Rhea, and with her, the father of Zeus, Hera, and other gods and goddesses. Hesiod tells Kronos' story in the Theogony *and in the* Works and Days.[5] *But we also find hints elsewhere about Kronos and the particularly happy age over which he presided, a time of ease, peace, and abundance.*

Hesiod (the poet is singing of the Golden Age during Kronos' rule) First of all, the immortals who have houses on Olympus made a golden race of speech-endowed human beings. They existed at the time of Kronos, when he was king in the sky. And they lived like the gods, with carefree spirits, far away from toil and suffering. Wretched old age never overtook them, but they were always the same from their feet up to their hands. They delighted in abundant feasts, apart from every evil. And when they died, it was as though they were overcome by sleep. They had all good things. For without envy, the grain-giving field spontaneously bore many fruit and grain crops. And willingly and peacefully they distributed the results of their work along with many good and noble things. Rich in sheep, they were dear to the blessed gods.[6]

Philodemus Life in the time of the god Kronos was happiest—as Hesiod and the poet of the *Alcmeonis* and Sophocles have written.[7]

Unknown (a late Greek interpolation within Hesiod's Works and Days *that describes Kronos' rule among the "happy heroes" who lived on the Islands of the Blessed.)* Kronos is king among the heroes. For Zeus himself, the father of men and of gods, released him. And now, as is fitting, Kronos perpetually has honor among them.[8]

Plato (the Athenian is speaking) "Long before those cities existed, the ones we've just discussed, it is said that during the Age of Kronos there was a very happy settlement and government. . . . Tradition lets us know that life during that time was blessed. Men were furnished with everything in abundance and spontaneously. The cause of this abundant bliss is said to be this. . . . The god Kronos, in his love and affection for human beings, set over us at that time a better race of daemonic spirits. And they, in a way that was easy for them and for us, took charge of us and supplied us with peace and reverence and good law and justice lacking envy. As a result, Kronos brought humankind to perfection in terms of freedom from political faction, and happiness."[9]

Plato (the Stranger is speaking to a young Socrates) "All these stories [about the rule of Kronos and how earlier people were earthborn rather than born from another human], and others even more astonishing than these, have their source in the same event. But in the lapse of time, some of them have been lost to memory. . . .

"The life and time about which you ask, when all the fruits of the earth sprang up spontaneously for men, did not belong to this present time and this present revolution of the cosmos. Rather, it belonged to the previous time. For then, before this time, the god Kronos ruled and supervised the turning of the cosmos as a whole. . . . No creature was wild. And creatures didn't eat one another. And war didn't exist or civil strife. . . . Under the god's rule, there were no states or separate citizenship. Nor did men possess women as wives or children. . . . They had fruits in abundance from trees, other bushes, and plants. The earth yielded these spontaneously, producing them without the work of farmers. And they lived for the most part in the open air, without clothing or beds. The climate was regulated for their comfort, and the abundant grass that grew up out of the earth made for them soft beds.

"That, Socrates, was the life of men during the Age of Kronos. As for life during this present time, which is said to be the Age of Zeus, you know it by your own experience."[10]

Plotinus (Plotinus is discussing the archetypal world of Intelligence, the realm of eternal intelligibles) Over them rules pure Intelligence with extraordinary wisdom. There is the true realm and life of Kronos, whose very name suggests abundance and intelligence. It encompasses all that is immortal, everything intelligent and divine, every soul. There is eternal stability, eternal rest.[11]

Apart from happy times, the ancient Greeks mapped out a geography of happy lands and happy places. Prominent among them are the Islands of the Blessed where there is an abundance of all good things.

Hesiod (Of the Heroic Age, Hesiod explains that some heroes perished fighting before the walls of Thebes and Troy, and so "terrible battle destroyed these men-heroes" as "the end of death covered over . . . them." As for the rest, he says the following.) Father Zeus, the son of Kronos, granted the other heroes life and an accustomed abode far apart from human beings, and he made them dwell at the limits of the earth. And these dwell with carefree spirits on the Islands of the Blessed by deep-eddying Ocean. They are the happy heroes for whom the grain-giving field bears honey-sweet fruit, flourishing three times per year.[12]

Pindar But those . . . preserving their souls from all unjust acts, follow the way of Zeus to the tower of Kronos. There, ocean breezes blow around the Island of the Blessed, and flowers of gold light up like fire . . . And with these flowers they weave bracelets for their wrists and crowns for their heads.[13]

Drinking song O dearest Harmodius! You can't be dead! They declare that you are in the Islands of the Blessed, where swift-footed Achilles is, and—they declare—Diomedes, the son of Tydeus.[14]

Plato (Socrates is speaking) "Every human who has lived a just and holy life departs when dead to the Islands of the Blessed, and he dwells there in all happiness apart from misfortune."[15]

Plato (Socrates is speaking) "Delivered from such things as gluttony and similar pleasures, the soul turns its vision from things below toward things that are real and true and thus a vision of higher things.... *The soul does so* in the pursuit of education and training.... *Consequently, these souls* will not willingly engage in practical activities such as the governance of a city-state. Why? It is because they believe they've been settled in the Islands of the Blessed while still alive.... *This education and training consists in studies having to do with* perceiving the idea of the Good, which is found in those studies that force the soul to turn itself to the place that is the happiest part of reality.... If the soul contemplates Being itself, it is doing what is proper.... *And finally,* the soul turns its vision upward to the goal of education. There it fixes its gaze on that which sheds light on all, ... the Good itself. *And after governing the city-state and educating others, such souls will* dwell in the Islands of the Blessed.[16]

In Lucian of Samosata's The True History *(or* The True Tale*), the narrator explains that the "Island of the Blessed" is ruled by* Rhadamanthus of Crete. *Entering the island's city, the narrator is* taken to the drinking party of the blessed.... The whole city, *the narrator explains,* is built of gold. Its wall is constructed of emerald. And each of its seven gates is made of a single plank of cinnamon. The ground within the walls, foundations and all, are ivory. The temples of all the gods are built of beryl, and the altar in each is a great monolith of amethyst upon which the inhabitants offer hecatombs. Around the city flows a river of the finest perfume, ... in which there is pleasant swimming. The baths are in great crystal houses heated by fires of cinnamon. Rather than ordinary water, though, these long tubs are filled with warm dew. *The people within this city* wear purple clothes made of the finest material (like that of a cobweb). *Strangely, though,* they do not have bodies. *Therein* a man does not grow old. *As for seasons,* it is always spring, with Zephyrus, the West Wind, *cooling the inhabitants. As for refreshment, there's abundant food and wine, with bread-producing plants, ample fruit trees, and rivers flowing with milk and wine.* During each meal, there is music and singing. *And nearby, there are* two springs—one of laughter and one of pleasure. *These add* a great deal to the inhabitants' enjoyment.[17]

Diogenes Laertius (reporting the response of the Cynic Diogenes of Sinope) The Athenians urged Diogenes to be initiated into the mysteries. They told him that in the nether world, initiates enjoy special privileges. "It would be laughable," he said, "if the Spartan king Agesilaus and the Theban general Epaminondas continue on in the mud while some worthless jokes who have been initiated will be in the Islands of the Blessed."[18]

Staying with the Islands of the Blessed for a moment, the following selections attempt to pinpoint where they are. Whereas Hesiod declares they are "far apart from human beings . . . at the limits of the earth," these other authors locate them in Africa or in the sky.

Herodotus As for those in Cambyses' army who were sent against the Ammonians, they set out from Thebes [in Egypt] and traveled with guides. What is known is that they came to the city of Oasis, a city inhabited by Samians, who are said to be of the Aeschrionian tribe. The city itself is a seven-day march from Thebes through the sand. This place is called the Island of the Blessed in the Greek language.[19]

Strabo The Islands of the Blessed are found at the extreme western edge of Maurusia [Morocco], near where its shore runs parallel to the opposite coast of Iberia [Spain]. It is clear Homer considered these regions happy given their contact with the Islands.[20]

Iamblichus (from his work, On the Pythagorean Life*) Question*: What are the Islands of the Blessed? *Answer*: The sun and the moon.[21]

Moving on, most Greeks identified Mount Olympus, the abode of the Olympian gods, as a place of perfect happiness.

Pseudo-Hesiod (describing the shield of Heracles) And upon the shield there was the holy dancing place of the immortal gods. And in the middle, Apollo, the son of Zeus and Leto, played a golden lyre so as to excite desire. There was also the dwelling place of the gods, holy Olympus, and their assembly place. And an unlimited abundance of wealth and happiness surrounded the immortals in their gathering. And just now, the goddesses, the Muses of Pieria, were beginning a song in the manner of clear-voiced singers.[22]

Homer Bright-eyed Athena departed for Olympus, where, they say, the abode of the gods stands firm, immovable forever. Neither is it shaken by wind, nor drenched with heavy rain, nor does snow fall there. But a clear sky spreads out cloudless like a great white sail, and the bright sun fills the sky. And there upon Olympus the blessed gods are delighted every day.[23]

Diogenes Laertius (reporting two epigrams carved on Plato's tomb) Here in the hollow of the earth, Plato's body is hidden, while his soul has its immortal station with the blessed.

   And: I, a flying eagle, am the image of the soul of Plato that has flown off to Mount Olympus, while Attic soil holds his earth-born body.[24]

Another happy land was the Elysian plain or the Elysian fields, also known as Elysium.

Homer (Proteus, the old man of the sea, is speaking to the hero Menelaus) "As for you, god-nourished Menelaus, it is not decreed for you to die and meet your destined doom in horse-grazing Argos. Rather, the immortals will escort you to the Elysian plain and to the limits of the earth where yellow-haired Rhadamanthus is. Here, life is the easiest for men. There's no falling snow or much of winter or thunderstorms. But a clear West Wind always blows—sent up by Ocean to cool and refresh the men there. You will not die because you hold Helen as your wife and so are the son-in-law of Zeus."[25]

As with the Islands of the Blessed, some attempted to locate the Elysian plain in the real world.

Strabo As for the people of the west, Homer makes it clear that they were happy and that they lived in a temperate climate. Homer had doubtlessly heard of the wealth of Iberia [Spain], and how, in pursuit of that wealth, Heracles invaded the country, and after him the Phoenicians—the people who in earliest times became masters of most of the country. . . . The gentle breezes of Zephyrus, the West Wind, blow in the west, and it is there that Homer locates the Elysian plain itself, where, he declares, Menelaus will be sent by the gods.[26]

We close with a number of other happy lands and cities, including the land of the Hyperboreans, the Lacedaemonians, and the Thessalians, as well as Libya, Troy, a city called "Happy City," various lawful cities, and what may be called "the city of Justice."

Pindar Neither by ship nor on foot will you find the fabled path to the land and assembly of the Hyperboreans. . . . Led on by Athena, Perseus, the son of Danae, once went to the land of these blessed men, the Hyperboreans.[27]

Pindar Happy is Lacedaemon! Blessed is Thessaly! The descendants of Heracles, best at fighting, reign over both lands.[28]

Homer (Menelaus is speaking) "I came to Libya where the lambs grow horns as soon as they are born and where the sheep bear their young three times per year. And whether he is a lord or a shepherd in that land, every man has plenty of cheese, meat, and sweet milk, for the ewes give their milk throughout the year. No one goes without."[29]

Ibycus The Achaeans . . . destroyed the great, glorious, happy city of Priam, the son of Dardanus.[30]

Herodotus The Greek colonists who live on the Hypanis River call themselves citizens of *Olbia*, Happy City.[31]

Diogenes Laertius (giving basic facts about the early wise man Bion) Bion was by birth a citizen of *Olbia*, Happy City.[32]

Xenophon (describing happy lawful cities) Those cities that live by and stay true to their laws are always the strongest and happiest cities.[33]

Hesiod (describing the happy city of Justice) Weeping and clothed with occluding mist, Justice follows along to the city and to the abodes of the people, and she brings evil to those human beings who drive her out of the city and do not make straightforward distributions. But those men who give straight judgments to foreigners and to those who live within the city and the surrounding land and do not swerve from justice at all, their city thrives and the people in it flourish. Then does Peace, who safeguards young men, come upon the earth, and far-seeing Zeus does not ordain painful war for them. Neither hunger nor bewildering blindness haunt straight-judging men, but in abundance they distribute every valued thing. For them, the earth bears much of what it takes to live. And upon mountains the topmost part of the oak tree produces acorns, and the middle part yields the bee's honeycomb. And wooly sheep are weighed down by wool. And the women give birth to children who are like their parents. Having good things, they thrive in every way and at all times. And they don't go away on ships, but the grain-giving field bears crops of fruit and grain.[34]

·   ·   ·

As we've seen, the Greeks spoke about some distant times and some faraway places as generally happy. As for times, there were the Age of Kronos, the Golden Age, and, for some, the Heroic Age—although it is possible to view these three as one. As for places, there were the Islands of the Blessed, Mount Olympus, the Elysian plain or fields, and a variety of other happy lands and cities.

To give a summary idea of the good life in these times and places, happiness was judged an easy, toil-free life with an abundance of good food and wine. It was a life filled with delight, a life lived in good weather, a peaceful life. It was one with good governance and laws, with neither political strife nor warfare. It was an ageless life—perhaps immortal. At very least, it was a life ending in the serenity of a sleep-like death.

If there were happy times and happy places, then surely there were beings, whether divine or human, who lived during those times and dwelled in those places. The following chapter offers a roster of happy gods and happy humans.

NOTES

[1] Perhaps "realist" is a better descriptive. Prior to being a poet, Hesiod was a shepherd and a farmer.

[2] "Iron Age," as well as "Golden Age" and "Heroic Age," is actually more a common extrapolation from Hesiod, who only refers to the "iron race or kind of men"—or golden, silver, bronze, and heroic race or kind of men.

[3] Hesiod, *Works and Days* 174-179. To some extent, Hesiod's vision of the Iron Age or iron race of men is no different from the voices we heard in Chapter 4 relative to "the problem with happiness."

[4] Hesiod, *Works and Days* 112-115.

[5] Kronos' nature is paradoxical in Hesiod's poems. On the one hand, he is "the one whose counsels are crooked, the most terrible of [Ouranos' and Gaia's] children"; he is the one who "hate[s] his expansive father," lopping off his penis with a sickle made of adamant; he is the one who swallows his own children, eventually battling them in the Titanomachy. On the other hand, he is "the king in the sky" during the Golden Age, the happiest of all times for human beings. Kronos' paradoxical nature is a mystery the ancient Greeks explored and gained much from—particularly those of the Orphic tradition.

[6] Hesiod, *Works and Days* 109-120.

7 Philodemus, *On Piety* B 6798 Obbink. For the Greek text, see Martin L. West, *Greek Epic Fragments* (Cambridge: Harvard University Press, 2003), 62-63.

8 The interpolation, which appears in two papyri, occurs after line 173 of Hesiod's *Works and Days*. Of the heroes, Hesiod explains in lines 170-173: "And these dwell with carefree spirits on the Islands of the Blessed by deep-eddying Ocean. They are the happy heroes for whom the grain-giving field bears honey-sweet fruit, flourishing three times per year." For the interpolation, see Glenn W. Most, *Hesiod: Theogony, Works and Days, Testimonia* (Cambridge: Harvard University Press, 2006), 100-101.

9 Plato, *Laws* 4.713a-e.

10 Plato, *Statesman* 269b, 271d-272b.

11 Plotinus, *Enneads* 5.1.4.

12 Hesiod, *Works and Days* 168-173.

13 Pindar, *Olympian* 2.69-74. Note that this place of happiness or blessedness sometimes shows up in the plural (islands) and sometimes in the singular.

14 *Drinking song* 894.

15 Plato, *Gorgias* 523b-c.

16 Plato, *Republic* 7.519b-c, 7.526e, 7.540a-b. Reading these parts of the *Republic* together, the Islands of the Blessed may be understood as having to do with the "idea of the Good" and with Being itself (*ousia*) or the "happiest part of reality." Thus, the islands are an abstraction or a state of mind or soul. As such, Socrates himself sometimes experienced the Islands of the Blessed—or moods of thought or abstraction. We see this, for example, in Plato's *Symposium* 174d, 175a-b, and 220c-d. The Victorian classics scholar and translator Benjamin Jowett translated these experiences or moods as "fits of abstraction."

17 Lucian of Samosata, *The True History* 2.6, 11-16. Though the description is meant to be humorous, exaggerated, and even deceptive (see Lucian's Introduction, where the narrator admits that he is a liar, and that his work relates what he has neither seen nor heard), it nevertheless resembles what many would have believed about the Islands of the Blessed—something like it, anyway.

18 Diogenes Laertius, *Lives* 6.39.

19 Herodotus, *Histories* 3.26.

20 Strabo, *Geography* 1.1.5.

21 Iamblichus, *On the Pythagorean Life* 18, in *The Pythagorean Sourcebook and Library*, 77.

22 Pseudo-Hesiod, *The Shield of Heracles* 201-206.

23 Homer, *Odyssey* 6.41-46.

24 Diogenes Laertius, *Lives* 3.44.

25 Homer, *Odyssey* 4.561-569.

26 Strabo, *Geography* 1.1.4.

27 Pindar, *Pythian* 10.29-30, 45-46.

28 Ibid., 10.1-3. Lacedaemon is Sparta.

[29] Homer, *Odyssey* 4.85-89. As a place of abundance, Libya, or northern Africa, is a happy place. As it is described in the *Odyssey*, the swineherd Eumaeus' home island of Syria is similar: "There's an island called Syria," he explains to Odysseus. "Perhaps you've heard of it? It sits above Ortygia, where the sun turns. Even though the island is not densely populated, it is nevertheless a good land—good for cattle and sheep, full of vines for wine, and rich in grain. Hunger and famine never enter the land, nor does any other hateful plague fall on wretched mortals. But when the tribes of men grow old throughout the city, Apollo of the silver bow arrives with Artemis, slaying them with their gentle shafts" (*Odyssey* 15.403-411). Compare Syria to the Golden Age, the Rule of Kronos, and the Islands of the Blessed.

[30] Ibycus, fragment 282. The city is Troy. When speaking to Priam, the ruler of Troy, in Book 24 of Homer's *Iliad*, Achilles says, "And you too, old man, I have heard that you were once happy. They say that in wealth and number of offspring you surpassed the rulers of all the lands surrounding your own. . . . But from the day when the Uranian gods unloaded this misery on you, war and slaughter have surrounded your city."

[31] Herodotus, *Histories* 4.18. The remains of the city are in present-day Ukraine on the Black Sea.

[32] Diogenes Laertius, *Lives* 4.46. This Olbia is the same as the Olbia mentioned by Herodotus.

[33] Xenophon, *Memorabilia* 4.4.16.

[34] Hesiod, *Works and Days* 222-237. We know the city of Justice or the just city is happy because of the peace and the abundance of good things it has. For Hesiod, happiness or happy prosperity is the same as working hard, "shunning transgressions," and living in a state of "blameless[ness] before the immortals" (see *Works and Days* 826-828).

HAPPY GODS & HAPPY PEOPLE
THE HAPPY FEW

"All who would win joy must share it. Happiness was born a twin."
—Lord Byron, *Don Juan*

TAKE A LOOK at the first part of Jesus of Nazareth's Sermon on the Mount, which begins the fifth chapter of the Gospel of Matthew. It's all about blessedness or happiness. After accounting for the location of the sermon (a mountain), his posture (he's sitting), and the nature of his audience (his disciples), Matthew reports Jesus' initial words, full of great promise: "Blessed are the . . ."[1]

Like Stesichorus' "HAPPY THE MAN WHO . . ." papyrus fragment we encountered in Chapter 2, the one that made us wonder *who* or *what*, exactly, the happy man is, the first words of the Sermon on the Mount are words that cause our ears to open wide with burning curiosity. *Who, exactly, is blessed? Who, exactly, is happy?*

Having kicked off the sermon, Jesus goes on for about a minute answering our *who* question, listing those people who are blessed or happy. In this way, he satisfies our curiosity in a way that Stesichorus' tantalizing junkyard scrap is forever unable to. As he does so, Jesus employs the plural of the Greek word *makarios*, the adjectival form of *makar* (blessed, happy). "*Makarioi* are the . . ."

Even at Jesus' time in the first half of the first century AD, *makar* was a word with a long history stretching back some seven hundred years to when Homer's poems were first recorded. Of all happy-related words, Homer liked *makar* best. Of the 38 times it shows up in the *Iliad* and the *Odyssey*, it is mostly used to describe the gods. Homer employs it as an "ornamental epithet." Such words are akin to beautiful jewelry that signifies something positive about the one wearing it. In this case, *makar* points to the being and life of the gods. It indicates strength, immortality, and a satisfying and easy life full of pleasure.[2]

Relative to Homer, Jesus' use of the term is quite different, a point easily confirmed by running down the list of those who are counted blessed or happy by him. They are the poor in spirit; those who mourn; the gentle or humble; those who hunger and thirst for righteousness; the merciful; the pure in heart; the peacemakers; and lastly, those who are persecuted because of righteousness.

Of course, if we were to trace the use of *makar* beginning with Homer, we would see that some Greeks used the term or equivalent terms to describe similar kinds of human beings. The just or righteous; those who are good; those who are pure in soul; those who are gentle. And so on.

The truth is that discovering who is blessed or happy among the Greeks is both an easy and a complicated task. It's easy because all that's involved is querying the authors that have survived from Homer on. It's complicated, however, because they all give different answers. For instance: Who's the happy one, Homer? The gods and those powerful, wealthy men who win glory. Who's happy, Plato? The one who lives well, the virtuous man. And what about you, Sextus Empiricus? The man who suspends all judgment and claims no knowledge, thereby finding tranquility. Not only that, but it's relatively rare to find an author who explicitly states, as Jesus does, precisely who is blessed or happy.

Even so, let's give it a go. Let's see who among the gods and men the Greeks judged happy. As we'll observe, while some are specific individuals, others are categories of men, somewhat akin to Jesus' "poor in spirit" or those who are "humble."

IN THEIR OWN WORDS

Let's begin with the gods. From Homer on, three "ornamental epithets" were regularly used of the gods. Two that were often paired were "immortal and ageless." (Afterall, think of being immortal without being ageless.[3]) The other was "blessed" or "happy." In short, the gods were happy, even if they suffered at times—something the poet Homer recognized and allowed for in his epic poems, but the later philosopher Epicurus refused.

Diogenes Laertius (giving details about Aristotle's successor Theophrastus)
Theophrastus has left behind him a very large number of scrolls . . . ,
which are full of every excellence. They are as follows: . . . *On Happiness*, one book, . . . *On the Happiness of the Gods*, one book.[4]

*In Homer, Hesiod, the Homeric Hymns, and much of Greek literature, as
we've already noted, "blessed" is a common epitaph for the gods. They are*
"the blessed gods . . ."[5]

*Homer (for Homer, "blessed" is often associated with immortality and
with an easy life or a life of pleasure)* The blessed gods, who live forever. . . . The gods, who live at ease. . . . The blessed gods are delighted every day.[6]

Aristophanes (the chorus leader is speaking) "At first, there was no race
of immortals (gods) before Desire (Eros) joined everything together.
Then, as one thing mixed with another, Sky (Ouranos) was born,
and Ocean (Ōkeanos) and Earth (Gē or Gaia), and the whole imperishable race of blessed gods."[7]

*Homer (the Achaean hero Achilles is speaking to the Trojan ruler and fa-
ther of Hector, Priam)* "For while the gods plan sorrow upon sorrow
for wretched mortals, they live without any sorrow or grief. Their
life is a life without care."[8]

Sophocles (unknown speaker) "Rows of happiness—these are the only
furrows tilled in the garden of the gods."[9]

Archytas To God belongs happiness and the happy life.[10]

Aristotle Above all other beings, we assume that the gods are
blessed and happy.[11]

*Epicurus (Epicurus advises his student and follower Menoeceus about the
nature of the god)* First, you should acknowledge that the god is an
indestructible and blessed living being. This is the commonly held

understanding of the god, the common epithet in writing. Accordingly, do not attribute to the god anything that is contrary to his indestructibility or incongruous with his blessed happiness. Instead, think about the god whatever can defend and uphold his blessed happiness and his indestructibility.[12]

Epicurus (Epicurus explains to Pythocles, his student and follower, what the happiness of the god or divine nature logically implies—that "perfect bliss" implies freedom from work) An eclipse of the sun or the moon may be due to the extinction of their light, even as we observe this in our own experience [*with other light sources*]. *Or, Epicurus explains, it may be due to other causes.* Furthermore, let the regularity of their orbits be explained in the same way as certain ordinary incidents within our own experience. Whatever the case, the divine nature must not be given to explain this. Rather, the divine nature must be kept free from the task and in perfect bliss.[13]

The Greeks recognized an assortment of happy human beings for a variety of reasons. They celebrated specific individuals and people groups, as well as a range of happy types, including the man who dies in battle; family with beautiful and wise family members; the poet; the just man; the good man; the simple man. Finally, they acknowledged the reality of happy dogs.

We'll begin with specific individuals and people groups—*Agamemnon, Peleus, Priam, Heracles, Periclymenus, Homer, Hesiod, Priscus, Socrates, Anaxarchus, Zeno of Citium, and the Hyperboreans.*

Homer (Priam, the ruler of Troy, is with beautiful Helen atop the walls of his city; they look down on the field of battle where Agamemnon is standing among other Achaeans) Priam called Helen to him and said, "Dear child, . . . tell me the name of the huge man there—the Achaean man who is noble and great. I've seen men taller by a head, but not one so fine looking and majestic. He looks like one of the chief men."

And Helen, a goddess among women, exchanged these words with him. . . . "I will tell you what you want to know. The hero you ask about is wide-ruling Agamemnon, the son of Atreus, both a good and noble king and a strong and mighty spearman. . . ."

That's what Helen said. And the old man Priam marveled at Agamemnon and said to Helen, "Blessed son of Atreus, offspring of Fate and happy-by-god! I see that many Achaeans are subject to you. When I was in Phrygia I saw many horsemen, the people of Otreus and Mygdon, who were camping upon the banks of the Sangrius. I was their ally with them when the Amazons, peers of men, came up against them. But even they were not so many in number as the Achaeans."[14]

Homer (Achilles is speaking to Priam, the ruler of Troy and father of Hector; while acknowledging their present wretchedness, an unhappiness contrasted with the gods' happiness, he describes the former happiness of his own father, Peleus, and the former happiness of Priam) Achilles addressed Priam with winged words. "Ah, wretched man, you have endured so much evil. Tell me: how did you take it upon yourself to . . . enter the presence of the man who has killed and stripped so many of your brave sons? Your heart must be made of iron! But come now and sit on this seat, and let us allow the pain of mourning in our spirits to rest—because weeping will do us no good. For while the gods plan sorrow upon sorrow for wretched mortals, they live without any sorrow or grief.

"On the floor of Zeus' house there are two jars from which he gives gifts. The one is filled with evil and the other with good. To whomever Zeus, who delights in thunder, mixes and gives out both, that man will meet now with good and now with evil fortune. But for the man who only receives evil gifts—ah, that man will suffer shameful treatment. Evil poverty and hunger will drive him back and forth over the earth, and neither the gods nor men will honor him.

"In a similar way the gods gave glorious gifts to Peleus from the moment of his birth. He ruled over the Myrmidons, surpassing all other men in happiness and wealth, and even though he was a mortal man, they gave him a goddess for his bride. But a god gave evil to him too, for he has no offspring in his halls except for one son who is destined to an unfortunate end. Nor may I take care of him now that he's growing old since I remain encamped here, far from my father at Troy, to be a distress and trouble for you and your children.

"And you too, old man, I have heard that you were once happy. They say that in wealth and number of offspring you surpassed the rulers of all the lands surrounding your own—Lesbos, the seat of Makar, toward the sea; Phrygia, inland; and all those men who dwell upon the boundless Hellespont. But from the day when the Uranian gods unloaded this misery on you, war and slaughter have surrounded your city."[15]

Hesiod (Hesiod is describing the happiness of Peleus, the father of Achilles) Peleus, the son of Aeacus, dear to the immortal gods, came to Phthia, the mother of flocks, bringing great possessions from wide open Iolcus. And all the people envied him in their spirits seeing how he had sacked the well-built city, and how he had accomplished his longed-for marriage. And so, they all spoke these words, "Three, no, four times blessed is the son of Aeacus! Peleus is happy and prosperous! You are blessed because far-seeing Olympian Zeus has given you a wife with many gifts, and the blessed gods have given you your marriage, and in these halls you step up into the holy bed of a daughter of Nereus. The father, the son of Kronos, has truly made you outstanding among the heroes. He's honored you above other men who eat bread and consume the fruit of the earth."[16]

Hesiod (Hesiod is reporting Heracles' happiness) And when he had finished his groan-causing tasks, mighty Heracles, the brave and strong son of beautiful-ankled Alcmene, made Hebe his highly regarded wife on snowclad Olympus—she who is the child of great Zeus and golden-sandaled Hera. He is happy! Having accomplished his great work, he dwells among the immortal gods, unharmed and ageless all his days.[17]

Scholiast on Apollonius of Rhodes and Hesiod (the following passage has to do with what the poet Hesiod declares about Periclymenus, the son of Neleus and grandson of Poseidon) But Hesiod says that Periclymenus changed himself into one of his usual forms. . . . He says the following: "Happy is high-minded Periclymenus! The Earth-shaker Poseidon furnished him with all sorts of gifts. Among birds, he would appear as an eagle. At another time he would become an ant—a wonder to see. And then a shimmering swarm of bees. And then a cold-hearted, dread serpent. And he possessed all sorts of gifts that cannot be named."[18]

Pseudo-Plutarch (the author gives Homer as both a happy and an unhappy man) But another oracular response of the god goes something like this: "Happy and unhappy one!—for you were born to both happiness and unhappiness."[19]

The Contest of Homer and Hesiod (the narrator is reporting what happened after the great contest between Homer and Hesiod, the contest Hesiod won thanks to his poetry centered on peace and farming) After the assembly broke up, Hesiod sailed across to Delphi to consult the oracle. . . . They say that as he was approaching the dwelling of the god [Apollo], the prophetess was inspired and said, "Happy is this man who serves my house!—Hesiod, the man honored by the immortal Muses! His glory will surely spread as far as the shining of the dawn!"[20]

Anonymous (the following is a funerary epigram for Priscus, a soldier and farmer) When the great battle was over and he had returned to the land of his fathers, he shone as a beacon to all men—above all to his own parents. Then he turned his mind to farming his father's land. And in doing everything, he directed his laborers according to Hesiod's advice for farmers, allowing them to reap much fruit. And he had everything good and lived comfortably for a long time, satisfied with happiness and wealth until his final rest.[21]

Herodotus (Croesus, the ruler of Lydia, is speaking with the wise man Solon of Athens, who offers him a few surprising examples of happy men—Tellus of Athens, and Cleobis and Biton of Argos) Croesus found the opportunity to say, "My Athenian guest, we have heard many accounts of your wisdom and your wanderings—how as one who loves wisdom, you have traveled much of the world for the sake of seeing it. Now, then, I desire to ask you who is the happiest man you have seen."

Croesus made the inquiry expecting that he himself would be judged the happiest man. Rather than flattering the man, though, Solon proclaimed the truth. "O King, it is Tellus of Athens." Croesus was amazed at what he had said and replied sharply, "Why do you judge Tellus the happiest man?"

Solon said, "Tellus was from a well-off city. And his children were noble and good. And he saw children born to them all, and all these children survived. His life was one of abundance by our standards, and his death was most glorious. When the Athenians were fighting their neighbors at Eleusis, Tellus came to help, routed the enemy, and died very nobly. Then the Athenians buried him at public expense on the spot where he fell, and they honored him greatly."

Hearing Solon's judgment, Croesus was upset. Still, he agreed to hear who, in Solon's view, was second happiest, fully expecting the answer to be Croesus himself. But it wasn't. Instead, it was two obscure youths from Argos, Cleobis and Biton, both "strong in body" and "victorious athletes," who were not rich but died well after serving their mother by pulling her for five miles from their farm to the Temple of Hera in Argos—which is to say they fell asleep in death after having done something glorious. How do we know this was the best end? Herodotus tells us their mother stood before Hera and asked "the goddess to give them whatever is best for a man to chance upon." After sacrificing and feasting, this death was "the best end of life." Later, "the Argives made images of them in stone, statues of them who had become the best of men, and dedicated the statues at Delphi." And so, we're told, "Solon gave the second place in happiness to these two."[22]

Xenophon (the historian depicts a happy Socrates) All who knew what kind of man Socrates was, and all who care for virtue, all these men continue even now to miss Socrates most of all as the most helpful man in the pursuit of virtue. As for me, I have described him as he was. He was so pious that he did nothing without a sign from the gods. He was so just that he did no harm, however small, to any man. Instead, he conferred the greatest benefits on all who dealt with him. He was so self-controlled that he never chose the more pleasant thing or way over the better thing or way. He was so wise that he never erred in judging between what was better and what was worse. He did not even have to ask others about these, but he relied on himself for his knowledge of them. He was skillful in explaining and defining such things—and in testing others, and in convincing them of error, and in urging them on toward virtue and noble goodness. For all these points, then, he seemed to me the best and happiest man.[23]

Diogenes Laertius (Diogenes reports on the early skeptic philosopher Anaxarchus) Anaxarchus was called *Eudaimonikos* or "Happy Man" on account of his freedom from passion and contentment in life.[24]

Antigonus of Macedonia (Antigonus declares the founder of Stoicism Zeno of Citium's happiness in a letter) King Antigonus to Zeno the philosopher, greeting. I consider myself superior to you in glory and wealth. But in reason and education, and in the perfect happiness you have attained, I acknowledge that I am far behind you.[25]

Pindar (the poet describes the blessed happiness of the Hyperboreans) Neither by ship nor on foot will you find the wondrous path to the land and assembly of the Hyperboreans. Perseus, the leader of men, once entered their houses and feasted with them when they were sacrificing glorious hecatombs of donkeys to the god. Apollo rejoices most in their praise and worship, and he laughs when he sees the animal's rather erect arrogance. Nor is the Muse a stranger to their customs. But everywhere the young girls move this way and that in the dance to the loud cries of the lyre and pipes. Binding golden laurel in their hair, they joyfully feast. Neither sickness nor old age abuse that hallowed people, nor do they toil or fight, and so Nemesis leaves them alone, unharmed. Led on by Athena, Perseus, the son of Danae, once went to the land of these blessed men, the Hyperboreans.[26]

Next, we move on to happy types. First up is the happy man who dies in battle, the man who has happily received his share of glory and fame.

Homer (Odysseus is speaking in recognition of his own wretchedness compared with the blessedness or happiness of the man who dies in battle) "Ah me! I am a wretched man! What will happen to me now? I fear that the goddess spoke the infallible truth when she said that I would suffer my fill of pain upon the sea before I came to my homeland. Now it's happening! Look at the many clouds Zeus has scattered in the wide sky. And see him stir the sea. And feel the winds that blast me now. Now I am utterly destroyed! My salvation is gone! Three times—no, four times blessed—were those Danaans who died upon the wide plain of Troy to benefit the sons of Atreus. I wish that I had died and met my allotted destiny on that day when a multitude of Trojans hurled bronze-tipped spears at me as we fought over the body of Achilles, the son of Peleus. Then I would have received my share of funeral gifts and honors, and the Achaeans would have broadcast my fame and glory. But now it is my portion to be conquered by a pathetic death."[27]

Simonides of Ceos Of those men who died at Thermopylae—glorious is the good fortune, and beautiful the destiny![28]

For the ancient Greeks, family was central to a good and happy life. Since one's identity was largely tied up with one's family, the excellence of an individual family member amounted to the excellence of everyone in the whole family.

Homer (Priam is speaking to the god Hermes, who is disguised as a royal young man) "You are so wonderful in bodily form and beauty and wise at heart. Blessed are the parents from whom you have sprung!"[29]

Homer (Odysseus is speaking to princess Nausicaa, the daughter of Alcinous and Arete) "I take your knees, O queen. Are you a goddess or are you a mortal? If you are a goddess, one of the gods who possess the wide sky above, then I say that you are most like Artemis, the daughter of mighty Zeus, in your looks, form, and stature. But if you are someone among mortals who live on the earth, then three times blessed are your father and queen mother, and three times blessed are your brothers, too. Surely their spirits forever grow warm with happy thoughts because of you, seeing such a beautiful flower entering the dance. But above all others, that one is blessed in his heart who prevails with wedding gifts and leads you home. For with my own eyes, I've never seen a mortal such as you are— whether a man or a woman. Awe holds me as I look at you!"[30]

Just as Homer does at the end of the last selection ("Above all others, that one is blessed in his heart who prevails with wedding gifts and leads you— Nausicaa—home"), Sappho of Lesbos recognizes happiness in the one who marries well.

Sappho of Lesbos Happy suitor! The wedding has happened just as you wanted. You have the girl you won. . . . [Her] form is full of grace, [her] eyes gentle and kind. [Her] delightful face is lit up with desire. Aphrodite has honored you above others.[31]

Then there is the poet. As the bringer of great delight and diversion, the Greeks believed the poet is happy.

Hesiod Happy is the man whom the Muses love! Sweet speech flows from that man's mouth. Even when some man is bearing sorrow, even when it is some brand-new care in his spirit that dries out his heart with weeping, even so, when the poet-singer, the servant of the Muses, sings about the glorious deeds of men from long ago and about the blessed gods who hold Olympus, that man suddenly forgets his concerns and does not remember his troubles. Quickly do the goddesses' song-gifts divert his mind![32]

Aristides (Aristides is recalling the happiness of Sappho, the celebrated poetess of the island of Lesbos) I imagine you too have heard Sappho bragging to some of those women thought to be happy, saying that the Muses had made her happy and enviable, and that when she dies, she will not be forgotten.[33]

Though a few Greeks, such as the sophist Thrasymachus, exalted the unjust man as the happy man, most believed the ideal and happy man was the just man. Similarly, the good man was also counted happy.

Hesiod Since justice is not among them, fish and wild beasts and large flying birds eat one another. But Zeus gave human beings Justice, which is by far the best thing that has come to be. If someone who knows what is just is willing to declare it in the assembly, then far-seeing Zeus gives him the happiness of wealth. But the man who intentionally lies in his testimony, swearing a false oath, he is incurably hurt in the very act of hindering Justice. In times to come, that man's family will be left in the dark, obscure, while the family of the man who swears well and truly will be better off.[34]

Bacchylides (Menelaus is speaking) "Trojans dear to Ares—Zeus ruling on high, who clearly sees all things, is not the cause of all the pains that distress mortals! Rather all men may come to know straight-judging Justice, the goddess who serves holy Eunomia (Good Order) and wise Themis! Happy are they whose sons take Justice home to live with them! Ah, but that other one, Hubris— shameless arrogance, insolence, and wanton violence! . . . It was Hubris who destroyed those arrogant sons of Earth, the Giants."[35]

Plato (Socrates is conversing with Thrasymachus, who earlier argued that "the life of the unjust man is better than the life of the just man," and that injustice is therefore more profitable and happy-making) Socrates: "Did we not agree that the overall excellence or virtue of the soul is justice? And that its vice is injustice?"

Thrasymachus: "That's what we agreed."

"Therefore, the just soul and the just man will live his life well, whereas the unjust man will live his life in an unfortunate manner."

"So it appears," Thrasymachus said, "according to your argument."

"But there's more. He who lives well is blessed and happy. By contrast, he who does not is the opposite."

"Of course."

"The just man, then, is happy, whereas the unjust man is wretched."

"Let it be so," Thrasymachus said.

"But surely it is not profitable to be wretched. No, that requires happiness."

"Of course."

"Never, then, O blessed Thrasymachus, is injustice more profitable than justice."[36]

Plato (Socrates is speaking to Cebes and Simmias on the final day of his life) "When a man dies . . . the soul, the invisible part of him, goes to another place that is, like itself, high-minded, pure, and unseen, to the realm of . . . the good and wise god. . . . The soul goes into that which is like itself, into the unseen, the divine, the immortal, and the wise. The soul is happy there, delivered from its wandering and error, and from its follies and fears, and from its wild, uncultivated desires, and from other evils and misfortunes typical of human beings. And as the initiated say, the soul lives on with the gods, following that which is true through the time that remains."[37]

Aristotle (he is praising Plato) He was the first among mortals to visibly show by his own personal life and the investigations of his dialogues how the good man is also a happy man.[38]

As we'll see in Part 2, many Greek philosophers believed that the key to happiness is a simple, frugal life. What follows is just one example. Keep in mind, however, that there are many others.

Epictetus Such is the Cynic *philosopher* who is honored by Zeus with the scepter and the diadem. He says, "So that you may see, O men, that you seek happiness and tranquility not where it is, but where it is not—look at me! God has sent me to you as an example—I who have neither property nor house, wife nor children. I do not even have a bed or a tunic or household furniture. And yet see how healthy I am!"[39]

Finally, the Greeks acknowledged the possibility of happy animals—more specifically, happy dogs. (Sorry to those of you who love cats.) Homer was the first to imply such a dog in reference to Odysseus' dog, Argos, who had, according to the swineherd Eumaeus, once been a fast and strong, well-cared for dog, happy while hunting. By contrast, Homer notes that now Argos is "miserable" and suffering—though when he sees Odysseus for the first time in twenty years, he's happy enough to "wag his tail."[40]

Epictetus You count a dog happy who is engaged in the chase or laboring hard—when you see him sweating, in pain and panting violently after running.[41]

▪   ▪   ▪

Where have we been so far in Part 1? What have we found out about what the ancient Greeks thought and said about happiness?

First, we learned that most Greeks viewed happiness as the end or goal of life. However it was understood, happiness was judged the target we humans shoot for, the highest good.

Next, we discovered a variety of early Greek formulas for happiness. Primed by Stesichorus' fragment, "HAPPY THE MAN WHO . . . ," we observed that different Greeks equated happiness with just as many happy-making things (the *what* of happiness). Broadly speaking, though, there was the notion that happiness is simply the satisfaction of desire for whatever we want (the further *what* of happiness).

The problem? Even though there are many ways to get happiness or what we want, from the gods and Fate to the intelligence and excellence of human activity (the *how* of happiness), we human beings are, in fact, often not satisfied—in a general sense, anyway. Or bad things happen. Therefore, as the poet Bacchylides observed, it is hard for us humans to be "completely happy."

Nevertheless, we see in Greek literature that there are happy times and happy places (the *where* of happiness), and so, there live those beings, whether divine, human, or canine, who are happy (the *who* of happiness) (what we've been exploring in this chapter).

With that, with a basic understanding of the *what, how, where,* and *who* of happiness, we move on to ancient Greek philosophers and, as we'll see, a far more systematic exploration and exposition of what happiness is—what its nature is, who is happy, and how a person becomes happy. See you in Part 2.

NOTES

[1] For the "Beatitudes" portion of the Sermon on the Mount, see Matthew 5.1-12. Though "blessed" strikes the right connotation given the context, the Greek of Matthew 5.3 ff., "*Makarioi hoi . . .*" (from the adjective, *makarios*: blessed, happy, prosperous), could just as well be translated, "Happy are the . . ."

[2] For a discussion of *makar* among the gods, see Tim J. Young, *A Hero's Wish: What Homer Believed about Happiness and the Good Life.* For an explanation of the "ornamental epithet" (*epitheta ornantia*), see M.L. West, *Indo-European Poetry and Myth* (Oxford: Oxford University Press, 2007), 83-85.

[3] Take, for example, the mortal man Tithonus. When his divine, immortal and ageless lover Eos (Dawn) asked Zeus to make him immortal, she forgot to ask him for agelessness. Thus, even though Tithonus lived on forever, he grew older with every disadvantage of old age.

[4] Diogenes Laertius, *Lives* 5.42, 43, 49. Unfortunately, neither of these works remain.

[5] See, for example, Homer, *Iliad* 1.339, 4.127, 8.550, 14.143; Homer, *Odyssey* 4.755, 8.281, 9.276, 9.521, 12.61, 14.83, 18.134; Hesiod, *Theogony* 101, 881; Hesiod, *Works and Days* 120, 139; *Homeric Hymn* 2.346, 4.71, 4.144, 4.251, 4.372, 5.35, 19.27.

[6] See, for example, Homer, *Iliad* 24.99 and Homer, *Odyssey* 5.7 (for the gods "who live forever"); *Iliad* 6.138 and *Odyssey* 4.805 (for the gods "who live at ease"); *Odyssey* 6.46 (for the gods who "are delighted every day"). For an extended discussion of the relationship between blessedness, on the one hand, and immortality and a life of ease or pleasure, on the other, see Tim J. Young, *A Hero's Wish: What Homer Believed about Happiness and the Good Life.*

[7] Aristophanes, *Birds* 700-703. "Mixed" can have both sexual and non-sexual connotations. For instance, one army can mix in battle with another, or a man can mix in love with a woman.

[8] Homer, *Iliad* 24.525-526.

[9] Sophocles, *Ion*, fragment from Johannes Stobaeus, *Anthology* 4.39.10. For the text (fragment 320), see Hugh Lloyed-Jones, *Sophocles: Fragments* (Cambridge: Harvard University Press, 1996), 178-179.

[10] Archytas fragments, *The Pythagorean Sourcebook and Library*, 187.

[11] Aristotle, *Nicomachean Ethics* 10.8.7 (1178b).

[12] Epicurus, *Letter to Menoeceus*, in Diogenes Laertius, *Lives* 10.123. "The commonly held understanding of the god, the common epithet in writing" expressed

from Homer on is the fact that the gods are immortal and ageless (that is, inde-structible) and happy or blessed.

[13] Ibid., 10.96-97.

[14] Homer, *Iliad* 3.161-190 (parts).

[15] Ibid., 24.517-548.

[16] Hesiod (or Pseudo-Hesiod), *Catalogue of Women* fragment 58. For the Greek text (Strasburg Greek Papyri 55), see H.G. Evelyn-White, *Hesiod, the Homeric Hymns, and Homerica* (Cambridge: Harvard University Press, 1914), 186-187.

[17] Hesiod, *Theogony* 950-955.

[18] Scholiast on Apollonius Rhodius and Hesiod (or Pseudo-Hesiod), *Catalogue of Women*. For the Greek text (Scholiast on Apollonius Rhodius, Arg. i. 156), see H.G. Evelyn-White, *Hesiod, the Homeric Hymns, and Homerica*, 160-161.

[19] Pseudo-Plutarch, *On Homer* 4.

[20] *The Contest of Homer and Hesiod* 322. For the text, see H.G. Evelyn-White, *Hesiod, the Homeric Hymns, and Homerica*, 586-587.

[21] *Titulus funerarius Prisci* (Testimony 51). For the Greek text, see Glenn W. Most, *Hesiod: Theogony, Works and Days, Testimonia* (Cambridge: Harvard University Press, 2006), 196.

[22] Herodotus, *Histories* 1.30-32.

[23] Xenophon, *Memorabilia* 4.8.11.

[24] Diogenes Laertius, *Lives* 9.60.

[25] Ibid., 7.7.

[26] Pindar, *Pythian* 10.29-46.

[27] Homer, *Odyssey* 5.299-312.

[28] Simonides of Ceos, fragment 531, in Diodorus Siculus, *World History* 11.11.6.

[29] Homer, *Iliad* 24.376-377.

[30] Homer, *Odyssey* 6.149-161. Odysseus calls Nausicaa "queen" (*anassa*) not be-cause she is in fact a human queen (rather, that is her mother, Arete) but be-cause he is unsure whether or not she is a human or a goddess. To be safe, then, he says, "O queen."

[31] Sappho of Lesbos, fragment 112.

[32] Hesiod, *Theogony* 96-103, part of which is repeated in *Homeric Hymn 25 to the Muses and Apollo* 4-5.

[33] Aristides, *Orations* 28.51 (ii 158 Keil).

[34] Hesiod, *Works and Days* 277-285. Note the implied tie of the happiness of the family with the man who is just and thus happy: "the family of the man who swears well and truly will be better off."

[35] Bacchylides *Dithyramb* 15, "The Request for the Return of Helen," 50-63.

[36] Plato, *Republic* 1.353e-354a.

[37] Plato, *Phaedo* 80c-81a.

[38] *Encomium* by Aristotle preserved in Olympiodorus on Plato, *Gorgias*.

[39] Epictetus, *Discourses* 4.8.30-31. In another discourse, Epictetus states it is the "true Cynic['s]" "responsibility" to appear on the "tragic stage" of our world,

and to, "like Socrates say, 'Where are you hurrying? What are you doing, you miserable men? Like blind people you are wandering up and down. You are going by another road and have left the true road. You search for prosperity and happiness where they are not. . . . Why do you seek it outside yourself? In the body?" In another discourse, Epictetus asks, "And how is it possible that a man who has nothing—who is naked, houseless, and without a hearth, who is squalid, without a slave or a city—how can such a man live a life that flows well?"—that is, a life that is happy. "Behold, God has sent you a man to show you that it is possible: 'Look at me,' he says, 'I who am without a city, without a house, without possessions, without a slave. I sleep on the ground. I have no wife, no children . . . ; rather, I have only the earth and the heavens, and one poor cloak. And what do I want? Am I not without pain and sorrow? Without fear? Am I not free?" (*Discourses* 3.22.26-27, 45-48).

[40] For Argos the dog, see Homer, *Odyssey* 17.291-335.

[41] Epictetus, *Discourses* 4.1.124-125. Epictetus' description of the happy dog is similar to Eumaeus' description of Argos.

PART 2

Thinking about Happiness—the Philosophers

8

ISOCRATES

<blockquote>

"Fair Isocrates, . . . his speeches are better than Lysias' speeches, and he possesses a nobler character. . . . A more divine impulse will lead him to greater things. I say this because there is a natural love of wisdom in his mind."

—Socrates (in Plato's *Phaedrus*)

</blockquote>

ISOCRATES (436-338 BC) WAS AN orator, philosopher, and teacher from Athens. He had a school in Chios that specialized in rhetoric, and later a school in Athens devoted to philosophy and the education of the whole person—the development of the mind, character, and judgment. On this, more in a moment. Thanks to shyness and a certain weakness of voice, Isocrates wrote, rather than presented, most of the speeches or discourses that have come down to us. We also have nine of his letters, which, scholars suggest, act as discourses.

As for happiness, and specifically *eudaimonia*, Isocrates seems to have had a rather conventional view—this, at least, where happiness shows up in his speeches and letters to others. There, happiness is equated with prosperity or good fortune; it is wealth, honor, reputation, and loyal friends; it is, in the case of Egypt, excellent land for farming and, therefore, an abundance and variety of agricultural products—that is, wealth.[1]

Despite his apparent conventionalism, Isocrates possibly hints at a true—or truer—kind happiness in at least one speech. There, he contends that "happiness is not merely the ability to do whatever you want." Rather, it involves restraint since true "freedom is not the same as licentiousness." Relative to context, Isocrates declares these few points about happiness in relation to the "most advantageous" kind of political constitution, which is to say "the rule of the people" (*dēmokratia*)—a constitution, he says, that consults "the rule of the best."[2] Happiness, then, according to Isocrates, is a kind of restraint or restriction that looks to what is best.

This latter view of happiness, in comparison with the more conventional view he seems to endorse in his speeches and letters, lines up with the counsel he offers about how to live a good or worthwhile life. It was this counsel, or something like it, that he presented in the teachings of his school that focused on the whole person (as mentioned above).

In what follows, we'll peruse some of this counsel. Beyond this, we'll glance at a warning Isocrates offers relative to those teachers who claim to be able to teach a sure way to happiness.[3]

IN THEIR OWN WORDS

We begin, as promised, with Isocrates' counsel. In this case, it is his advice to Demonicus, the son of Hipponicus, who was Isocrates' friend. The imperative is to be excellent or virtuous—for virtue, Isocrates declares, is "that possession which is most holy and secure." While beauty, riches, bodily strength, and a noble birth may or may not be advantageous, virtue is always helpful.

I intend to counsel you on the things which young men should reach out for and grasp and on what actions they should keep away from, as well as what kind of men they should associate with and how they should manage their own lives. For only those who have passed over this road in life have been able truly to reach virtue—that possession which is most holy and secure.

For beauty is spent by time or wasted away by disease. Riches are better at serving vice than the noble and good man. They make it possible to live a lazy life, summoning young men to pleasure. Bodily strength accompanied with practical wisdom is, indeed, an advantage, but without this ally it harms those who possess it more than it helps. And while it adorns the bodies of those who exercise, bodily strength gets in the way of the care of the soul.

But virtue, when it authentically increases in our thoughts and purposes, is the one possession that remains with us in old age. It is better than riches and more useful than a noble birth. It makes possible that which is for others impossible. It endures with confidence that which is fearful to most people. It holds that being sluggish is blameworthy, and that engaging in hard work is praiseworthy.[4]

Isocrates goes on to offer many "noble maxims" or "serious and excellent sayings" to Demonicus. Included are the following.[5]

Show devotion to the gods.

Conduct yourself toward your parents as you would have your children conduct themselves toward you.

Train your body with exercises that lead not to bodily strength but to health.

Consider that no adornment is more appropriate for you than a sense of shame, justice, and moderation. For as all men believe, the character of the young is ruled by these virtues.

Fear the gods, honor your parents, respect your friends, obey the laws.

Hunt after pleasures that enjoy a good reputation. For enjoyment with honor is the best thing—but without it, enjoyment is absolutely worthless.

Guard yourself against accusations—even if they are false.

If you love learning, then you will learn much.

Be affable in your manner and courteous in the way you speak.

Train yourself in self-imposed toils and hardships so that you may be able to endure those that are contrary to your choosing.

Practice self-control in all the things by which it is shameful for the soul to be controlled—namely, in those things related to gain, impulse, pleasure, and pain.

Faithfully guard the secret that is given to you.

Make no man your friend before looking into how he has used his former friends.

Be slow to give your friendship, but when you have given it, strive to make it long-lasting.

You will best serve your friends if you do not wait for them to ask for your assistance but willingly go at the crucial moment of need to offer them your help.

In matters of clothing, be a man who loves beauty but not one who puts all his faith in looking good.

Do not be fond of the excessive acquisition of goods but enjoy your possessions with measure.

Be satisfied with present circumstances—still, seek improvement.

Do well to good men.

Hate flatterers as you would deceivers.

Be affable in your relations with those who approach you—never haughty.

Beware of drinking parties. But if there is a time you must be present, then stand up from your seat and depart before you get drunk.

Cultivate the thoughts of an immortal by being great in soul, but of a mortal by enjoying in due measure your possessions.

Consider education and culture to be a good far superior to the lack of education and culture.

Praise is the foundation of friendship, just as blame is that of enmity.

In your deliberations, let the past be a pattern for the future, for the unknown may be discerned by reference to the known.

Be slow in deliberation but quick to carry out your resolutions.

The best thing we have in ourselves is good judgment.

Whenever you consult someone about your own affairs, first observe how he has managed his own.

When you are placed in authority, do not employ any base or unworthy person in your administration.

Neither stand by a base deed nor plead for a base man in court.

Prefer honest poverty to unjust riches; justice is better than wealth.

Give careful consideration to all that concerns your life. But above all, exercise yourself in practical wisdom. For the greatest thing in the smallest place is a good mind in a human body.[6]

When you are about to say anything, always first consider it in your mind—for with many the tongue outruns the understanding. Let there be only two occasions when you speak: one, when the subject is one that you know clearly and well, and two, when the subject is one about which you are compelled to speak. Speech on these occasions alone is better than silence. At all other times it is better to be silent than to speak.

Consider that nothing in human life is certain or secure. That way you will neither feel too joyous when there is good luck nor too sad when luck turns bad.

Finally, we end with Isocrates' warning regarding those who claim to be able to teach a sure way to happiness.

If everyone involved in education were willing to speak the truth rather than make promises greater than they could fulfill, then people wouldn't say so many bad things about educators. . . .

I think it is clear to all that foreknowledge about what is destined to happen is not something we humans possess by nature. No, we are so far removed from this practical wisdom that Homer, who has been granted the greatest reputation for wisdom, has even made it so that the gods themselves deliberate about what is destined to happen. It's not that Homer knew their minds, but he wanted to point out that such knowledge is impossible for human beings.

And yet these educators[7] have gone so far in their daring that they attempt to persuade the young that, if they will only follow them, the young will know what must be done in life, and through this knowledge they will become happy.

There's more. Although they set themselves up as teachers and masters of such amazing goods, they are not ashamed of asking three or four *minae* for them. But if they sold anything else for so tiny a fraction of its actual worth, no one would deny their senseless folly. Even so, while they hardly value the whole of virtue and happiness, they act as if they are full of good sense and thus they are worthy to teach the rest of us. Then, although they say they have no need for money, disparaging wealth as nothing but "silver and gold coins," they stretch their hands out for a tiny profit, promising to make their students all but immortal! . . .

When, therefore, individuals add all the following observations together, . . . they have good reason to look down on such studies, regarding them as idle talk and logic chopping rather than true care of the soul. Which observations? When, for instance, they notice that these so-called "teachers of wisdom" and "transmitters of happiness" themselves lack so much and demand so little of their students. Or they look out for logical contradictions while overlooking inconsistencies in behavior. Or they pretend to know about what is destined to happen, but they're unable to say anything significant—let alone counsel a student—regarding what's going on right now.

NOTES

[1] Isocrates likely presents a conventional view not only because he himself adhered to such a view (in broad outlines, anyway) but also in order to persuade his audience. For examples of his mention of happiness (*eudaimonia*), see *To Demonicus* 1.48-52; *To Nicocles* 2.39; *Nicocles or the Cyprians* 3.32; *Panegyricus* 4.20, 75-77, 187; *To Philip* 5.67-71; *Busiris* 11.12-14; *Panathenaicus* 12.106, 126-129, 228, 254, 260; *Antidosis* 15.307; *Letter To Philip* 2.3, 22-24.

[2] See *Panathenaicus* 12.130-131.

[3] It is important to note that Isocrates counted himself a philosopher—though many have denied him this title. Regardless, unlike the other philosophers or teachers in Part 2, we will not summarize Isocrates' view of happiness since we've already summarized what remains of his teaching, which is, anyway, so little.

[4] Isocrates, *To Demonicus* 1.5-7.

[5] The maxims are found in ibid., 1.13-43. They have been offered here in the order they appear in the text. That said, we have not included all the maxims. The reader should be aware that, even though we have not employed ellipses, some text is missing.

[6] Compare the Roman satirist Juvenal's later (first or second century AD) recommendation that Romans ought to pray for "a sound mind in a sound body" (*mens sana in corpore sano*) rather than other desiderata (see *Satire* 10.356 ff.).

[7] "These educators" are not *all* educators, and certainly they are not educators in the sense that Isocrates is an educator. They are the sophists. Who were the sophists? Early on, the term "sophist" signified a wise man, someone who was knowledgeable and clever about reality and human life. For example, the seven wise men of Greece were labeled sophists. Other sophists were simply teachers for pay—experts in things like public speaking, politics, and how to live a successful life. Later, however, sophists acquired a negative reputation (among some) for being argumentative about things simply for the sake of winning an argument. Or worse, they argued to deceive. And some taught a kind of excellence or success devoid of morality. And, as Isocrates says, some claimed to have a kind of knowledge or expertise that they could not possibly actually possess.

PLATO
& SOCRATES

"If Phoebus Apollo had not sent Plato to the Greeks, then how would they have been healed by learning? But he did send him. And just as Apollo's son Asclepius is a healer of the body, so Plato is a healer of the immortal soul."
—Diogenes Laertius, *Lives and Opinions of Eminent Philosophers*

PLATO (c. 428/7-347[1] BC) WAS DREAMER. That stated, we must acknowledge that he was not only a man with his thoughts in the sky —in the realm of Being itself, of the Ideas, of absolute things like Beauty itself or the Good. No, he was also a man of action.

In fact, beginning when he was about forty years old, Plato ventured three times across the sea from Athens in Attica to Syracuse in Sicily in order to spread the benefits of philosophy and try to implement a good—if not ideal—form of government. The goal was a regime of laws in place of the whims of men, one that aimed at true liberty. The problem? To realize his plan, he had to work with a series of tyrants—with Dionysus I of Syracuse; his brother-in-law, Dion; and Dionysus' out-of-control son, Dionysus II.

Here are the highlights of Plato's effort according to one version of the story that has come down to us. When Plato criticized tyranny as a form of government, declaring that "the self-interest of the ruler alone is not the most important thing," Dionysus angrily told Plato that he was going on "like a foolish old man." In response, Plato suggested that Dionysus himself was going on "like a tyrant." This according to the ancient biographer Diogenes Laertius. Unsurprisingly, the tyrant was not at all pleased. Instead, furious with the philosopher, he threatened him with death, and when he was finally talked down from murdering Plato, he sold him into slavery.[2]

Whether the story is true or not, a few facts remain. One, dealing with tyrants is a dangerous business. Two, Plato nevertheless believed it was his obligation to help when and where possible. This was true not only for the politics of governing a city but also for the business of living well and happily.

We observe the latter in Plato's seventh letter, where he boldly announces that he is not a fan of the typical Syracusan way of life, the so-called "happy life," one dedicated to the pursuit of pleasure, characterized by daily feasts and nightly sexual romps.[3] In the *Republic*, Plato designates this lifestyle the life of the majority, one in which they "graze and copulate" like cattle.[4] It is a way of life, he asserts, that will inevitably lead to an unending succession of bad forms of government and to a similar succession of unhealthy kinds of soul. The last will end with a tyrannical soul, one in which the ever-shifting whims of desire oppress the ruled—that is, oneself.

Instead of letting matters get out of hand in this way, Plato recommends a monarchical soul, one in which reason rules through practical wisdom, the desires justly obey, and, consequently, the whole of life is contentedly harmonious since it is ordered toward what is good. This kind of soul, says Plato, is happy. As he expresses the point in his seventh letter, no "man can ever become happy unless he spends his life allied with practical wisdom and justice."[5]

It's hard to know if Plato himself was happy. An Athenian by birth who was born when the Peloponnesian War between Sparta and Athens was raging in the latter third of the fifth century BC, and related by his mother to the great Athenian law reformer and statesman Solon, Plato's first choice in life had been to engage in politics, that most Athenian of sports. In the end, however, he pursued the life of philosophy because *post bellum* Athenian politics left him feeling dizzy, madly shifting one way and then another with revolutionary change and violence. Moreover, he witnessed the men of Athens put Socrates to death in 399 BC, the man he considered "the most just of men then alive."[6]

Fortunately, Plato didn't let Socrates die. Rather, he took the man who taught him how to ask questions and pursue a line of thought to its very end, and he wrote him in to most of his dialogues as the main character. Therein, we encounter Socrates fully alive again, with the "power to charm the souls of men."[7] Therein, he's conversing with a whole cast of other well-drawn characters, and, indeed, he's dialoguing with us, as we read along and participate in the discussion.

The fact that Plato included Socrates as the main character in most of his dialogues raises the so-called "Socratic problem." When Socrates speaks, it is hard to know whether Plato is giving Socrates' position or his own. It's a question that scholars have long debated and perhaps one that is too complex for a short introduction. Presently, let's just note the problem and agree to return to it when we meet up with Xenophon's presentation of Socrates in the next chapter. For now, we'll let "Plato" stand for both Plato and Socrates, fully acknowledging the fact that we really don't know who thought and said what.[8]

A final point before we get to Plato himself. Unless otherwise noted, all of the following selections come from Plato.

IN THEIR OWN WORDS

We'll begin with Plato's basic formula for happiness, that happiness equals living and doing well and nobly.[9]

Socrates: He who lives well is blessed and happy. It's the opposite for the man who does not.[10]

Socrates: In whatever he does, the good man does well and nobly. And he who does well is blessed and happy.[11]

But what does it mean to live and do well and nobly? It is to be good, to be virtuous. Happiness, then, comes about by means of virtue, which is the same as being good and thus living and doing well.

Aristotle (praising Plato) He was the first among mortals to visibly show by his own personal life and the investigations of his dialogues how the good man is also a happy man.[12]

Diogenes Laertius Plato held that the goal of life is to become godlike, and that virtue is sufficient in itself for happiness.[13]

The Athenian: One kind of life is sweeter than the other . . . In short, in comparison with a vicious life, the virtuous life in body and soul is not only more pleasant, but it also rises above the other in terms of beauty, correctness, excellence, and good reputation. Consequently, if a man lives with virtue, he will live with complete happiness.[14]

Socrates: Will the soul be able to perform its own function well if it is lacking its own virtue? Or will it be unable?

    Thrasymachus: Unable.

    Socrates: Necessarily, then, a bad soul rules and manages things badly, and a good soul does everything well?

    Thrasymachus: Necessarily. . . .

    Socrates: But he who lives well is blessed and happy.[15]

If happiness comes about by means of virtue, then what is virtue?[16]

Socrates: In the first place, virtue signifies ease of motion, and secondly, that the flow of the good soul is always unimpeded.[17]

Socrates: It appears, then, that virtue is a kind of health and beauty and good condition of the soul.[18]

Socrates: Virtue is the means by which a thing performs its function well.[19]

If, among other descriptives ("ease of motion," "unimpeded . . . flow of the good soul," "health and beauty and good condition") virtue is "the means by which a thing performs its function well," then what is a thing's function or work? With the first statement that follows, Socrates offers a simple definition of "the function of a thing." The second selection explains "function" with several examples, ending with the prior simple definition.

Socrates: The function of a thing is that which it alone can do, or what it does better, than anything else.[20]

Socrates: Would you say that a horse has a specific function or work?

Thrasymachus: Sure.

Socrates: Would you be willing to define the function or work of a horse—or of anything else for that matter—to be that which one can do only with it or best with it?

Thrasymachus: I don't understand.

Socrates: Well, let me express it this way. Apart from the eyes, is there anything else by which you can see?

Thrasymachus: Of course not.

Socrates: Again, can you hear with anything other than the ears?

Thrasymachus: There's no other way.

Socrates: Isn't it right, then, to say that seeing is the function of the eyes and hearing the function of the ears?

Thrasymachus: Yes, by all means.

Socrates: Once more, you could use a dagger, a sword, a butcher knife, and many other instruments to trim vine branches. . . . But I imagine that nothing will work or perform as well in comparison with a pruning knife.

Thrasymachus: True.

Socrates: Must we not assume, then, that pruning is the function of a pruning knife?

Thrasymachus: We must.

Socrates: I imagine you will now better understand that the function of a thing is that which it alone can do, or what it does better, than anything else.[21]

Since for Plato happiness corresponds to virtue, and virtue corresponds to a thing's function as "the means by which a thing performs its function well," and because a thing's function corresponds to its nature (a point Plato makes in the Timaeus *and the* Cratylus[22]*), then we must investigate what a human being is, that is, what human nature is. We'll begin with the basics— that is, general human nature, which is a composite of body and soul.*

Socrates: The whole [human being], composed of a soul and a body, is called an animal—that is, a living being.[23]

What is the body? The body serves the soul as its means of locomotion; it is, as it were, the soul's chariot upon the earth.

Timaeus: The mortal body was made to be the chariot of the soul. . . . It is the means of easy transportation . . . upon the earth, which has all manner of heights and hollows.[24]

What is the soul? The soul itself has three parts, here (in the Phaedrus) *compared to a charioteer with his chariot hitched to two horses. One of the horses is good and noble; the other is not. We'll discover more about these three parts of the soul in a moment.*

Socrates: The soul is like the composite union that arises from a yoked pair of winged horses and their winged charioteer. . . . As for human beings, the charioteer of the soul holds the reigns, driving and guiding the pair of horses. Yet another point: one of the horses is good and noble, of noble stock, whereas the other horse is quite the opposite. This is why driving the chariot of the soul is necessarily difficult and troublesome for us.[25]

Plato offers another image of the soul in the Republic, *a dialogue that explores the nature of justice. In order to understand what justice is, Socrates and his interlocutors search for it in an imaginary city. The city itself has three basic parts: the ruling part, the auxiliary guarding and law-enforcing part, and the producing-trading-money-making part. The question is whether the soul is like the city, and so, whether the soul similarly has three parts.*

Socrates: Our inquiry is to see whether the soul possesses these three parts or forms [of the city] or not. We are agreed that the same number and same kinds, or parts, are in both the city and the soul.[26]

Shortly after their agreement, Socrates and Glaucon (Plato's brother) attempt to discover —by means of argument and a process of asking and answering questions—the three parts of the soul. Corresponding respectively to the three parts of the city mentioned a moment ago, they are the rational, the spirited, and the desiring parts.

Socrates: It would be reasonable, then, to state that these two parts of the soul are different from each other. We'll call the part of the soul by which it calculates and reasons the rational part. And the part with which it desires, hungers, and thirsts, and feels the passionate excitement of other longings, we'll call the non-rational and desiring part of the soul—the companion of various fill-me-ups and pleasures.

Glaucon: Yes, it would be reasonable. . . .

Socrates: Let us assume, then, that these two parts, or forms, have been separated from each other and marked off in the soul. Still, is the *thumos*—the heart or spirit, that by which we are provoked and feel angry—a third, spirited part, or is it the same as the rational part or the desiring part? . . . Again, is this high-spirited *thumos* a third part in the soul just as we found three separate kinds of people that held the city together—the counselor-deliberators, the auxiliary guardians, and the money-makers?

Glaucon: It must be a third part.[27]

If there are three parts of the soul, then each part must have its own function ("what it alone can do, or what it does better, than anything else") and virtue ("the means by which it performs its function well"). The same must be true for the body, as well as for the whole of human nature operating as a unity, body and soul (just as a city as a whole may operate well).

Keeping in mind that, for Plato, living well or virtuously amounts to happiness, let's look at each of these happy-making virtues or excellences in turn, beginning with the body and working our way through each part of the soul until we get to the virtue or excellence of the whole. As for the body, health by means of physical training and medicine is its virtue.

Socrates: Physical training and medicine combine into a single art to care for the body.[28]

Socrates: Simplicity in physical training or exercise begets health in bodies.[29]

And now, the soul. The general nature of the soul is self-motion—that is, by nature, the soul is something that can move itself. To do so, however, the soul must decide where to go. Consequently, the general function of the soul is to deliberate and direct in order to get the soul moving in the best or most excellent direction.[30]

Socrates: The very nature of the soul is self-motion.[31]

Socrates: The function of the soul is . . . management, rule, deliberation, and the like.[32]

But what is the function of each part of the soul? And following upon the function, what is the virtue of each part?

The function of the rational part is to rule and direct the whole soul. It does this by means of wisdom, its virtue.

Socrates: It is the rational part's function to rule since it is altogether wise and exercises foresight on behalf of the whole soul. . . . *The rational part* will rule the desiring part . . . and guard the whole soul and body . . . by taking counsel and by deliberating. . . . We call a man wise because of the small part in him that rules and delivers these orders and exhortations, and by its knowledge of what is beneficial for each part and for the whole soul, the community of the three parts.[33]

Socrates: The truth is that when wisdom is present, he who has it has no need for good luck.[34]

The function of the spirited part of the soul is to listen to, obey, and carry out the rational part's directives. Given the fight put up by the oftentimes disobedient desiring part (that unruly horse), as well as the agitation caused by pleasure and pain (what the desiring part moves toward or away from), the performance of this function requires courage, the spirited part's virtue.

Socrates: The spirited part's function is to listen to, obey, and be allied with the rational part of the soul. . . . *With the rational part, it will guard the whole soul and body . . . by carrying out the rational part's resolutions by means of courage.* . . . We call a man courageous, I suppose, because of the spirited part in him—when the spirited part carries out, through both pleasure and pain, the orders and exhortations of the rational part regarding what is to be feared and what is not.[35]

Next, the desiring part of the soul. As we see in the Symposium, *for Plato, desire itself is a kind of poverty or lacking. Desire wants what it doesn't have. Generally speaking, what is lacking is what is necessary. Therefore, the function of the desiring part of the soul is to seek what is generally necessary for survival and sufficient for well-being.*

As Plato sees it, the problem with desire is not the yearning we may feel for wisdom (this is philosophy, the desire for or love of wisdom) or the desire we may feel to know and experience truth or the good or the beautiful. Instead, for most people the desire-problem appears relative to things like honor, money, food, wine, and sex. Rather than desiring enough food for health, for instance, or enough sex for reproduction and the continuation of the species, humans desire and seek these things in excess, in ways that are often positively unhealthy and harmful. We humans go beyond the necessary to the, strictly speaking, unnecessary.[36]

Corresponding to the above function, then, the virtue of the desiring part of the soul is moderation, that excellence by which the desiring part listens to and obeys the ruling part of the soul and so properly directs desire toward what is necessary for each person's survival and well-being. When this happens, the whole soul operates together well.

Socrates: Moderation is some kind of order—power over and control of certain pleasures and desires. It is what people mean when they use the term, "self-control." . . . The intended meaning of speaking this way seems to me to be that the soul of a man has a better part and a worse part, and to say "self-control" or "having power over oneself" means the control of the worse part by the naturally better part of the soul.[37]

Socrates: The most significant features of moderation for most people are the following: one, listening to and being obedient to the rulers, and two, ruling over the pleasures of eating, drinking, and having sex.[38]

Socrates: Moderation spreads throughout the whole soul, making the strongest, weakest, and intermediate parts sing in unison.[39]

Socrates: The wise man is moderate because of the friendship and concord of the three parts of the soul, when the ruling part and the ruled agree that reason should rule.[40]

The aforementioned "friendship and concord" point to the function and virtue of the soul as a whole. The whole soul is to operate in such a way that each part performs its own function well and does not interfere with or do the work of the other parts.

It may be useful to recall the imaginary city that runs well when each part does what it is supposed to do. Some in the city rule. Some enforce the directives of the ruling part. And some produce goods and trade these goods for the survival and well-being of the city. When each part functions well and does not interfere with the work of the other parts, the whole city thrives with harmony and well-being.

The same is true for the soul as a whole. When the rational part rules with wisdom, and the spirited part listens to and enforces the directives of the rational part with courage, and the desiring part desires with moderation, heeding the rule of the rational part, then the whole soul operates in harmony. Like a string trio, it is a harmonious unity. This harmony is justice, the virtue of the soul as a whole, the means by which the soul does well.

Socrates: Justice is doing one's own work and not doing this, that, and the other thing that are not one's own.[41]

Socrates: The just man does not allow each part of the soul to perform the function or do the work of another part, or to interfere and meddle with another part's function or work. Rather, the just man does a good job arranging what is his own—ruling, ordering, and befriending himself, and harmonizing the three parts of the soul like three notes or intervals in a musical scale, high, low, and middle. And having joined and bound all three together, and all those in between, he himself becomes a harmonious unity, entirely one. . . . The just man believes that in everything the just, noble, and beautiful action is the one that preserves and brings about this harmonious condition of the soul, and that wisdom is the knowledge that presides over and supports such action."[42]

Socrates: When the whole soul follows the wisdom-loving part and there is no dissension within, the result for each part is that in every way it performs its own act and is just. Each part also enjoys its own pleasures—the most excellent pleasures and, so far as possible, the truest pleasures.[43]

To offer a kind of summary, we see in the report of the biographer Diogenes Laertius how wisdom (or to be more specific, practical wisdom), courage, moderation, and justice were the key virtues for Plato.

Diogenes Laertius (reporting Plato's view) There are four forms or kinds of perfect virtue: practical wisdom, justice, courage, and moderation. Of these, practical wisdom is the cause of right conduct, and justice is responsible for straight dealing in partnerships and commercial transactions. Courage is the cause that makes a man not give way but stand his ground in alarms and perils. Moderation causes mastery over desires, so that we are never enslaved by pleasure but live in an orderly manner.[44]

One final point about desire. It follows from the above remarks, and more specifically from the notion of moderation, that well-being or happiness is not (merely) the satisfaction of any and every desire for any and every pleasure (or whatever it is we desire). To put it directly, happiness is not getting whatever we want. Rather, such a position, if taken to its logical end, leads to absurd conclusions. Plato demonstrates the point by recalling the conversation Socrates had with the businessman Callicles, representative of the—even if here exaggerated—sophist position.

Callicles believes that true virtue or excellence is the ability to intelligently and courageously satisfy any and every desire. This excellence, he claims, is true happiness. Consequently, the virtuous man marshals wisdom and courage in the service of unrestrained desire rather than its control. In response, Socrates suggests that Callicles' belief is no different from suggesting that the one who has an itch and can best scratch it is happiest. We may do better, he argues, to deal with the itch by means of moderation rather than inflaming it with our clawing attention.

Socrates said, "Tell me, friend, what about a man himself? What is his relation to himself? Is he a ruler or one who is ruled?"

Callicles responded, "What are you talking about?"

"What I mean to say is that each man rules himself—or is there no need for self-governance . . . ?"

"What exactly do you mean by 'self-governance'?"

"Nothing complex. I mean just what the many do when they talk about such things: moderation and self-control when it comes to things like our desires or longings and pleasure." . . .

Callicles countered, "But how can a man be happy if he is any man's slave? . . . The man who wants to live happily should let his desires be as strong and as big as possible and not check them. Furthermore, he should be able to serve them when they are strongest thanks to his manly courage and intelligence—he should always be able to satisfy each desire as it comes. Ah, but this, I imagine, is not possible for the many. . . . And since they are unable to furnish for themselves the pleasures that would satisfy their desires, the many approve of and praise moderation and justice . . . But truly, Socrates, luxurious living, immoderation, and freedom are excellence and happiness. . . ."

Socrates responded, "I admire the way you march out and make your argument, Callicles. No holds barred! What freedom of speech! The truth is you're now declaring freely and clearly what others have in mind but are unwilling to say aloud. So don't give up. Keep on going so that we may clearly understand how to live. Now tell me this: are you saying that the desires should not be moderated or restrained in any way, . . . but that a man should let his desires grow as large as possible and then find some way to satisfy or fulfill them, from one source or another? Is this excellence?"

"That's right, Socrates. That's what I'm saying."

"In that case, it is not correct to say, as people do, that those who lack and need nothing are happy."

"It's not at all correct. If that were true, then stones and corpses would be happiest."

"Life as you describe it is strange, Callicles—the dead are the happiest ones! In that case, I wouldn't be surprised if Euripides spoke truthfully when he said, 'Who knows if living is actually dying, and dying is actually living?' It may be true that we are dead in this manner. I once heard wise men say that we are now dead. The body is our tomb, they said. And the part of the soul where the desires are located is easily persuaded to waffle back and forth. And so, some clever man—one of those bards of mythical tales, a Sicilian or an Italian man—told a story . . . in which he called this part of the soul the immoderate and leaky part. He said it was like a jar with holes because of its insatiate desire. . . . The soul was like a sieve, he said, unable to hold anything. Doubtlessly all this seems absurd. Nevertheless, the story gets to the point I wish to make in order to persuade you to make a change—so that you might take hold of a well-ordered, moderate life, one that is satisfied with what is fitting and sufficient, rather than a life that is greedy and immoderate." . . .

Callicles doesn't budge. So, after offering another analogy, Socrates said, "Then you're suggesting [*contrary to what I've said*] that the unrestrained, immoderate life is happier compared to the well-ordered, moderate life. . . ."

"I do for this reason, Socrates. The man who has filled himself will no longer experience pleasure. Such a life, after all, is the one that I just now likened to the life of a stone—the one that is all filled up and no longer feels delight or pain. Instead, the pleasant life is made up of the greatest inflow."

". . . And outflow?"

"Certainly." . . .

Socrates said, "Tell me, then, if this man is happy—the man who has an itch and wants to scratch it. But not only that, the one who is freely able to scratch the itch now and throughout his life." . . .

Callicles replied, "Then, yes, I say that the man who is able to scratch lives his life pleasantly."

"And if pleasantly, then happily—he lives a happy life?"

"By all means, yes." . . .

By means of a long argument, Socrates explains why he disagrees. He concludes by saying—

"In whatever he does, the good man does well and nobly. And he who does well is blessed and happy. The base man, by contrast, who does not do well and thus behaves in an evil manner, is miserable. . . . This is what I put to you, Callicles, what I say is the truth of the matter. And if it is true, then anyone who wishes to be happy must practice moderation and must flee immoderation as fast as his feet will carry him."[45]

We've seen that true happiness has to do with the condition of our souls. Each part must perform its natural function well with virtue so that the whole may be well. In the final selection, we hear Socrates call on his fellow Athenians to care for their souls. If they do, they will live well and be happy since, as we know, "he who lives well is blessed and happy."

Socrates: Men of Athens, I greet and love you, but I will obey the god rather than you. And while I live and can continue, I will never give up philosophy. Nor will I stop exhorting you and pointing out the truth to any one of you whom I happen to encounter. Rather, in my accustomed way, I will say, "Best of men, you who are a citizen of Athens, the greatest of cities and the most famous for wisdom and power—are you not ashamed to care for the acquisition of the most wealth possible, and for reputation and honor, when you neither care for nor worry about wisdom and truth and your soul, that it may be in the best possible condition?"[46]

Summary of happiness for Plato & Socrates

For Plato (and Socrates), happiness is not about getting what we want; it is not about satisfying any and every desire. Rather, happiness is a matter of living well or virtuously—with excellence. To be virtuous, therefore, is to be happy.

Virtue itself is "the means by which a thing performs its function well," where a thing's function is "that which it alone can do, or what it does better, than anything else."

Happiness, or living well, has to do with the whole human person, which is a composite of body and soul. The most important part to consider, however, is the soul. When the soul does well, the whole person does well. Therefore, each part of the soul must perform its function well so that the whole person may do well.

The soul has three parts. Each part has its own function and corresponding virtue. The rational part of the soul rules by means of wisdom. The spirited part takes orders from and enforces the rule of the rational part by means of courage. The desiring part obeys the rational part and thus moves toward what is necessary and sufficient for the body and soul by means of moderation. Together, when each part of the soul performs its own proper function well without interfering with the work of the other parts, the soul harmoniously operates as a whole. This soul harmony is justice.

When soul justice (harmony) occurs, the whole person is living well and happily, deliberating, directing, and acting in accord with wisdom. So it is that Plato concludes that virtue, or living well, is central to happiness and human flourishing. If the goal or work of human life is to "live well" or to be happy, then virtue is the means by which we live such a life.[47]

NOTES

[1] Though most give 428 or 427 BC as Plato's date of birth, some scholars, including *The Oxford Classical Dictionary*, give 429 BC.

[2] For this account of Plato's time in Sicily, see Diogenes Laertius, *Lives* 3.18-23, which covers his interaction with the three men. Diogenes Laertius further reports that Anniceris the Cyrenaic "ransomed Plato" when he was being sold on the island of Aegina and "sent him on to his friends in Athens." According to the same account, Plato later turned to the "younger Dionysus" for "land and men" to help him (Plato) establish a new city and constitution (a republic). But Dionysus didn't keep his promise to supply Plato as he desired because, it seems, the younger tyrant suspected that Plato was conspiring with Dion to overthrow him and liberate the whole of Sicily. It was only by the intervention of Archytas the Pythagorean that Plato secured his own liberty to return to Athens. Plato's third visit to Sicily finished the whole project. "Plato came to Sicily a third time to reconcile Dion with Dionysus. But he returned home without success. And from then on he did not engage in political matters—that even though his writings deal with the art of government."

[3] Plato, *Letter* 7.326c-d.

[4] Plato, *Republic* 9.586a-b.

[5] Plato, *Letter* 7.335d.

[6] Ibid, 324e.

[7] Plato, *Symposium* 215c.

[8] The fact that Socrates shows up as a character in many of Plato's dialogues is the reason for the title of this chapter, "Plato & Socrates." For a similar reason, the next chapter is called, "Xenophon & Socrates." Again, we'll briefly explore the "Socratic problem" in the introduction to the next chapter. For the moment, suffice to say that Plato's Socrates is somewhat different from Xenophon's Socrates and other contemporary presentations of Socrates, such as that of the comic playwright Aristophanes.

[9] Note: given the close connection in Plato's thinking between happiness and virtue, much of what follows may also be found in Chapter 7 of the Cave's *Aretē: Excellence or Virtue—What the Ancient Greeks Thought and Said about Aretē.*

[10] Plato, *Republic* 1.354a.

[11] Plato, *Gorgias* 507c.

[12] Encomium by Aristotle preserved in Olympiodorus' *Commentary on Plato's Gorgias* 41.9.

[13] Diogenes Laertius, *Lives* 3.78.

[14] Plato, *Laws* 5.734d-e. In this case, both "excellence" and "virtue" are *aretē*.

[15] Plato, *Republic* 1.353e, 1.354a. Note the last line in this selection is the simple formula for happiness given in the first selection above, that happiness equals living well. Rather than a feeling or a thought, happiness is an act, something we do (living well).

[16] The word behind "virtue" is *aretē*. It may also be given as "excellence," not to mention many other words (valor, merit, goodness, success, fertile, and so on). To learn more, see the Cave's *Aretē: Excellence or Virtue—What the Ancient Greeks Thought and Said about Aretē.*

[17] Plato, *Cratylus* 415c-d.

[18] Plato, *Republic* 4.444d-e.

[19] Ibid., 1.353c. Faithful to Plato's intention (evident in Socrates' overall position), the line has been modified by transforming Socrates' question or query into a positive statement. The question-query: "I am asking about whether a thing that has a function performs it well by means of its own virtue? . . ."

[20] Ibid., 1.353a. This definition of function appears at the end of the next selection. The Greek for function or work is *ergon*.

[21] Ibid., 1.352d-353a.

[22] For example, see Plato, *Cratylus* 386d-387a, where Socrates states, "It is clear that things have some fixed reality (being or essence) (*ousia*) of their own, not in relation to us or under our control or fluctuating according to how they appear, but things exist according to themselves, in relation to their own reality (being or es-

sence), which they possess from nature (in a natural manner)." Socrates next argues that "actions" (the singular is *praxis*) are also "things" with their own nature or way of being. Consequently, actions should also be "performed according to their own nature." For example, in order to cut "well" or "rightly," we must "cut each thing according to the nature of cutting and being cut."

23 Plato, *Phaedrus* 246c.

24 Plato, *Timaeus* 69c and 44d-e.

25 Plato, *Phaedrus* 246a. For a similar comparison, where the mortal body is compared to a chariot, and the soul is put within the body, see Plato, *Timaeus* 41e and 69c. Interestingly, a similar analogy appears in Indian philosophy in the *Katha* Upanishad 3.3 ff. Relative to the comparison we'll look at next from the *Republic*, the "charioteer" is the rational part of the soul, the "good and noble" horse is the spirited part, and the "opposite" troublesome horse is the desiring part.

26 Plato, *Republic* 4.435c.

27 Ibid., 4.439d-e, 4.440e-441a. Socrates further compares the three to a guiding shepherd (the rational part), his sheep that follow him (the non-rational desiring part), and the sheepdogs that help the shepherd guide the sheep (the spirited part) (see ibid., 4.440d).

28 Plato, *Gorgias* 464b. "Care for the body" refers to health and fitness.

29 Plato, *Republic* 3.404e.

30 The best or most excellent direction, which goes along the path of virtue or excellence, is toward survival and well-being, on the one hand, and being itself, truth, goodness, beauty, and similar realities on the other.

31 Plato, *Phaedrus* 245e.

32 Plato, *Republic* 1.353d.

33 Ibid., 4.441e, 4.442a-c. "Wise" is *sophos*, the adjectival form of *sophia* (wisdom).

34 Plato, *Euthydemus* 280b. Wisdom is *sophia*.

35 Plato, *Republic* 4.441e, 4.442a-c. Courage is *andreia*.

36 For desire being a kind of poverty or lacking, see Plato, *Symposium* 203c-d. Somewhat more exactly, desire is "for good things and to be happy"; humans "desire the good" (Ibid., 205d and 206a). For a discussion of "necessary and unnecessary desires or appetites," see Plato, *Republic* 8.558.d-559d, where the "desires that we cannot turn away from may rightly be called 'necessary,'" and those "desires [we] may free [ourselves] from by practice" are "unnecessary." For example (the one given by Socrates), necessary desire is the desire for simple food whereas unnecessary desire is the desire for a variety of food.

The distinction between necessary and unnecessary desires, as well as between natural and groundless desires, is one that shows up later in Greek philosophers such as Epicurus. For instance, in Epicurus' *Letter to Menoeceus*, he states, "We must consider that of the desires, some are natural, and some are groundless. Of the natural desires, some are necessary, and some are merely natural. And of the necessary desires, some are necessary for happiness, some for freeing the body from disturbance, and some for living itself." In the *Principal Teachings*, Epicurus observes that "unnecessary desires are those that lead to no pain if they remain unsatisfied. They involve an appetite that is easily relieved whenever its satisfaction is hard to procure or when it seems likely to cause harm." For both, see Diogenes Laertius, *Lives* 10.127, 148.

[37] Plato, *Republic* 4.430e, 4.431a. Moderation is *sōphrosunē*. Self-control is *enkrateia*.

[38] Ibid., 3.389d-e.

[39] Ibid., 4.432a.

[40] Ibid., 4.442c-d. The "ruled" here refers to both the spirited and desiring parts, those parts that listen to and obey the rational part. The spirited part does so by means of courage; the desiring part does so by means of moderation.

[41] Ibid., 4.433a-b. Though this definition of justice is intended for justice in general, it may equally be applied to the soul and its parts. Justice is *dikaiosunē*.

[42] Ibid., 4.443d-e.

[43] Ibid., 9.586e-587a. "Performs its own act" is the same as "function."

What are the "most excellent" and the "truest pleasures"? If we look back a few sections, we get some idea: "To be filled with what is proper to nature is pleasure. . . . That which is more actually filled with real things" —that is, things that truly, actually *are* versus merely apparent, shadowy things—"would more actually and truly cause us to delight in a true pleasure."

The opposite is also true. Therefore, "Those who have no experience of wisdom and virtue but are ever devoted to feastings and that sort of thing are swept downward . . . and wander here and there throughout their lives. . . . They have never been filled with real things—things that truly are—, nor have they tasted stable or pure pleasure. Instead, with eyes ever bent upon the earth and heads bowed down over their tables, they feast like cattle, grazing and copulating, ever greedy for more of these delights." See ibid., 9.585d-586b.

[44] Diogenes Laertius, *Lives* 3.90-91. Note how some virtues are externally oriented, some internally oriented, and some are both.

[45] Plato, *Gorgias* 491d-494d, 507c-d. As we've already noted, the Greek behind "excellence" is *aretē*, which may also be given as "virtue."

[46] Plato, *Apology* 29d-e. Wisdom, here, is practical wisdom (*phronēsis*).

[47] One final point. Notice how it takes wisdom or right knowledge for every part of the soul to do its job, that is, to work with excellence or to be virtuous. The rational part rules with knowledge and wisdom, and the other parts perform their roles well in conjunction with the rational part's knowledge and wisdom. It is in this manner that Socrates (or Plato through Socrates) suggests, as he does, that "knowledge is virtue." In this way, knowledge as wisdom is happiness, and so knowledge as wisdom is the most significant good we can possibly pursue.

XENOPHON
& SOCRATES

"Xenophon was a modest man and quite handsome. . . . In general, he was a good man, who liked horses, hunting, and military tactics. . . . He was religious, with an affection for making sacrifices to the gods and a competency in discerning signs in the victims. He was also a zealous admirer and follower of Socrates." —Diogenes Laertius, *Lives and Opinions of Eminent Philosophers*

LIKE PLATO, XENOPHON (c. 430-354 BC) was an Athenian citizen born during the first few years of the Peloponnesian War. Unlike Plato, however, he was not in Athens when that politically turbulent city put Socrates to death. Instead, he was off with a large Greek mercenary force, the Ten Thousand, fighting for the Persian throne on behalf of Cyrus the Younger against his brother Artaxerxes II. Things didn't go so well. Though the Greeks and their Persian allies fought well enough during the Battle of Cunaxa (401 BC), Cyrus was killed. After, when the Persians slaughtered the higher-ranking Greeks, Xenophon boldly stepped up to lead the remaining men northward to the Black Sea. This harrowing march is the subject of his later account, the *Anabasis* or *The Expedition Up*. In the years that followed, Xenophon battled on in Asia Minor, allied with the Spartans against the Persians. His association with Sparta eventually resulted in his exile from Athens. He consequently spent the next few decades supported by the Spartans, living and writing on a country estate near Olympia in the Peloponnese.

It was an unfortunate turn of events for Xenophon but fortunate for us since, during those years, he authored a few histories, an array of essays, and the *Cyropaedia* or *The Education of Cyrus*. Otherwise, he wrote several memoirs featuring Socrates—a point that returns us to the Socratic problem mentioned in the introduction to the last chapter ("Plato & Socrates").

The problem? It is that the Socrates in Plato's dialogues is different—at least *somewhat* different—from the Socrates in Xenophon's memoirs. And to add to the problem, the comic playwright Aristophanes presents a very different Socrates from both in the *Clouds*.[1] So which Socrates is the *real* Socrates? What did he actually feel, think, say, and do? The short answer is we can't say for sure. That admitted, and assuming that Plato and Xenophon both present Socrates as they actually experienced him in their works, we may conclude we are getting therein something that approximates the *real* Socrates through two sets of spectacles, as it were—those of Plato and Xenophon.

If this conclusion is something close to the truth, then what we have with Xenophon is the presentation of a man he greatly admires. In fact, at one point Xenophon declares that "Socrates seemed to me the best of men, a truly happy man."[2]

To conclude, let's hear Diogenes Laertius' account of Xenophon's introduction to Socrates in Athens. "The story goes," he reports,

> that Socrates met Xenophon in a narrow passageway in the marketplace. Holding out his staff to prevent him from going on, Socrates asked him where each kind of food was sold. Upon receiving an answer, he further inquired, "And where do men go to become noble and good?" Puzzled, Xenophon had no idea. "Then follow me," Socrates responded, "and learn." From then on he was Socrates' student.[3]

Let's imitate Xenophon. Let's hear Socrates—at least Xenophon's Socrates—talk about how we can become "noble and good." In doing so, we'll learn about happiness.

One final note. As with Plato, all passages are from Xenophon's own work unless otherwise noted.

IN THEIR OWN WORDS

The following are Socratic conversations recorded by Xenophon. In the first, the sophist Antiphon criticizes Socrates' approach to philosophy and happiness as unduly harsh. In defense, Socrates suggests that training to endure hardship and to go without things is the only way to reduce our needs or what we lack—our wants or desires. This needs-reduced life, he argues, approximates that of the gods, who have no needs. As such, Socrates' training program in enduring hardships and going without things, and thereby reducing needs and desires, is a sensible path to happiness.

The sophist Antiphon came to Socrates wishing to lure his students away from him. Therefore, in their presence he said, "Socrates, I thought that philosophy necessarily produces happiness. But the benefit you get from philosophy seems the opposite to me. For example, you're living a life that would drive even a slave to abandon his master. Your meat and drink are cheap and second-rate. And the outer clothing you wear is not only in a sorry state, but you never change it, whether it be summer or winter. And you never wear shoes or underclothes.[4] Moreover, you refuse to take money—something that, merely to get it, causes good cheer, while having it makes one freer and life pleasanter. If students are meant to copy their teachers, . . . then you must think of yourself as a teacher of unhappiness."

Socrates responded, "Antiphon, it seems you suppose that my life is troublesome and painful. I'm convinced that you'd rather choose death than a life like mine. Come on, then, let's examine what hardships you've observed in my way of life.

"Is it that those who take money are obliged to carry out the work for which they're paid—while I, because I refuse to take it, am not compelled to engage with anyone if I do not want to? Or do you think my food is second-rate because it is not as healthy as or less nourishing than yours? . . . Or less enjoyable? . . .

"Do you not know that the more one takes pleasure in eating, the less is his need for seasoning and sauce? And the more one enjoys drinking, the less is his longing for drinks that are unavailable? As for outer clothing, we change it, as you know, due to cold or hot weather. And shoes are worn to protect the feet from pain and to provide greater convenience in walking. Now, let me ask you, have you ever seen me staying inside more than others because of the cold?—or scuffling with anyone for a shady spot on account of the heat?—or failing to walk anywhere due to sore feet?

"Do you not know, Antiphon, that by training, practice, and exercise, those who are by nature weak in the body grow mightier than the very strongest man who doesn't train, practice, and exercise? And that the training itself becomes easy and bearable? Since, then, I am always training my body to bear patiently whatever happens, don't you think that I am more able to bear everything with ease than you are without training? . . .

"My dear Antiphon, you seem to imagine that happiness is living luxuriously and with extravagance. As for me, I hold that it is divine to lack or need nothing. And so that which has the fewest needs is nearest to God. And since that which is divine is the best, then that which is nearest to God is nearest to the best."[5]

In the second conversation, Socrates attempts to convince his friend and follower Aristodemus that, relative to other animals, the gods have given human beings many good things for living well and happily. Among them are an erect posture, hands ("the very things that bring our superior happiness to completion"), speech, the life-long enjoyment of sex, and an excellent soul that is skilled at living and cognizant of the gods. All in all, thanks to the gods' care for us, "we humans live like gods." We are by nature "the most excellent creatures both in body and in soul."

Aristodemus said, "Truly, Socrates, I don't despise the divinity. But I judge it too great to need my attention or service."

In turn, Socrates said, "Certainly, then, the greater the being that judges it worthwhile to attend to and serve you, the more you should honor it."

"I assure you," Aristodemus said, "that if I believed the gods cared about humans, I would not neglect them."

"So, you think they do not care for humans? First, humans are the only living creature that the gods have made to stand upright. And this upright position gives a man a wider view in front of him and a better vantage point for things above, and it exposes him less to injury and suffering. Second, whereas the gods give feet to other animals, feet that allow them to move from one point to another, they endow humans with hands, the very things that bring our superior happiness to completion. Third, though every animal has a tongue, the human tongue is the only one made by the gods that can touch different parts of the mouth, enabling us to articulate the voice and indicate our wishes to one another. Fifth, whereas a fixed time is given to other animals for the enjoyment of sex, old age is our only limit.

"Moreover," Socrates said, "the gods are not merely content to care for and manage the human body. What's even greater and far more important is that the gods implant a first-rate soul in human beings. What other animal's soul is there that perceives the existence of the gods who order the cosmos—the greatest and most beautiful of things? And, besides human beings, what other group of animals attend to and serve the gods? And what soul is more competent than the human soul to make provision against hunger and thirst, cold and heat? And to help in times of sickness? And to exercise toward bodily strength? And to work hard to learn things, and then to remember all that is heard or seen or learned?

"Therefore, is it not obvious to you now that, relative to the other animals, we humans live like gods—that by nature we are the most excellent creatures both in body and in soul?"[6]

In the third conversation, Socrates attempts to convince the hedonist Cyrenaic philosopher Aristippus that self-control and the ability to endure hardship are better than an unrestrained life of pleasure.[7] His case hinges upon the fact that well-trained leaders or rulers are disciplined and able to put up with hunger, thirst, and other wants. Socrates finishes by citing Hesiod on the way of virtue and vice, and by recounting Prodicus' story about Heracles, who, as a young man, had to choose between Lady Virtue and Lady Vice and their corresponding ways to happiness.

(Xenophon is speaking) In other conversations, Socrates encouraged his companions to practice self-control relative to a longing for food, drink, sex, and sleep, and the experience of cold, heat, and hard work.

Observing that one of his associates was rather unbridled in such matters, Socrates said, "Tell me, Aristippus, if you were required to take charge of two youths in order to train them so that the one would be competent to govern—to lead or rule others—while the other would never even seek an office, how would you train them?[8] Shall we contemplate this question together, beginning with the fundamental question of their food?"

"Yes," Aristippus said, "it seems to me that food does come first—since we can't live without food."

"Well, now, won't the desire for food naturally take hold of both of our youths at certain times?"

"Yes, it seems likely."

"Which of the two young men, then, should we accustom to plodding on with pressing business before satisfying his own hungry belly?"

"Clearly the one who is being trained to govern," Aristippus said. "Otherwise, the affairs of the city might be neglected during his rule."

"What about thirst? Should the same one be given power to endure thirst when both want to drink?"

"Doubtlessly," he said.

"What about training with sleep? Which young man should receive the capacity to limit his sleep so that he can sleep late and rise early—and even go without sleep, if such is the need?"

"The same one again," he said, "the would-be ruler."

"What about sex, the business of Aphrodite? Who should have self-control regarding sexual pleasures, so that he won't be hindered in doing what is necessary?"

"The same one again," he said.

"Well, what about this point—not fleeing from hard work but willingly taking it on? To which youth should we make this addition?"

"We'll add that one as well to the one we're training to rule." . . .

"Tell me, Aristippus, does it seem to you that with this training our youth will be less likely to be caught by the enemy in comparison with other animals? As you know, some of these animals are so greedy and grasping that . . . they cannot resist their longing for food, and so they are caught in traps, while others are taken with drink."

"Doubtlessly," he said.

"And does it seem to you that other animals—consider quails and partridges, for example—are so sex-crazed, that when they hear the call of the female, they are so carried away by yearning and a hope for Aphrodite's gifts, that they lose all sight of danger and fall into the nets?"

Aristippus agreed to this as well.

"Tell me, then, what you think. Is it shameful that a man would find himself in the same predicament as a mindless wild animal? But isn't this what happens with an adulterous man? He slips into a woman's bed in the same way, knowing he's in danger of being punished by the law, and so he's in danger of being trapped, caught, and mistreated. Must not such a man be out of his mind, considering the fact of impending misery and shame, and the fact that, if he so desired, he could find a way to satisfy his longing for sex without any danger?"

"So it seems to me," he said.

"More. Since the most important human occupations—fighting, farming, and many others—are done outside in the open air, then do you think it the height of carelessness that so many men are un-trained to endure cold and heat?"

He agreed.

"Don't you believe, then, that our would-be ruler should train so that he is able to bear them with ease?"[9]

"Doubtlessly," he said.

"If then we judge those with self-control in all these matters as fit to rule, then should we not judge those who cannot control them-selves as men with no prerogative to rule?"

He agreed.

"Well, then, since you now know each category and which one belongs where, have you ever thought about where you belong? That is, where would you put yourself?"

"I have considered it. And let me say that the last place I see myself is with the rulers—those who actually want to govern. Considering how challenging it is to provide for my own needs, I judge it no less than crazy for someone to want to supply the city's wishes in addition to his own. Again, it is the height of thoughtlessness for anyone not only to go without much of what he wants but also to submit himself to the city's judgment merely because he hasn't satisfied the preferences of the city's citizens. I tell you, Socrates, city-states assert the right to deal with their leaders just as I deal with my own household slaves. I expect them to furnish me with abundant provisions. At the same time, I demand that they keep their hands off these goods. That's how it is with city-states. It's the business of the rulers to supply the city-state with everything good and beneficial without enjoying these same things themselves. To conclude, Socrates, I'll say this. If anyone wants a great deal of trouble—for himself and for others—, then I would train him as you suggest. And I would categorize him with those fit to lead—yes, with the rulers. On the other hand, I place myself with those who desire to live in the easiest way possible and with the greatest pleasure."

Socrates said, "Now, then, should we look at which of the two men lives a more pleasant life? Is it the ruler or the one ruled?"

"Let's do it," Aristippus said.

Socrates mentions the ruling Persians in Asia, Scythians in Europe, and Carthaginians in Africa, and those they rule, before passing to the Greeks. "And what about the Greeks? You're one. Which group among us Greeks seems to enjoy a more pleasant life—those with the power to rule or those ruled by the powerful?"

"Don't look at me!" Aristippus objected. "I wouldn't put myself with the slaves either. As for me, there's a middle path that I try to walk. It is a path that goes neither through rule nor through slavery but through freedom, which surely leads one to happiness."

Having observed how human beings behave in the real world, particularly the strong relative to the weak, Socrates is doubtful about Aristippus' path to happiness. Still, Aristippus attempts to defend himself by declaring that he remains aloof and a "stranger" everywhere. We might today say "off the grid" or "below the radar." Socrates is not convinced.

Finally, Aristippus asks, "What about those, Socrates, who are trained in the art of ruling or kingship, which you seem to identify with happiness? How are they better off than those whose distress and suffering come about by the force of necessity?" . . .

"Don't you think, Aristippus," Socrates said, "that there is some difference between voluntary and involuntary sufferings? For example, if you willingly endure hunger or thirst, you can eat and drink and do whatever you like whenever you want to, whereas the man who suffers against his will cannot end the suffering whenever he wants. Not only that, but the one who voluntarily endures hardship is heartened in his work by hope. To give an example, men who hunt enjoy their weary toil because they hope to ensnare wild animals.

"Sure, prizes like these are worth little after all that work. But what about those who toil to win good friends?—or to conquer enemies? Or what about those who train their bodies and souls in order to manage their own households well—or to help their friends?—or to serve their own homeland? Doubtlessly these men find pleasure in toiling for these goals. And doubtlessly they live a happy life, content with themselves, approved and envied by others.

"Moreover, self-indulgence and enjoyment will never have the power to bring the body into its highest conditioning and health, as the trainers of athletes say. Nor does such sluggish satisfaction produce any knowledge in the soul worth talking about. Rather, as good men say, it is patient, enduring attention and work that leads to noble and good results.

"For instance, Hesiod somewhere says, 'It is easy to have Vice. She's there in abundance for you. The way to her is smooth, and she dwells very near to you. But the immortal gods have put sweat in front of Virtue. The path to her is long and steep, and so it is rough going at first. Nevertheless, when one comes to the highest point, then the path becomes easy—however hard it is at first.'[10]

"We also have the witness of Epicharmus' with the line, 'The gods ask for toil as the high price of every good thing.' . . .

"Yes, and the wise man Prodicus makes the same point regarding virtue in his tale about Heracles. When Heracles was making his way from boyhood to young manhood, and so he was on the path to becoming his own master, he came to the point where he had to choose between a life of virtue or one of vice. So, he went out to a quiet spot and sat there puzzling over which path he should take. Sitting there, two very tall women appeared and walked up to him. One was fitting and noble in appearance—her body ordered with purity, her eyes adorned with modesty, and her bearing generally expressing discretion. She wore a white robe. But the other! She was plump and soft, with an unnatural pink and white face all made up, and an upright spine to exaggerate her height, and eyes wide open. As for her robe, it hung so as to reveal everything—all her charms. She eyed herself and looked away to see if anyone noticed her. She would also glance at her own shadow."

Socrates explains that it is these two women who approach Heracles, each making their case to him. The latter woman speaks first. Heracles should be her friend, she urges—if, that is, he wants to follow along the easiest and most pleasant road. He'll have the best of everything—food, drink, sex, sleep, scents, and every other pleasure. All sweets! No hardship! No war or worries! And no toil because he'll simply seize what he wants from others.

"So then," Socrates said, "when Heracles had heard her claims, he asked, 'Lady, what is your name?' She responded, 'My friends call me Happiness, but those who hate me have nicknamed me Vice.'"

Now the other woman speaks. She promises a good result if Heracles will only follow her path. Yet, she says, it won't be easy.

"She said, 'Of all that is truly good or noble, the gods give nothing to men without toil and effort.'"

This woman goes on to explain what a man must do to get various goods. Favor from the gods requires worship. Goodwill from friends calls for kindness. A city's honor demands service. Greek admiration involves the hard work of virtue. Fruits require cultivation; an increase in flock numbers, shepherding; and defense and power, training in the art of war. Lastly, a strong body demands the mind's command and much toilsome, sweaty training.

Socrates went on, saying, "As Prodicus tells it, Vice here interrupted and said, 'Have you considered, Heracles, how long and hard this road to enjoyment is that this woman Virtue is mapping for you? I will lead you along a short and easy road to happiness.'"

Virtue strongly disagrees and declares, "'But I associate with the gods and with good human beings, and no fine action, whether the deed of a god or of a human being, is done without me. . . . So, Heracles, child of good parents, if you toil hard along the path that I, Virtue, have mapped for you, you can acquire the most blessed happiness.'"

Finishing Prodicus' story, Socrates said, "In any case, Aristippus, you would do well to think about these matters and consider the life ahead of you."[11]

In the fourth conversation, Socrates works to persuade Euthydemus that happiness, as an indisputable good, should only include that which is truly good. Consequently, things such as beauty, strength, wealth, reputation, and the like should not be included in one's understanding of true happiness.

Euthydemus said, "It seems that happiness is an indisputable good, Socrates."

"It is, Euthydemus, as long as it's not made up of disputed goods."

"But what part of happiness is disputed?"

"No part—as long as we do not include in it beauty or strength or wealth or reputation or any other things such as these."

"But my god—of course we'll include them!" Euthydemus said. "How can anyone be happy without them?"

Sighing to god, Socrates said, "By including them, we'll be including that which causes a great deal of trouble to human beings. Beauty—in the form of a pretty face, for example—frequently brings destruction to those who steal a look at it. And strength leads many to overestimate themselves and engage in tasks that are truly too much for them. And wealth destroys others with all the plotting it demands. Finally, reputation and political power cause many to suffer great misfortune."

Euthydemus said, "Well, Socrates, if I'm wrong to praise this manner of being happy, then I must say that I don't even know what to pray to the gods for!"[12]

In the fifth conversation, Socrates tells Critobulus a story about the Spartan naval commander Lysander and his visit to Cyrus the Younger's gardens. There he declares the nature of Cyrus' happiness, which has to do with being a good man, which in turn involves discipline and hard work.

Socrates explains that when Lysander visited the Persian prince Cyrus the Younger in Sardis, he was amazed by his extensive, well-ordered, and beautiful garden. And so, when he heard Cyrus claim that he had planned and planted much of it himself, Lysander looked at all his jewelry and fine clothing and protested—

"Did you truly plant this garden with your own hands?"

Defending himself, Cyrus said, "Does that astonish you, Lysander? I swear by the Sun god Mithras that whenever my health is good, I never sit down to eat without first sweating by working hard at some task, something I take pride in—whether it be something related to the art of war or farming."

To congratulate him, Lysander declared, "It seems to me, Cyrus, that you deserve to be happy. You are happy because you are a good man."[13]

We'll end with a brief selection from Xenophon's On the Cavalry Commander *that ties a city's happiness to training for war. To state the obvious, perhaps, Xenophon is speaking.*

Far more honor is won with victory in war than with boxing with your fists. Here's why. Both the city-state and the warriors share in the glory since the gods usually crown such cities with happiness in prosperity. It is fitting, then, for men and cities to train in the art of war.[14]

SUMMARY OF HAPPINESS FOR XENOPHON & SOCRATES

For Xenophon (and Socrates), happiness is a matter of desire, wants, or needs reduction. The fewer things a person needs or wants, the more that person is like the gods, who need nothing and are perfectly happy (in keeping with Greek tradition positing happy and immortal gods). Therefore, as the person's desires, needs, or wants decrease, happiness increases.

But how can a person curb his or her desires, needs, or wants? The answer is a program of rigorous training that will help the person learn how to endure hardship—little food, little wine, in short, little that affords pleasure. Not only that but such a program will also accustom such a one to pain.

The key to happiness, then, is strength—it is self-control and the ability to endure. This is the path that leads to virtue, the path that the hero Heracles chooses to follow. This is also the way of life that Cyrus the Younger exemplifies in his choice to work hard before eating or relaxing.

NOTES

[1] The *Clouds* was first performed in 423 BC, making Aristophanes' presentation of Socrates the earliest we have in writing. How accurate was it? It's hard to know. But it seems to represent what some in Athens, including those who brought him to court in 399 BC, believed about him. That said, Plato has Socrates deny the Aristophanic, as we may call it, presentation. "None of it is true," asserts Socrates before the men of Athens in Plato's *Apology*. For the Aristophanic presentation and Socrates' denial, see Aristophanes, *Clouds* 188 ff., and Plato, *Apology* 19a-e.

[2] Xenophon, *Memorabilia* 4.8.11.

[3] Diogenes Laertius, *Lives* 2.48.

[4] The difference between "outer clothing" (often given as a "cloak") and "under-clothing" (often given as a "tunic") is that between the *himation* and *chitōn*.

[5] Xenophon, *Memorabilia* 1.6.1-10. The notion that "it is divine to lack or need nothing" has a long history in ancient Greek philosophy.

[6] Xenophon, *Memorabilia* 1.4.10-14.

[7] For more on Aristippus of Cyrene, see Chapter 12, "Aristippus & Cyrenaicism."

[8] When you read "train" or "to train" (*paideuō*) in this selection, know that it also means "to raise" or "to educate."

[9] In this instance, "train" or "to train" is *askeō*, which means to practice, exercise, train—as in the training of an athlete and, much later, the training of a monk. It (*askeō*) is behind the term "asceticism."

[10] See Hesiod, *Works and Days* 287-292.

[11] Xenophon, *Memorabilia* 2.1.1-34 (parts).

[12] Ibid., 4.2.34-35.

[13] Xenophon, *Economics* or *The Estate-Manager* 4.20-25. The Greek word for "garden" here is *paradeisos* or *paradisos*, which may also be given as "paradise."

[14] Xenophon, *On the Cavalry Commander* 8.7.

ARISTOTLE

"Aristotle was Plato's most outstanding student, surpassing all the others. . . . When he left Plato and the Academy, he selected a covered walkway in the Lyceum in which he used to walk back and forth with his students pursuing philosophical matters. This is why Aristotle and his students are called 'Peripatetics'—those who walk while teaching and learning."

—Diogenes Laertius, *Lives and Opinions of Eminent Philosophers*

ARISTOTLE (c. 384-322 BC) WAS AN avid collector of facts. Whether spending time with a beekeeper in his apiary, or riding along with a fisherman in his boat, or observing Athenian or Macedonian politics (he lived for a time in Macedon and was tutor to the future Alexander the Great), or studying the flora and fauna of Lesbos with his colleague and friend Theophrastus, he was always gathering information. Diogenes Laertius declares that Aristotle surpassed others in the study of nature, and that he compiled "not a few" notebooks filled with data related to the cause and reality of all things, including the smallest of things.

Born in Stagira, in present-day northern Greece, Aristotle made his way to Athens when he was about seventeen or eighteen. There he joined Plato's Academy, where he studied for twenty years, gathering content to convert into systematic knowledge. Near the end of Plato's life, Aristotle left the Academy, venturing out on his own as a naturalist and philosopher. Though he often disagreed with his former mentor, Aristotle continued to admire and love him.

Toward the last decade of his life, Aristotle set up and taught in his own school in Athens. Since it was organized in an area dedicated as a public sanctuary and gymnasium to "Apollo Lykeios," the school came to be called the Lyceum. Many secondary schools in Europe still incorporate some version of the term into the names of their own schools today.

By the time he died, Aristotle had written a very large number of books. If we still had them all, not to mention his many notebooks, they would fill a whole bookshelf. Diogenes Laertius claims that his writings added up to some 445,270 lines, which amounts to something like 3 million words and so about 40 or 50 books. The books—now mostly lost, though we still have their titles—covered a plethora of subjects including love, wealth, prayer, pleasure, beauty, music, education, plants, kingship, household management, dramatic victors at various Dionysian festivals, and athletic victors at the Olympic and Pythian games. Most significant are those works still extant concerned with logic, physics, metaphysics, ethics, politics, poetics, rhetoric, zoology, and more.

In a way, all of Aristotle's collecting, classifying, and systemizing is not surprising. After all, he believed that such activity—study and contemplation—was the highest kind of activity for a human being. In fact, as we will see, Aristotle identified such activity with happiness itself.

Before turning to his thoughts about happiness, though, let's briefly note that Aristotle's writing is significantly different from Plato's and Xenophon's. Scholars tell us that we only possess what amounts to his lecture notes. As such, his works can be rather dry. The speaker is Aristotle himself, whose primary activity is to think through whatever problem he's hoping to address step by step. Fortunately, if we're willing to endure the slow pace, then one ponderous step usually and logically leads to others that end in a worthwhile conclusion—in this case, a conclusion that reveals something more about happiness.

IN THEIR OWN WORDS

In his most significant work on ethics, the Nicomachean Ethics, *Aristotle begins by exploring what it is we humans act for.[1] Depending on the activity, he observes, there are many ends or goals we seek to accomplish and many goods we hope to attain. Still, what is the highest goal or good we live and act for? Most people, he says, call it "happiness." Even so, everyone disagrees about what happiness is. Consequently, Aristotle steps back to further investigate the notion of the highest goal or good. Doing so, he discovers that the highest goal or good is final, which means that it is chosen for itself rather than as a means to other goals or goods. As such, it is sufficient in itself. Such a thing, Aristotle concludes, is happiness.*

Every art and every methodical investigation, and, similarly, every act and moral choice, seem to aim at some good. Consequently, the notion that "everything aims at the good" is well proven.[2]

If then, our every act has some end or goal that we desire for its own sake, . . . then clearly this must be the good—indeed, it must be the best of goods. Will not the knowledge of this good have a tremendous influence on our lives? Won't this knowledge better enable us, like archers, to hit upon what is right?[3]

Whatever the good is, it seems as though it is different in different actions, activities, and arts—in medicine, military strategy, and the rest. What is the good of each activity and art? Is it not the end for the sake of which everything is done? In medicine, it is health. In military strategy, it is victory. In the art of building, it is, for example, a house. . . . In every activity and in every choice, the good is the end for the sake of which men do whatever they do.[4]

The highest good is evidently something final. Consequently, if there is only one final good, this will be the one end we are seeking. But if there are many ends, then the most perfect or final of these will be the one we are looking for.

Now, we call the thing that we pursue in and for itself more final than another thing that we pursue for the sake of, or as a means to, something else. Moreover, the thing that is never chosen for the sake of something else is more final than things chosen both for themselves and for something else. Therefore, we call something "absolutely final," or "final without qualification," if it is always chosen for itself and not as a means to something else.

Given the above, we can conclude that happiness appears to be such an end since we always choose happiness for itself and not for the sake of something else. By contrast, we choose things like honor, pleasure, understanding, and every excellence or virtue, not only for themselves . . . but also for the sake of happiness, seeing them as the means by which we can be happy. On the other hand, no one chooses happiness for the sake of honor and the like, nor, generally speaking, for anything other than itself.

The same conclusion seems to follow from the vantage point of self-sufficiency since the final good appears to be an independent or self-sufficient thing. . . . Now, we define "self-sufficient" as that which, when known or experienced alone, makes life desirable and lacking in nothing. This is the kind of thing we judge happiness to be.

Moreover, happiness is the most desirable and choiceworthy of all things.[5]

Since all knowledge and moral choice aims at good of one kind or another, . . . *the question is this*: what is the highest good that action can achieve? As for its name, nearly everyone is agreed—for both the crowd of men and the few who are educated and refined call it happiness, and they assume that "living well" and "doing well" is the same thing as "being happy."

But they argue about what happiness is. The account given by the many is not the same as that given by the wise. Most people associate happiness with obvious things that can be seen and felt, such as pleasure or wealth or honor. . . . But quite often the same man declares happiness one thing and then another—health when he is sick and wealth when he is poor.[6]

Aristotle further seeks to understand what the highest goal or good is for humans by investigating "man's proper function." In this way, he is like Plato (and Socrates) in associating the goal or good of human existence with human nature and its various functions. He concludes that proper human function is "an activity of the soul in accord with reason." This rational soul activity is itself excellent or virtuous. Therefore, he concludes, "happiness is an activity of the soul that accords with perfect virtue."

To call happiness the highest good is perhaps to speak in terms of clichés. Therefore, what we need is a clearer account of what, exactly, happiness is. It is possible we will be able to do this when we have grasped man's proper function [*wherein the human good is found*].[7] . . .

What can this function possibly be? Can it be living itself? No, life and the act of living is clearly something that men have in common with plants—and what we are seeking is something that mankind alone does. Let us therefore eliminate the life-act of nutrition and growth. The next possibility is sense perception, that is, some form of perceptive living or life. But this form of living also seems to be something common to horses, oxen, and every other animal.

There remains, then, a kind of active or practical life that follows reason or some rational principle. . . . Therefore, man's proper function is an activity of the soul in accord with reason—at the very least not independent of reason. [*Thus, to function well in accord with reason is to function well as a human being—excellently or virtuously.*] . . .

The function of an excellent man, therefore, is to perform these activities well and finely. . . . The human good, then, is the activity of the soul that accords with virtue. And if there happens to be more than one human virtue, then it is that activity which accords with the best and most complete or perfect virtue.[8]

Happiness is an activity of the soul that accords with perfect virtue. Accordingly, we must now consider the nature of virtue. . . .

Now the kind of virtue we must study is human virtue, and the happiness we must discover is human happiness. By human virtue, we are not referring to virtue of the body but to that of the soul. So it is that we define happiness as an activity of the soul.[9]

If, as Aristotle concludes, the highest human good is happiness, and happiness is an excellent or virtuous activity of the soul that accords with reason, then we must next grasp Aristotle's understanding of the soul—its parts and their corresponding virtues. The following sketch presents his views in summary form.[10] Afterward, and letting Aristotle speak for himself, we will explore in greater detail what he calls the moral or ethical virtues and the intellectual or thinking virtues.

Aristotle taught that the soul has two major parts, the rational and the non-rational part. (By the way, he left aside the question of whether these parts are real. At the very least, he judged, they are real in terms of function and activity.) The rational part itself has two parts or aspects with corresponding virtues. One is reason itself, which knows for the sake of knowing. Its general virtue is theoretical wisdom (sophia) (philosophical or intellectual wisdom), whereby we understand truth or what is — that is, the necessary and universal truth of things and that which follows from this truth. The other part shares in reason by listening to it. It knows for the sake of guiding and acting. Its virtue is practical wisdom (or prudence) (phronēsis), the ability to deliberate well about and thus apprehend how best to act toward an end or goal. Other virtues corresponding to the rational part include scientific knowledge (epistēmē), which has to do with the understanding and demonstration of truth; art or applied science or skillful knowledge (technē), which is the ability to produce things; and intelligence (nous), which apprehends fundamental principles.

As for the other part of the soul, the non-rational, it also has two parts or aspects. One is the appetitive or desiring part, the part that feels desire or aversion. It may or may not participate in reason — that is, it may or may not listen to and obey reason. This part has a number of moral or ethical virtues, including courage, moderation, justice, generosity, magnificence, magnanimity, gentleness, truthfulness, wittiness, friendliness, and proper shame. The other is the nutritive, or vegetative (plantlike), part. It has no virtue in itself since it operates automatically, having no part in reason.

Now that we've seen the general nature of the soul in terms of its parts and virtues, let's take a closer look at virtue itself and the soul's virtues.

Regarding virtue itself, Aristotle concludes that there are two general kinds.

So then, there are two kinds of virtue — intellectual or thinking virtue and moral or ethical virtue.[11]

Let's first turn to the moral or ethical virtues and a summary definition. Aristotle offers the following digest of the general nature of moral virtue — a summary that will make more and more sense as we proceed.

We have now discussed the common properties of the [moral] virtues. We've looked at an outline of their general nature — that they are means that fall between two extremes, and that they are habits, which is to say a trained ability or disposition. Further, we've shown that the virtues render us apt to do the same actions as those by which they are produced, and to do them in a manner commanded by right reason, and that the virtues depend on us and are voluntary.[12]

The next question has to do with how a person becomes virtuous—and thus, keep in mind, happy. Aristotle explains that we acquire the moral virtues by means of training, habituation, and doing what is morally excellent. Acts of virtue lead to further acts of virtue, which ultimately result in the habit of being virtuous, the possession of a virtuous disposition. Therefore, it is important for children to grow up practicing virtue and for city-states to enact legislation promoting it.

Moral or ethical virtue is born thanks to habit, which is to say customary behavior. In fact, moral virtue gets its name, with a slight variation of form, from that word.[13]

The [moral] virtues are engendered in us neither by nature nor yet in a way contrary to nature. Rather, nature disposes us to receive them, perfecting them by means of habit.[14]

We acquire the [moral] virtues . . . by doing them, by putting them into action, just as we do with the various arts or skills. For we learn an art or skill by doing that which we wish to do when we have learned it. We become builders by building and harpers by harping. And so, by doing just acts we become just, and by doing acts of moderation and courage we become moderate and courageous. This conclusion is confirmed, as well, by what occurs in city-states. Those who craft the laws make the citizens good by means of accustomization or habituation, that is, by getting used to good habits. This is the purpose of all legislators, and if they don't do this well, then they miss the mark. Indeed, this is what distinguishes a good from a bad constitution.[15]

In a word, moral habits or dispositions are formed as a result of similar activities or actions. So it is that we should control the nature of our activities since the quality of our habits depends on the quality of these. Consequently, it is no small thing whether, from when we are young, we are trained up in one habit or another; rather, it is a great difference—in fact, all the difference.

So then, unlike other branches of study, our present inquiry does not merely have a speculative aim. We are not looking into the nature of virtue only to know what it is. On the contrary, we are doing so in order to become good. Otherwise, the whole enterprise would be without an advantage.[16]

Returning to the "summary definition" cited a moment ago, including the fact that moral virtue is a "mean that falls between two extremes," let's look at what this "mean" is. Generally speaking, the mean between two extremes produces, increases, and preserves moral habits (virtues). By contrast, whatever is extreme, that is, any deficiency or excess, degrades and ultimately destroys them.

Let us observe that moral habits are such that both deficiency and excess destroy them. To illustrate what we cannot see by what we can see, this is clear in the case of strength and health. Too much and too little exercise alike destroy strength. Similarly, to take too much or too little food and drink is ruinous to health. By contrast, an appropriate amount, that is, one of due measure, produces and increases and preserves them. The same holds true for moderation and courage and the other virtues. The man who runs away from everything in fear, and never makes a stand or endures anything, becomes a coward, while the man who fears nothing at all but marches on toward everything is overly bold, rash. Similarly, the man who enjoys every pleasure and abstains from none is undisciplined. So it is that moderation and courage are destroyed by whatever is excessive and whatever falls short or is deficient, whereas they are preserved by whatever is in the middle, the mean.[17]

How do we know where we stand relative to moral virtue? Aristotle explores how, while engaged in specific behaviors, our experience of pleasure and pain reveals who we are in terms of the virtues. Moral virtue is some-thing that exists—or not—relative to pleasure and pain. As for happiness and pleasure, we'll further explore their relationship in time.

The pleasure or pain that accompanies our actions may serve as a sign indicating our moral habits or dispositions. For instance, the man who abstains from bodily pleasures and rejoices in the absti-nence is moderate, whereas the one weighed down by or annoyed by such an abstinence is undisciplined. More: a man is courageous who is glad to take a stand before danger or endure it—or at least it does not distress him. But the distressed man is a coward.[18]

Moral virtue is concerned with pleasure and pain. . . . We may pro-pose, then, that moral virtue makes us do what is best in things that entail pleasure and pain, while moral badness, which is to say vice, has the contrary effect.[19]

Men become worse through pleasures and pains, that is, either by pursuing and fleeing from the wrong pleasures and pains, or by pur-suing and fleeing from them at the wrong time or in the wrong man-ner or in any other way of going wrong that may be distinguished. This is why some people go so far as to define the virtues as a kind of impassivity and quietude or rest. But they err in stating this abso-lutely instead of qualifying their definition by the addition of "right and wrong manner," and "time," and all the rest.[20]

Next, Aristotle explains how virtuous acts must be done with knowledge, deliberate choice, and from a permanent disposition. In this way, they are different from the various arts or crafts or skills.

The case of the arts (or crafts or skills) is not really analogous to that of the virtues. Works of art possess wellness or excellence in them-selves, so that it is enough if they are produced so that they have a certain quality of their own. But virtuous acts, that is, acts done in conformity with the virtues, are not done justly or moderately, for example, if they themselves are merely of a certain kind of act; rather, they are so only if the agent, the doer, is also in a certain condition or state. First, he must act with knowledge, knowing what he is doing. Second, he must deliberately choose the act, and choose it for its own sake. Third, the act must be the expression of a firm and unchangeable habit or disposition.[21]

Considering virtue and the various states of the soul in terms of genus or general kind, Aristotle suggests that virtue must be either an emotion (feelings such as desire, anger, fear, or joy, most of which are accompanied by pleasure or pain), or a capacity (the means by which we feel the various emotions), or a habit or disposition (by which we are well- or ill-disposed to the emotions). Of the three possibilities, he concludes that virtues are habits or dispositions.

The virtues are neither emotions nor capacities. It remains that they are habits or dispositions. So then, we have stated what virtue is in terms of its genus.[22]

Aristotle further explains what it means to feel (that is, experience emotion) or to act in an excessive or defective manner, or, by contrast, to act in accord with the mean.

Moral virtue has to do with emotions and actions in which there is the possibility of an excess and a deficiency, as well as a mean. For instance, one can feel afraid or be bold, feel desire or anger or pity, and generally experience pleasure and pain either too much or too little—not well in either case. By contrast, to feel these feelings at the right time, on the right occasion, toward the right people, for the right purpose, and in the right manner, is to feel them in the best way according to the mean—the very thing that is virtue. The same holds true for actions—there is an excess, a deficiency, and a mean.[23]

In the next few selections, Aristotle briefly offers the various aspects and a more complete definition of moral virtue. Virtue is both that which allows a thing to perform its function well and a kind of perfection or excellence. It involves reasoned choice that determines the mean.

Notice the role that "a wise and sensible" person plays in bringing reason to life. Although Aristotle doesn't explicitly say it, and despite his oftentimes tedious academic approach, his is not a dry, rational virtue that works everything out by cold logic or categorical imperative, but one founded on human beings who think and act excellently. We might even say they are heroes. But that may be going too far for Aristotle. If they are heroes, then their feet are planted firmly on the ground. Regardless, to know what is good, we must look to exemplars, to model men and women.

Every virtue has a twofold effect on the thing to which it belongs: it not only makes the thing well or good in itself, but it also allows the thing to perform its function well.[24]

Virtue is a habit or disposition involving deliberate choice, consisting in the observance of a mean relative to us, as determined by reason, that is, as a wise and sensible man would determine it. Virtue is a mean that falls between two vices, that which is excessive and that which is deficient.[25]

There are three dispositions: two vices, one of excess and one of defect, and one virtue that is the observance of the mean.[26]

Aristotle observes that for some behaviors and feelings, such as adultery and shamelessness, for example, there is no mean, no excellent middle ground.

Some actions and emotions do not permit the observance of the mean. In fact, the very names of some directly imply that which is bad. Take, for example, malice, shamelessness, and envy, and, of actions, adultery, theft, and murder. All these and similar actions and emotions are judged bad in themselves—but not for their excess or deficiency. No, it is impossible to remain upright with them. Rather, in feeling or acting in such a way, one always misses the mark. Nor in their case does doing well or not depend on the circumstances—for instance, whether one commits adultery with the right woman, at the right time, and in the right manner. No, to act in any of these ways whatsoever is to miss the mark.[27]

As for other emotions, actions, and areas of life, what we may call the field of virtue (that which the virtue is "relative to"), there is a mean that falls between the excess and the defect.

The observance of the mean relative to fear and boldness is courage. The man who is excessively fearless is not designated by any special name (such is the case with many virtues and vices). By contrast, the man who is overly bold is rash. He who is too fearful and not bold enough is a coward.

Relative to pleasures and pains, though not all of them, and less so relative to pain, the observance of the mean is moderation. The excess is immoderation or licentiousness. Though there are few who are deficient regarding the enjoyment of pleasures, and so such a condition has not been given a name, we may nevertheless call it insensibility or a lack of sensation or feeling.[28]

In addition to courage and moderation, Aristotle catalogs other virtues (other means), along with their fields and their vices, their excesses and defects, as follows (summarized). Relative to getting and spending money, liberality or generosity is the mean, prodigality or extravagance is the excess, and illiberality or meanness is the defect. There's also magnificence (the mean), tastelessness or vulgarity (the excess), and stinginess (the defect).

Relative to honor and dishonor there are magnanimity and proper ambition (means), vanity and over ambition (excesses), and pusillanimity and a lack of ambition (defects).

Regarding anger, there is gentleness or mildness (the mean), irascibility (the excess), and spiritlessness or a lack of spirit (the defect).

The mean regarding self-expression is truthfulness; the excess is boastfulness; the defect is self-deprecation.

The mean, excess, and defect regarding conversation is wittiness, buffoonery, and boorishness, respectively.

Regarding social conduct, they are friendliness, obsequiousness or flattery, and quarrelsomeness.

Regarding shame, they are modesty or proper shame, shyness or bashfulness, and shamelessness.

Finally, relative to indignation, they are righteous indignation, envy, and malice or malicious enjoyment or spitefulness.[29]

Aristotle recognizes that the mean (and so the virtue) does not always fall precisely between the excess and defect.

In some cases, the defect is more opposed to the mean. In others, it is the excess. For instance, relative to courage, the defect cowardice is more opposed to the mean than is the excess rashness or over-boldness. With moderation, the excess immoderation or licentiousness is more opposed than the defect insensibility.[30]

Aristotle fully recognizes the challenge in knowing what the mean is and in achieving moral excellence. It is hard work. Accordingly, he offers several tips regarding how to hit the target of the mean.

Moral virtue is a mean . . . between two vices—one vice that is marked by excess and the other by defect. It is a mean insofar as it is able to hit the midpoint amid emotions and actions. This is why it is hard work to be morally excellent. It is hard work to apprehend the middle of anything. For example, not everyone is able to find the center of a circle. Only one with knowledge can do so. So then, anyone can get angry. That's easy. . . . But to be angry . . . at the right person, and in the right amount, and at the right time—this is not easy for everyone. Rather, to do so well is rare, praiseworthy, and noble.[31]

The first rule in aiming at the mean is that we should point ourselves away from the extreme that is more opposed to the mean. . . . The second rule is that we should look into and examine the errors that we are most likely to commit. . . . Then we must drag ourselves away in the opposite direction. . . . The third rule is that we must in everything be on guard against pleasure and what is pleasant. . . . These are the things we may do that will best enable us to hit the mean.[32]

According to Aristotle, one may move from what he terms "brutishness" to virtue, or moral excellence. What does such a movement on what we may call "the ladder to virtue" look like? In short, one moves from acting on irrational impulse (brutish, animal-like behavior) to moral viciousness, where one mistakes evil for good. Next one knows the good but is unable to pursue it consistently, given one's own moral weaknesses. With long practice, however, one is finally able to overcome various unhealthy desires, and so one comes to a place of moral strength. Beyond this is virtue or excellence, where the unhealthy desires vanish altogether, and good habit is the rule. In brief, the rungs on the ladder go from brutishness (the lowest rung) to moral viciousness, moral weakness, moral strength, and, finally, up to virtue.[33]

Given that virtues have to do with actions, Aristotle investigates what it means for an action to be voluntary or involuntary. The question is: What makes for a voluntary or involuntary act?

An involuntary act is one that is done under compulsion or because of ignorance, whereas a voluntary act would seem to be an act of which its beginning is in the agent himself, who knows the particular circumstances in which he is acting.[34]

Aristotle moves on to the nature of choice, which "appears to be something voluntary," *he says.*[35] *Choice is not the same as desire, passion, wish, or opinion. As for the latter, Aristotle states,* "It is our choice of the good or the bad that determines who we are, not the opinions we hold."[36]

After determining that choice is not any of the above four (desire, passion, wish, opinion), Aristotle explores the relationship between choice and deliberation, and then the nature of deliberation itself.

What, then, is the nature of choice? . . . On the one hand, it appears to be something voluntary. . . . Perhaps it is a kind of deliberation since choice involves reasoning and some process of thought. And this is indicated by the term itself, *prohairesis,* which means something taken or chosen *before* other things.[37]

We deliberate about things that are in our control and are attainable by action.[38]

Matters of deliberation, then, are matters in which there are rules that generally hold good, but in which the result is uncertain or there is an element of indeterminacy. In important matters, we distrust our own powers of judgment and call on others to assist us in our deliberations.[39]

We deliberate not about ends but about means to ends. A physician does not deliberate about whether he is to heal his patient . . . ; rather, [he] takes the end for granted.[40]

Choice, then, is a deliberate desire for things that are within our power. For we first deliberate, and then, having decided based on the deliberation, we desire according to the deliberation.[41]

Along with the many moral or ethical virtues cataloged above (with their mean, excess, and defect), Aristotle also discusses the general nature of justice and its various kinds.

It is clear that the law-abiding man and the fair man are both just. "The just man or thing," therefore, signifies that which is lawful and that which is equal or fair.[42]

Justice that is coextensive with the whole of virtue is the practice of virtue in general toward another.[43]

The parts of justice include two kinds—distributive justice (concerning the distribution of honor, wealth, and the other divisible assets of the community of citizens that may be allotted to its members in equal or unequal shares), . . . and corrective justice, which offers a corrective principle in private transactions.[44]

Such were Aristotle's views regarding moral or ethical virtue. Next, we must look at what he thought about intellectual virtue.

In the first lines of Book 6 of the Nicomachean Ethics, *Aristotle recognizes that we choose the mean and avoid excess and deficiency with the help of "right reason." The conclusion begs several points of discussion.*

As Aristotle states them, they are: What is the "exact definition of right reason"? *and,* "What is the standard that determines it?"[45]

As for the latter question, the general answer is the intellectual virtues, which have to do with the rational part of the soul and its two rational faculties, "one whereby we contemplate those things whose first principles are invariable, that is, they cannot be other than they are, and one whereby we contemplate those things that allow for variation."[46] *Aristotle calls the first the* "scientific faculty," *the part which is capable of knowledge. He terms the second the* "calculative faculty," *the part which is endowed with reason and is practiced in calculating.*

The attainment of truth is the function of both intelligent or intellectual parts of the soul. Accordingly, their respective virtues are those habits or dispositions that will allow each to best attain the truth.[47]

The virtues by which the soul achieves truth in terms of assent and denial are five in number. These are skillful knowledge (or art), scientific knowledge (or science), practical wisdom (or prudence), theoretical wisdom (or wisdom), and intelligence.[48]

Let's look at each intellectual virtue in turn—scientific knowledge, skillful knowledge, practical wisdom, intelligence, and theoretical wisdom. When we get to practical wisdom, notice the reference again to people, to the example of virtuous individuals—in this case, to a prudent person, one who possesses and practices practical wisdom.

Scientific knowledge . . . may be made clear as follows. We all suppose that a thing that we can know with scientific knowledge cannot vary, that is, it cannot be other than it is. . . . A thing known by scientific knowledge, therefore, necessarily exists. Accordingly, it is eternal . . . and thus ungenerated and incorruptible, having no beginning or end. Further, we suppose that all scientific knowledge is teachable, and so what is scientifically knowable is learnable. . . . Scientific knowledge is the habit or disposition whereby we make demonstrations or construe explanations.[49]

Scientific knowledge is conviction about universal and necessary truths. And demonstrated truths and all scientific knowledge are derived from first principles (since scientific knowledge operates by means of reason). . . . First principles are apprehended by intelligence.[50]

Skillful knowledge (or art) is a habit or disposition that produces or makes things by means of reason or calculation that is truthful. . . . Architectural skill, for example, is an art or skillful knowledge.[51]

As for practical wisdom, we may grasp it by considering the nature of those people we say have practical wisdom. Now, we suppose that those who have practical wisdom are those who can deliberate well and nobly about those things that are good and useful for themselves. We suppose this not only relative to one area of life—for instance, to those things that are good and useful for health or strength—but relative to living well in general.[52]

Practical wisdom is not scientific knowledge since matters of conduct *(what practical wisdom is concerned with)* allow for variation.[53]

Practical wisdom is a truth-attaining rational habit or disposition concerned with action, that is, matters of conduct, relative to things that are good and bad for human beings. . . . This point accounts for the word "moderation," which means "preserving practical wisdom." Moderation does indeed preserve our conviction regarding what is good and bad. For pleasure and pain do not destroy or pervert all our convictions. For example, they do not destroy or pervert the conviction that three angles of a triangle are, or are not, together equal to two right angles. They only do so relative to those things having to do with action or matters of conduct.[54]

Of the two parts of the soul that have reason, practical wisdom is the virtue of one part, namely, the one that forms opinions or judgments, since, as practical wisdom does, opinion deals with that which can vary.[55]

First principles are apprehended by intelligence.[56]

It is clear that theoretical wisdom (or wisdom) must be the most perfect, that is, precise, kind of knowledge. The wise man, therefore, must not only know the conclusions that follow from the first principles, but he must also know the truth about these first principles. Thus, theoretical wisdom must be a combination of intelligence and scientific knowledge—it is the crowning completion of knowledge, as it were, the knowledge of those things most valued and honored.[57]

Given the skepticism and even derision of others, Aristotle explains how men such as Thales and Anaxagoras (two early Presocratic philosophers or natural scientists) may be counted wise in terms of theoretical wisdom but not so in terms of practical wisdom. This is because theoretical wisdom is not concerned with those things that are good and useful for human beings, whereas practical wisdom is.

Practical wisdom is concerned with the affairs of men. *Aristotle goes on to assert,* Practical wisdom is in fact the same habit or disposition as political knowledge, though their essence, to be sure, is different.[58]

As Aristotle seems to admit, there is still some question as to why practical wisdom and theoretical wisdom are useful. Nevertheless, he goes on to affirm their benefit. Each is part of happiness as the virtue of part of the soul. Consequently, each is the means by which the soul functions well and, thus, humans act well. This doing or being well is happiness.

We have stated, then, what practical wisdom and theoretical wisdom are—what each has to do with, that is, its proper sphere of activity, and that each is the virtue of a different part of the soul.

Even so, one may raise further questions about the usefulness of these two virtues. For one, since theoretical wisdom is only concerned with *what is* rather than *what is coming to be*, it contemplates none of the things that make a man happy. And even though practical wisdom does consider *what is coming to be*, or changing, varying realities, we may nevertheless ask why we need it. True, practical wisdom concerns itself with just, noble, and good things for a man. But these are the things that a good man *does*. Therefore, since the virtues are habits or dispositions, we are no more able to act in such a manner simply because we know about them—just as we are not actually healthy and well simply because we know about such things. . . .

First, let us say that, even *if* neither one of them produces anything, theoretical wisdom and practical wisdom are necessarily desirable and choiceworthy in themselves because they are virtues corresponding to different parts of the soul. Second, in point of fact they *do* produce something. They do so not as the art of medicine produces health, however, but as health itself produces health. In this way, theoretical wisdom produces happiness since theoretical wisdom is part of virtue as a whole, and so it makes a man happy by being possessed and by actualizing itself. Third, a man performs his proper function, or brings his work to completion, by means of both practical wisdom and moral or ethical virtue. This is so because moral virtue makes us aim at the right target, and practical wisdom makes us hit it by choosing the right means.[59]

Finally, friendship. As it was for many ancient philosophers, for Aristotle friendship is indispensable for a good life and happiness. As such it is a virtue—at least closely related to virtue.

Friendship is a virtue—or involves virtue. Moreover, it is one of the most indispensable requirements of life, for no one would choose to live without friends.[60]

We've now investigated virtue with Aristotle, and so we've grasped virtue's relationship to happiness, that "happiness is an activity of the soul that accords with perfect virtue."

Let's turn now to pleasure. How does pleasure fit in with Aristotle's view of happiness?

According to Aristotle, pleasure completes an activity, perfecting and giving it a kind of fullness. Consequently, it is possible to judge or evaluate pleasure based on the activity it completes. Activities in turn may be judged or evaluated relative to the aspect of human nature they engage. Since the soul (its rational part) is more properly human than the body, activities engaging the soul are superior to those engaging the body.

Still, we must measure activities against the moral yardstick of goodness or badness. How can we know the difference between the two? Apart from the obvious, perhaps, Aristotle turns to the "morally good man." Such a man serves as the measure of what is truly and morally pleasurable, and what is not. For such a man, the morally pleasurable is that which is "in accord with virtue."

Pleasure completes an activity. . . . One might believe that all men desire pleasure because all men wish to live. Life is an activity, and each man is active relative to his favorite faculties and activities. For example, the man who is musical actively listens to music. Or take the student thinking about theoretical questions. Or other activities. Now pleasure completes these various activities. As such, it completes life, which these men desire. It is with good reason, then, that they also aim at pleasure since for everyone pleasure completes life, which is desirable. . . .

The activities of thought or the understanding differ from those of the senses, . . . so that the pleasures that complete them are different. . . . The pleasures of thought or the understanding are superior to the pleasures of sensation—of seeing, hearing, smelling, tasting, and touching. . . .

Since activities differ relative to goodness and badness, and since some activities are choiceworthy, others are to be shunned, and still others are neutral, so too are pleasures good or bad, choiceworthy or unprofitable, or neither. Each activity has its own proper pleasure. Therefore, the pleasure proper to morally good activity is morally good, and the pleasure proper to morally bad activity is morally bad. . . .

Things that are both valuable and pleasant to a morally good man *are* actually valuable and pleasant. . . . A morally good man judges activity in accord with virtue the most desirable. . . . And the happy life is one that accords with virtue.[61]

And what about amusement or having fun? For Aristotle, amusement is "a kind of rest" from activity. Since happiness is an activity, amusement cannot, in itself, be happiness. Still, amusement is important for happiness in that it is the "rest or relaxation" that permits us to get back to the relatively serious activity that happiness is.

The happy life is a serious life spent in effort rather than a less serious life engaged in various amusements.[62]

Amusement is a kind of rest or relaxation. We need rest because we cannot work continuously. Rest itself, then, is not an end or goal; rather, we rest for the sake of further activity. . . . In this way, Anacharsis' maxim seems right: "Play and amuse yourself in order to be serious and busy."[63]

As mentioned, happiness is an activity. It is a goal or end in itself insofar as it is an "activity in accord with virtue," and so we desire and choose happiness in and for itself rather than some result beyond happiness.

Happiness is not a habit or disposition. . . . Rather, happiness is an activity, . . . the kind of activity that is desired and chosen for itself rather than as a means to something else. Happiness does not lack anything, but it is self-sufficient. Now, those activities that are desirable and choiceworthy in themselves are ones that do not seek any result beyond doing the activity itself. Activity in accord with virtue appears to be this kind of activity.[64]

It is better to be happy as a result of one's own care and activity than by the gift of chance.[65]

In terms of what may be called a hierarchy of happiness, the highest kind of happiness is that of contemplation. "Happiness is coextensive with contemplation." As proof for this, Aristotle offers the life of the gods as well as other considerations. The happiness of practical wisdom and moral virtue is secondary. Finally, even though contemplation is the highest form of happiness, and the happiness corresponding to moral virtue is second, happiness nevertheless requires external goods. Therefore, happiness has to do with external goods in a tertiary way.

If happiness is an activity in accord with virtue, it is reasonable that it should accord with the highest virtue. And this activity will be the virtue of the best part of us. . . . It is the activity of the rational part of us—whether we call it the mind or intellect or by some other name—in accord with its own proper virtue that will be perfect happiness. . . . As we have already stated, this activity is contemplation—*which may be described as the act of observing and knowing what is with no practical goal in view.*[66]

The following considerations will show that happiness is a contemplative activity. Above all other beings, we assume that the gods are blessed and happy. Still, what sort of activity or actions should we assign to them? Acts of justice? But won't the gods seem absurd in making contracts or returning deposits, and so on? What about acts of courage, then, such as standing up to fear and taking risks because it is noble to do so? Or what about generosity and other acts of liberality? But to whom will they give? And it will be odd if the gods have money or anything like that. And acts of moderation and self-control? But such praise is vulgar since they have no low-ranking desires. If we went through every possible action we would find that they would seem trivial and unworthy of the gods.

Still, everyone supposes that the gods live and that they are therefore active in some way. . . . Now, if we take action away from a living being, as well as production, what is left but contemplation? Therefore, the operation of the god that surpasses all others in blessedness must be contemplative.

As for human activity, the activity that is most similar to this divine activity of contemplation must be essential to happiness. The point is also indicated by the fact that other animals have no share in happiness since they are completely deprived of such contemplative activity. While the whole life of the gods is blessed, and also the life of men inasmuch as the likeness of such an activity belongs to them, no other animal is happy since they do not share in the act of contemplation.

In conclusion, we can say that happiness is coextensive with contemplation—where there is contemplation, there is happiness. The more one is able to engage in contemplation, the more one is happy—not as something extrinsic to contemplation but as something intrinsic to it since contemplation is valuable in itself. Happiness, therefore, is some kind of contemplation.[67]

In comparison with contemplation, the life of moral virtue is happy in a secondary way since its activities are human activities. For we engage in justice and courage and other virtuous acts in relation to other human beings, observing our respective duties relative to contracts and services and many other actions having to do with the passions. And all of these appear to be typically human.[68]

Being a human being, one will also need external goods and advantages since our nature is not self-sufficient for the purpose of contemplation. Instead, our body must also be healthy. Further, it must have food and other attention. Nevertheless, we must not imagine that the happy man will require many or great things.[69]

Some believe that the happy man will not need friends. They say that those who are supremely happy and self-sufficient have no need for friends. . . . Nevertheless, it seems strange to ascribe every good thing to the happy man but then to leave out friends, who are thought to be the greatest of all external goods.[70]

We finish with the biographer Diogenes Laertius' summary of Aristotle's beliefs about the goal of life and happiness. Note the same hierarchy of happiness as that which is presented by Aristotle himself.

Diogenes Laertius Aristotle held that the exercise of virtue in a completed life is the goal of life. He said that happiness is made up of three categories of goods. First are those goods of the soul, which, in fact, he calls the primary goods because of their power. Second are those goods of the body—health, strength, beauty, and similar things. Third are external goods—wealth, good birth, reputation, and the like.

Moreover, he regarded virtue as not of itself sufficient to ensure happiness. Rather, bodily and external goods are also necessary.[71]

Diogenes Laertius Of the three kinds of life, the contemplative, the practical, and the pleasure-loving life, Aristotle preferred the contemplative life.[72]

SUMMARY OF HAPPINESS FOR ARISTOTLE

For Aristotle, happiness is the final goal or good that humans act for, the one that is chosen for itself rather than the means to some other goal or good. This goal or good is itself an ongoing act. It is "an activity of the soul in accord with reason," which is "man's proper function." But such an activity must be excellent or virtuous. Therefore, "the happy life is one that accords with virtue," with excellent activity.

There are two general kinds of virtue, each corresponding to different parts of the human soul. They are the moral or ethical virtues and the intellectual or thinking virtues.

The moral virtues exist relative to what we humans do. In general, they enable humans to perform human functions well relative to themselves and others, in the right manner, at the right time, and in the right place. More specifically, virtues are neither emotions nor capacities.[73] Rather, they are habits (trained abilities or dispositions) that are cultivated and established by means of acting—by doing acts of one virtue or another until we finally possess the habit or disposition.[74] Our habits (virtues) are revealed by "the pleasure or pain that accompanies our actions." Virtue helps us to do well, "what is best," relative to "things that entail pleasure and pain."

Each moral virtue is a mean that falls between two extremes, the excess and defect. For example, courage is the mean that falls between rashness and cowardice. Similarly, moderation falls between immoderation or licentiousness and insensibility or a lack of sensation or feeling.

Finally, moral virtue involves a voluntary act and choice. As such, and given the indeterminate nature of human life, it involves deliberation, which is the process by which we rationally consider the means by which we may achieve some goal or hit some target that is "in our control" and "attainable by action." We deliberate and therefore choose the mean and avoid the excess and deficiency with the help of right reason.

This brings us to the intellectual virtues. The intellectual virtue that primarily helps us deliberate and choose well is practical wisdom, which is "a truth-attaining rational habit concerned with action relative to things that are good and bad for human beings." Other intellectual virtues are scientific knowledge, skillful knowledge, intelligence, and theoretical wisdom.

Returning to "the happy life," which is a life "that accords with virtue," Aristotle holds that there are different levels of happiness. The highest happiness corresponds to the highest activity, which in turn engages the highest part of human nature, the rational part of the soul. This activity is contemplation. Next down is the happiness of human activity, such as living wisely, moderately, courageously, or justly. Although this sort of activity participates in and is directed by reason, it is nevertheless oftentimes aimed at goals or goods that have no direct relation to the activity of contemplation. As such, it is inferior to contemplation but excellent in that it participates in reason. Finally, there is the happiness of external goods, things that are necessary to support the life of the body and, therefore, the life of the mind.

As for pleasure, something that many associate with happiness itself (see, for instance, Aristippus of Cyrene or Epicurus in the following chapters), it is only good or happy insofar as it completes a superior human activity, such as contemplation or behaving with magnanimity. We must ultimately look to the example of excellent human beings, those who are morally good, to know what is superior and what is inferior.

Finally, amusement or having fun is not happiness because it is not the final goal or good that humans shoot for. Rather, amusement is simply giving serious activity a break so that we may get back to the same. As such, it plays a role in happiness, but it is not happiness itself.

NOTES

[1] For the following points regarding the scope of ethics and what kind of person benefits most from studying ethics, see Aristotle, *Nicomachean Ethics* 1.3.1-7 (1094b-1095a). First, the scope of ethics. It is important to note that, for Aristotle, moral philosophy or ethics is not an exact science or kind of knowledge. We should not expect the same level of precision as we would expect in, say, a mathematical investigation. Aristotle's goal, therefore, is to present "a broad outline of the truth" in the *Nicomachean Ethics*. Given the various topics involving broad notions and generalities (for instance, the goal of human action and life, the good, happiness, and the like), he says that "it is enough if we come to generally valid conclusions." This "enough," Aristotle judges, is sufficient for those who have been educated, for "it is the mark of an educated person to look for precision in each kind of thing only so far as the nature of the particular topic allows." This point leads us to the kind of person that benefits most from studying ethics. The educated person is one who has received an "all-around education." Such a person has experience relative to life and human action. For Aristotle, this bars most—if not all—young people from engaging in serious moral philosophy or ethics since, given their young age, they have neither received an all-around education, nor do they have sufficient experience relative to life and human action. Moreover, he declares, young people often live more according to their feelings or passions than they do from rational principles. But then again, he observes, many who are not young also do so. Take those who "lack self-control." Therefore, whether young or old, the key is to live according to the knowledge one has.

[2] Aristotle, *Nicomachean Ethics* 1.1.1 (1094a).

[3] Ibid., 1.2.1-3 (1094a). The Greek behind "end or goal" is *telos*, a term that, in this context, may also be given as "target" or "purpose." In the broadest sense, *telos* is "the fulfillment or completion of anything."

Otherwise, for Aristotle, "the knowledge of this good" is closely tied to the science or knowledge of politics—that is, knowledge having to do with the city-state (*polis*) and "the human good" of everyone within the city-state. Significantly, this is a communal or city-wide good since, as Aristotle puts it, "the good of the city-state is manifestly more important and more perfect" than "the good of one person," even though "the good in both cases is the same."

[4] Ibid., 1.7.1 (1097a).

[5] Ibid., 1.7.3-8 (1097a-1097b).

[6] Ibid., 1.4.2-3 (1095a).

[7] Aristotle goes on to say that "the good of man is associated with the function of man." He assumes that humans have some "natural" general function beyond specific functions such as those governing our eyes (seeing), hands (grasping), feet (walking), and so on. This general function is "unique" to humans. For Aristotle, as we will see, this function is the active exercise of reason.

[8] Ibid., 1.7.9-16 (1097b-1098a). In the interest of space, we have slightly changed the language of Aristotle to be more declarative (it *is*) than conditional (*if . . .*). That said, be assured that the declarative points are Aristotle's.

To better grasp *aretē*, the Greek term behind "virtue," see the Cave's *Aretē: Excellence or Virtue — What the Ancient Greeks Thought and Said about Aretē.* Given the tie, in Aristotle's mind, of happiness to virtue, much of the following content relating Aristotle's view of virtue comes from *Aretē: Excellence or Virtue.*

[9] Ibid., 1.13.1, 5-6 (1102a). For Aristotle, soul goods are the best of goods: "Good things are commonly divided into three groups," he says. "Some are given as 'external goods.' Others are related to the soul or the body. We call those things belonging to the soul most properly and truly goods." See ibid., 1.8.2 (1098b).

[10] The sketch itself is derived from Aristotle's *Nicomachean Ethics*. For more on Aristotle's understanding of the soul, see his *On the Soul.*

[11] Aristotle, *Nicomachean Ethics* 2.1.1 (1103a). The Greek for "intellectual or thinking" is *dianoētikos*, and for "moral or ethical" it is *ēthikos*. The "or" should not be read as *either* one *or* the other, for instance, moral *or* ethical; rather, the two terms are, in this case, equivalent — that is, one can translate *ēthikos* with both words. So it goes with "intellectual or thinking" and *dianoētikos.*

[12] Ibid., 3.5.21 (1114b).

[13] Ibid., 2.1.1 (1103a). The Greek term *ēthikos* (ethical) is related to the Greek term *ēthos* (custom, usage, manner; disposition, character, habit). The term "moral" similarly comes from the Latin *mōs* (custom, manner; character; habit). In some forms of *mōs*, the root is *mōr-* (as in the genitive, *mōris*).

[14] Ibid., 2.1.3 (1103a).

[15] Ibid., 2.1.4-5 (1103a-b).

[16] Ibid., 2.1.7-2.2.1 (1103b). Having said all this, Aristotle observes the complicated nature of discussing moral virtue — excellence having to do with conduct. Any such discussion must necessarily be a sketch, an outline, offering generalities rather than specifics, what is more-than-likely rather than certain. "Let it be understood that all reasoning relative to matters of practice, of conduct, must merely be offered in the form of an outline rather than with any precision. For, as we said at the beginning, we should realize that the kind of reasoning used in any inquiry will vary according to the subject. Accordingly, there is nothing fixed or invariable about practical matters and questions of expediency — any more than with matters of health. And if our general conclusions are inexact in this way, still more will be our reasoning about particular cases. For these fall under no established skill or art or set of rules or precepts. Instead, the one acting, the agent, must always consider for himself what the specific occasion demands, just as with medicine and navigation." Ibid., 2.2.3-4 (1104a).

[17] Ibid., 2.2.6-7 (1104a).

[18] Ibid., 2.3.1 (1104b).

[19] Ibid., 2.3.6 (1104b).

[20] Ibid., 2.3.5 (1104b).

[21] Ibid., 2.4.3 (1105a).

[22] Ibid., 2.5.6 (1106a). "Habit or disposition" is *hexis* (a possession; a permanent state or condition; a trained habit or skill).

[23] Ibid., 2.6.10-12 (1106b).

[24] Ibid., 2.6.2 (1106b).

[25] Ibid., 2.6.15-16 (1106b-1107a).

[26] Ibid., 2.8.1 (1108b).

[27] Ibid., 2.6.18 (1107a). Again, keep in mind that "Happiness is an activity of the soul that accords with perfect virtue." Therefore, the very fact that the "actions and emotions" mentioned in this selection "do not permit the observance of the mean" signifies that such "missing the mark" is not only vicious but also that people feeling and acting in such a way are not happy. To state it plainly, according to Aristotle, those who feel "malice, shamelessness, and envy" and those who engage in "adultery, theft, and murder" *cannot* be happy.

[28] Ibid., 2.7.2-3 (1107b).

[29] For Aristotle's rather brief discussion of these virtues, see ibid., 2.7.4-15 (1107b-1108b). For his detailed discussion, see 3.5.23-4.9.8 (1115a-1128b).

[30] Ibid., 2.8.6 (1109a).

[31] Ibid., 2.9.1-2 (1109a).

[32] Ibid., 2.9.3-7 (1109a-b).

[33] For Aristotle's discussion of these rungs or states, see ibid., 7.1-10. For an image of the ladder and a description of each rung, see the Cave's *Aretē: Excellence or Virtue—What the Ancient Greeks Thought and Said about Aretē.*

[34] Ibid., 3.1.20 (1111a).

[35] Ibid., 3.2.1, 2 (1111b).

[36] Ibid., 3.2.11 (1112a).

[37] Ibid., 3.2.16-17 (1112a).

[38] Ibid., 3.3.6 (1112a).

[39] Ibid., 3.3.10 (1112b).

[40] Ibid., 3.3.11 (1112b).

[41] Ibid., 3.3.19 (1113a).

[42] Ibid., 5.1.8 (1129a).

[43] Ibid., 5.2.10 (1130b).

[44] Ibid., 5.2.12 (1130b-1131a).

[45] For the general conclusion and two points of discussion, see ibid., 6.1.1, 3 (1138b).

[46] Ibid., 6.1.5 (1139a).

[47] Ibid., 6.2.6 (1139b).

[48] Ibid., 6.3.1 (1139b). The parenthetical "or" simply points to another word that may be used to translate the Greek, which is, respectively, *technē, epistēmē, phronēsis, sophia,* and *nous.*

[49] Ibid., 6.3.2-4 (1139b).

[50] Ibid., 6.6.1-2 (1140b-1141a).

[51] Ibid., 6.4.3 (1140a). The post-ellipsis part is actually prior to the first part in

Aristotle's text, but since it is an illustration of *technē*, we have placed it second.

⁵² Ibid., 6.5.1 (1140a).

⁵³ Ibid., 6.5.3 (1140b). The italicized material in parentheses is explanatory (not Aristotle's).

⁵⁴ Ibid., 6.5.4-6 (1140b). Aristotle seems to combine the words *sōzein* (to save, preserve) and *phronēsis* (practical wisdom) to get *sōphrosunē* (moderation). Hence, his remark, "This point accounts for the word 'moderation,' which means 'preserving practical wisdom.'"

⁵⁵ Ibid., 6.5.8 (1140b).

⁵⁶ Ibid., 6.6.2 (1141a).

⁵⁷ Ibid., 6.6.2-3 (1141a). Aristotle again makes the last point a few lines later.

⁵⁸ Ibid., 6.7.6, 6.8.1 (1141b).

⁵⁹ Ibid., 6.11.7-6.12.1, 6.12.4-6 (1143b, 1144a).

⁶⁰ Ibid., 8.1.1 (1155a).

⁶¹ Ibid., parts from 10.4.8-10.6.6 (1174b-1177a). "Completes" (from *teleō* or *teleioō*) can also be given as "fulfills" or "perfects." Otherwise, compare the "morally good man" to the "wise and sensible man" in ibid., 2.6.15 (1107a) cited above.

⁶² Ibid., 10.6.6-7 (1177a).

⁶³ Ibid., 10.6.6 (1176b-1177a). For the Scythian Anacharsis, see Diogenes Laertius, *Lives* 1.101-105.

⁶⁴ Ibid., 10.6.2-3 (1176a-1176b).

⁶⁵ Ibid., 1.9.5 (1099b).

⁶⁶ Ibid., 10.7.1 (1177a).

⁶⁷ Ibid., 10.8.7-8 (1178b). "Contemplation" is *theōria* (the act of seeing, viewing, beholding, inspecting; consideration).

⁶⁸ Ibid., 10.8.1 (1178a).

⁶⁹ Ibid., 10.8.9 (1178b-1179a).

⁷⁰ Ibid., 9.9.1-2 (1169b).

⁷¹ Diogenes Laertius, *Lives* 5.30.

⁷² Ibid., 5.31.

⁷³ To expand the point: Happiness is neither a feeling (emotion) nor the capacity for a feeling (emotion); rather, happiness is an activity in accord with the habit-disposition (virtue) that enables us to do well relative to our feelings (emotions).

⁷⁴ As such, although Aristotle does not explicitly make the point, we may distinguish between "acts of virtue" and "virtuous acts" — the former being an act independent of one's ongoing disposition (or habits) and the latter stemming from one's ongoing disposition (or habits). For instance, one may perform an act of courage while nevertheless generally being a coward, or one may perform a courageous act due to one's ongoing, habitual courage. Thanks to Dr. Mark Lowery, late professor at the University of Dallas, for this distinction (in the context of Thomas Aquinas on the virtues).

12

ARISTIPPUS OF CYRENE
& CYRENAICISM

"Aristippus was a Cyrenian by birth. According to Aeschines, he came to Athens thanks to the fame and reputation of Socrates. . . . When someone asked him what advantage philosophers have over other men, he answered, 'Even if all the laws are repealed, philosophers will go on living in the same manner.'"
—Diogenes Laertius, *Lives and Opinions of Eminent Philosophers*

ARISTIPPUS (c. 435-356 BC) ANNOYED MANY men in the ancient world. One was Socrates. Diogenes Laertius tells us that Socrates—the very man who trained to endure hunger, thirst, and cold—found it hard on occasion "to endure" Aristippus because what Aristippus did "annoyed" him. We're further told that Aristippus' contemporary Xenophon was positively "hostile" toward him—so much so, that in his *Memorabilia*, he pitted Socrates against him and his life lived in pursuit of pleasure. Nor did Plato care for him; rather, he "reproached" Aristippus in his book *On the Soul*. If we can trust Diogenes Laertius on the point, there were others.[1]

Regardless, the significance is not so much the relational soap opera starring these men of antiquity as it is the underlying issue, the disputed point, which is to say the nature of the good and happy life. Whereas Socrates and those he influenced—Xenophon, Plato, and Aristotle, to name a few—associated happiness and the good life with wisdom and virtue, Aristippus went with the far more obvious choice—pleasure.

But more. For Aristippus, the most significant pleasure was that of the body. Soul pleasures, or mental pleasures, are fine, he judged, but bodily pleasures are clearly what we humans long for. Offer a child an interesting scroll to read versus a honey-sweetened cookie to eat, and the child will go for the cookie every time. It's obvious, isn't it? Or so Aristippus urged.

Whatever we may decide, one point is fairly certain from the anecdotes we have concerning Aristippus' life. He was one of the most colorful characters in antiquity. Part of this color is the fact that he seems to have had a witty quip ready for every situation, however controversial or delicate. Shacking up with a prostitute? Blowing money on gourmet food? Groveling to tyrants? Spending a little too much time with rich men? Taking fees for teaching (something Socrates refused to do)? Aristippus had a clever answer for each.

Born in Cyrene along the northern coast of Africa in what is now Libya, Aristippus traveled to Greece and eventually to Athens to learn from Socrates. In time he founded or inspired the Cyrenaic school, which got its name from his hometown. After Aristippus died, his daughter, Arete, and his grandson—Arete's son, also called Aristippus—carried on his teachings and way of life in pursuit of pleasure-related happiness. So it was that the Cyrenaic school, or Cyrenaicism, came to be associated with hedonism.

In the selections that follow, we present the general Cyrenaic teachings on happiness (those of Aristippus), as well as the views of those who continued the Cyrenaic school after or alongside Aristippus (his daughter, Arete; his grandson, Aristippus; and his followers Hegesias, Anniceris, and Theodorus).

IN THEIR OWN WORDS

The first selections from the fourth century AD *Christian bishop and historian Eusebius of Caesarea, the third century* AD *biographer Diogenes Laertius, and the second century* AD *physician and philosopher Sextus Empiricus present the views of Aristippus and the Cyrenaics on the goal of life, happiness, pleasure, and pain. In short, both the goal of life and happiness are fundamentally connected to pleasure or pleasures.*

Eusebius of Caesarea Aristippus was a companion of Socrates and the founder of the so-called Cyrenaic school. . . . His life was entirely luxurious, and he was fond of pleasure. . . . He used to say that the essence of happiness is found in pleasures.[2]

Eusebius of Caesarea Aristippus of Cyrene says that pleasure is the goal of life, the highest good, and that pain is the worst of evils.[3]

Diogenes Laertius Aristippus and the Cyrenaics hold that there is a difference between "the goal of life" and "happiness." The goal is a particular pleasure, whereas happiness as a whole is made up of all the particular pleasures.[4]

Diogenes Laertius A particular pleasure is chosen for itself, whereas happiness is not chosen for itself but for its particular pleasures.[5]

Diogenes Laertius Aristippus and the Cyrenaics prove that pleasure is the goal of life with this fact: from our childhood on we are unconsciously attracted to it, that is, we don't even have to think about it. And when we get it, we wish for nothing else. And we flee from nothing else as much as we flee from pain, the opposite of pleasure. . . . Still, they say that some people may fail to choose pleasure because they are confused.[6]

Diogenes Laertius While pleasure is choiceworthy in itself, Aristippus and the Cyrenaics nevertheless recognize that the means by which some pleasures are attained are oftentimes troublesome in themselves, which is to say, the very opposite of pleasure. Therefore, the business of collecting together the pleasures that make up the whole of happiness appears to them to be quite unpleasant.[7]

Diogenes Laertius Aristippus and the Cyrenaics argue that there are two modes of feeling—pleasure and pain. Pleasure is a smooth, soft motion, whereas pain's motion is rough and harsh. . . . Pleasure is agreeable, attracting all living beings, whereas pain is repugnant, repelling them.[8]

Sextus Empiricus Cyrenaicism differs from skepticism. It declares that pleasure and a certain smooth motion of the flesh is the goal for human beings, whereas we skeptics say that it is tranquility, which stands in opposition to their goal.[9]

Diogenes Laertius Aristippus and the Cyrenaics call the absence of pleasure and the absence of pain intermediate conditions.[10]

Diogenes Laertius When it comes to the nature of pleasure, Epicurus and the Cyrenaics differ. The Cyrenaics only accept kinetic pleasure, that is, pleasure in motion; they do not accept static, or katastematic, pleasure. By contrast, Epicurus accepts both.[11]

Diogenes Laertius Contrary to Epicurus' position, the removal of pain does not seem to the Cyrenaics to be a pleasure any more than the absence of pleasure is a pain. The reason is this: both pleasure and pain consist in motion, whereas neither the absence of pleasure nor the absence of pain is motion. Indeed, the absence of pain is similar to the condition of a sleeping person.[12]

Diogenes Laertius Aristippus said, "Rather than going without pleasures, it is best to be their master and not their slave."[13]

Diogenes Laertius No one pleasure is different from or more pleasant than another pleasure.[14]

Diogenes Laertius Aristippus and the Cyrenaics say that bodily pleasures are much better than soul pleasures, including those of the mind, and that bodily distress is worse than soul distress. This is why those who do wrong are punished with bodily pain.[15]

Diogenes Laertius Not all soul pleasures and pains arise from bodily pleasures and pains. For example, we delight in the health, wealth, and happiness of our homeland as if this health, wealth, and happiness were our own.[16]

Diogenes Laertius Aristippus and the Cyrenaics say that pleasure does not arise from seeing and hearing things alone.[17]

Diogenes Laertius We listen with pleasure to the imitation of mourning, while the real experience of mourning is painful.[18]

Diogenes Laertius Contrary to the doctrine of Epicurus, Aristippus and the Cyrenaics do not admit that pleasure comes from the memory of good things or the expectation of good things.[19]

Diogenes Laertius Aristippus and the Cyrenaics say that although wealth is capable of producing pleasure, it is not choiceworthy in itself.[20]

Diogenes Laertius Aristippus and the Cyrenaics do not fully admit the idea that every wise man lives pleasantly and every simple man painfully. Still, it is mostly true. What is sufficient is when a man enjoys each pleasure as it comes.[21]

Diogenes Laertius In his book, *On the Philosophical Schools*, the historian Hippobotus reports the Cyrenaic belief that even those pleasures arising from shameful things—that is, from shameful deeds and situations—are good.[22]

The second set of selections in the form of brief reports, anecdotes, and sayings demonstrates Aristippus' views regarding happiness and pleasure.

Diogenes Laertius Aristippus took pleasure from things that were present and ready at hand. He did not hunt around and toil to enjoy something that was not present.[23]

Vitruvius Pollio They say that when the Socratic philosopher Aristippus was shipwrecked and cast ashore on the coast of the Rhodians, he observed geometrical figures drawn there. Turning to his traveling companions, he called out and spoke in this manner: "Let us be full of good hope, for I see signs indicating the presence of human beings."

When Aristippus came to the town of Rhodes, he went directly to the gymnasium. There he began discussing philosophical matters. Consequently, the people donated gifts to him so that he could not only provide clothing, nourishment, and whatever else it takes to live for himself but also for those who accompanied him.

When his companions wanted to return home, and they asked him what message he wanted them to convey, Aristippus instructed them to say this: that children should be provided with the sort of possessions and resources that will make them equal to free persons—the sort they can swim with and retain even after a shipwreck.[24]

Diogenes Laertius Aristippus was capable of adapting himself to a particular time, place, and person, and of playing his part appropriately under any circumstance. . . . He could always arrange a situation for his own well-being.[25]

Horace (in speaking about himself, Horace reveals Aristippus' own practice—at least as understood by Horace) Now I secretly fall back to Aristippus' precepts, and I try to adapt circumstances to myself and not myself to circumstances.[26]

Diogenes Laertius Bion tells the story in his *Discourses* that when his servant was on the road carrying a sack of coins that was too heavy, Aristippus said, "Dump it. Carry only as much as you are able."[27]

Diogenes Laertius When some man was puffed up with pride because of his extensive learning, Aristippus said, "Just as those who eat and exercise most are not healthier relative to those who eat what is necessary and exercise when they have to, so too it is not broad learning that leads to excellence but useful learning."[28]

Diogenes Laertius To the man who bragged that he could drink a lot without getting drunk, Aristippus said, "And so can a mule."[29]

Diogenes Laertius When Dionysus offered him his choice of three courtesans, he took all three, saying that even Paris obtained no good by preferring one beauty to the rest.[30]

Diogenes Laertius To the man who faulted him for living with a courtesan, Aristippus asked, "Is there any difference between taking a house that many have lived in before versus one that nobody has lived in?"

The man replied, "No."

Aristippus went on, saying, "Let's take another example. What about a ship that countless people have sailed in versus one that nobody has sailed in?"

"There's no difference," the man answered.

And so Aristippus concluded, "Well then, there is no difference between a woman who has lived with many versus one who has lived with no other men."[31]

Diogenes Laertius When Plato reprimanded Aristippus for his extravagance, Aristippus asked, "Do you think Dionysus is a good man?"

Plato said, "Yes."

Aristippus replied, "And yet he lives more extravagantly than I do. Therefore, there is nothing that prevents a man from living extravagantly and living well."[32]

Diogenes Laertius Once, when Diogenes [the Cynic] was washing vegetables, he saw Aristippus passing by and ridiculed him, saying, "If you had learned to use vegetables for food, you wouldn't be a slave in a tyrant's palace."

Aristippus replied, "If you had learned to associate with men, you would not be washing vegetables."[33]

Diogenes Laertius To the man who reprimanded him for spending too much on luxury food, Aristippus queried, "If you could have bought these things for three obols, would you have?"

The man said, "Yes."

"Well then," Aristippus responded, "I am no more the lover of pleasure than you are the lover of money."[34]

The remaining selections introduce Aristippus' later students, and thus later Cyrenaics, including his own daughter, Arete; her son and his grandson, Aristippus; and other followers. Among the latter were Hegesias, Anniceris, and Theodorus. We'll first turn to Arete and her son, Aristippus.

Diogenes Laertius Aristippus gave his daughter Arete the best guidance, training her to look down on excess.[35]

Eusebius of Caesarea Among his other hearers, there was his own daughter, Arete. She gave birth to a son and named him Aristippus. He was called his mother's own student since she introduced him to philosophical studies.

Now this Aristippus, *the son of Arete,* clearly said that the goal of life is pleasure, defining pleasure as a kind of motion. He said that there are three states affecting our constitution. There's one in which we feel pain. It's like a storm at sea. There's another in which we feel pleasure. It may be likened to the rolling of a gentle wave since pleasure is a gentle movement comparable to a favorable breeze. The third is an intermediate state in which we feel neither pain nor pleasure. This one is similar to a calm.[36]

Next up is Hegesias, who began his own Cyrenaic school, the so-called "Hēgēsiakoi." Though the Hēgēsiakoi also held that pleasure is the aim of life and connected to happiness, they "denied the possibility of complete happiness" thanks to the bodily suffering we humans inevitably experience.

Diogenes Laertius The Hēgēsiakoi proposed the same aims of life *as Aristippus and the Cyrenaics*—namely, pleasure and pain.[37]

Diogenes Laertius The Hēgēsiakoi denied the possibility of complete happiness. This is so because the body is infected with much suffering. And since the soul shares in the sufferings of the body, it is therefore troubled when the body is troubled. And luck prevents many things that we hope for. From all this it follows that complete happiness is non-existent.[38]

Diogenes Laertius The Hēgēsiakoi suppose that there is nothing naturally pleasant or unpleasant. Rather, when some men are pleased by something and others are not, this is because of the novelty or scarcity or even the oversupply of such things.[39]

Diogenes Laertius The Hēgēsiakoi say that poverty and wealth have nothing to do with pleasure. Rich men do not feel pleasure any better than poor men.[40]

Diogenes Laertius The Hēgēsiakoi say that slavery and freedom are neither good nor bad when it comes to measuring pleasure. The same is true for a noble and a low birth as well as a good and a bad reputation.[41]

Diogenes Laertius The Hēgēsiakoi say that the wise man will not be overly concerned with pursuing good things as he will be with shunning bad things. This is so because the goal is to live free from all trouble and pain.[42]

Cicero If then, we want to know the truth, death takes us from evil not from good. In fact, this proposition was maintained by Hegesias, the Cyrenaic philosopher, with such a solid argument that Ptolemy is said to have prohibited him from lecturing in the schools of philosophy because many of his hearers committed suicide. . . . The book of Hegesias to which I refer is called, *The Man Who Starves Himself.* It tells the story of a man who is stopped by his friends when he is starving himself to death. When asked why he's behaving in such a manner, he answers by listing all the pains and discomforts of human life.[43]

Next are teachings from the Cyrenaic school of Anniceris.

Diogenes Laertius Even if the wise man experiences distress, he will be no less happy even though his actual pleasures are few.[44]

Diogenes Laertius The happiness of a friend is not in itself choice-worthy since it is not felt by his neighbor.[45]

Diogenes Laertius Anniceris declares that a friend should be accepted not merely for the advantages he offers . . . but for the goodwill the friend engenders in us, on account of which we will even put up with suffering. Even though the men of this school make pleasure the end, and they are annoyed when deprived of it, they nevertheless willingly put up with suffering because of affection for their friends.[46]

Finally, there are the views of the Cyrenaic Theodorus, who was called "the Atheist" since he "totally rejected the usual opinions about the gods."

Diogenes Laertius Theodorus understood joy to be the goal of life and pain or grief to be the greatest evil. The one is brought about by thoughtfulness, the other by thoughtlessness.[47]

Diogenes Laertius Theodorus said that the wise man would satisfy his desires out in the open without any concern for the circumstances.[48]

HAPPINESS FOR ARISTIPPUS THE CYRENAIC & CYRENAICISM

For Aristippus and Cyrenaicism, "the essence of happiness," as Eusebius of Caesarea wrote, "is found in pleasures." More specifically, happiness consists of a collection of particular pleasures.

Pleasure itself—or more precisely, individual, specific pleasures—is the goal or good of life. We know this because pleasure is what children naturally choose without being aware of what they are doing. Pleasure is choiceworthy in itself.

Pleasure and pain are two modes of feeling. Pain is the opposite of pleasure. Both pleasure and pain are motions rather than static or motionless phenomena. Pleasure is "a smooth and soft motion, whereas pain's motion is rough and harsh." The absence of pleasure is not pain, just as the absence of pain is not pleasure. The absence of each is a condition that falls somewhere between pleasure and pain. There are bodily pleasures and pains and soul pleasures and pains. The former are superior to the latter.

Since happiness consists of a collection of particular pleasures, and "the means by which some pleasures are attained are oftentimes troublesome in themselves," the "business of collecting together the pleasures that make up the whole of happiness" can be, paradoxically, "quite unpleasant." Still, it's what we humans naturally do—we aim for pleasure.

NOTES

[1] For the response of Socrates, Xenophon, and Plato to Aristippus, see Diogenes Laertius, *Lives* 2.65. For Socrates' conversation with Aristippus in Xenophon's *Memorabilia*, see Chapter 10, "Xenophon & Socrates."

[2] Eusebius, *Preparation for the Gospel* 14.18.

[3] Ibid., 1.8.

[4] Diogenes Laertius, *Lives* 2.87.

[5] Ibid., 2.88.

[6] Ibid., 2.88, 89.

[7] Ibid., 2.90.

[8] Ibid., 2.86-87.

[9] Sextus Empiricus, *Outlines of Pyrrhonism* 1.215.

[10] Diogenes Laertius, *Lives* 2.90.

[11] Ibid., 10.136. For discussions on the nature of and differences between kinetic and katastematic pleasure, see A.A. Long, *Hellenistic Philosophy: Stoics, Epicureans, Sceptics*, 2nd ed. (London: Duckworth, 1986), 64-65, and J.M. Rist, *Epicurus: An Introduction* (Cambridge: Cambridge University Press, 1972), 170-172. In short, kinetic pleasure is that which accompanies the ongoing act of satisfying some desire, whereas katastematic pleasure is that of being satisfied after the act. For example, when one is thirsty, one drinks water. The ongoing act of quenching thirst is satisfying—pleasing (a kinetic pleasure). When one stops drinking, one is satisfied (no longer thirsty), which is also pleasing (a katastematic pleasure). We might call the former "acting" (or "active") pleasure and the latter "standing" (or "static") pleasure.

[12] Diogenes Laertius, *Lives* 2.89. For "Epicurus' position," see Chapter 15, "Epicurus & Epicureanism," which includes Diogenes Laertius, *Lives* 10.128-132, 138, 139. See also Cicero, *On the Ends of Good Things and Bad Things* 37, 38. Both may be found in the Cave's *The Best of Epicurus: The Life, Writings & Teachings of Epicurus the Greek Philosopher*, 124-125, 137.

[13] Diogenes Laertius, *Lives* 2.75.

[14] Ibid., 2.87.

[15] Ibid., 2.90. See also ibid., 10.137: Cyrenaics "believe that pains of the body are worse than pains of the soul. Their evidence is that wrongdoers are punished with bodily pain."

[16] Ibid., 2.89.

[17] Ibid., 2.90.

[18] Ibid., 2.90.

19 Ibid., 2.89. For "the doctrine of Epicurus" (including the fear of bad things to come), see Chapter 15, "Epicurus & Epicureanism," which includes Diogenes Laertius, *Lives* 10.137 and *Vatican Sayings* 19, 35. See also Cicero, *On the Ends of Good Things and Bad Things* 55, 57. Both may be found in the Cave's *The Best of Epicurus: The Life, Writings & Teachings of Epicurus the Greek Philosopher*, 133-134, 145, 146, 181.

20 Diogenes Laertius, *Lives* 2.92.

21 Ibid., 2.91.

22 Ibid., 2.88.

23 Ibid., 2.66.

24 Vitruvius Pollio, *The Ten Books on Architecture* 6.1 (Introduction).

25 Diogenes Laertius, *Lives* 2.66.

26 Horace, *Epistle* 1.18. Horace claims that he himself is a member of no particular school of philosophy; rather, he visits each school as a guest. Sometimes he is an "observer of true virtue." Sometimes, as he admits, he follows the lead of Aristippus.

27 Diogenes Laertius, *Lives* 2.77.

28 Ibid., 2.71.

29 Ibid., 2.73.

30 Ibid., 2.67.

31 Ibid., 2.74.

32 Ibid., 2.69. Dionysus, here, likely refers to Dionysus I of Syracuse. For more, see the introductory content for Chapter 8, "Plato & Socrates."

33 Ibid., 2.68. For more on Diogenes the Cynic, see the next chapter, Chapter 13, "Diogenes of Sinope."

34 Ibid., 2.75.

35 Ibid., 2.72.

36 Eusebius, *Preparation for the Gospel* 14.18.

37 Ibid., 2.93.

38 Diogenes Laertius, *Lives* 2.94.

39 Ibid., 2.94.

40 Ibid., 2.94.

41 Ibid., 2.94-95.

42 Ibid., 2.95.

43 Cicero, *Tusculan Disputations* 1.34.

44 Diogenes Laertius, *Lives* 2.96.

45 Ibid 2.96.

46 Ibid 2.96-97.

47 Ibid 2.98.

48 Ibid 2.99.

                                    13

DIOGENES OF SINOPE
THE CYNICS & CYNICISM

"When someone asked Plato, 'In your mind, what kind of a man does Diogenes seem to be?' he said, 'A Socrates gone mad.'"

—Diogenes Laertius, *Lives and Opinions of Eminent Philosophers*

"The man speeding on to happiness must go on even if it is through fire and sword." —Diogenes of Sinope, *Letter to Hicetas*

PAIN IS GOOD. Not in itself, perhaps, but it is good to be challenged, to toil and sweat, to go without, to suffer. Or so judged Diogenes of Sinope (c. 410-323 BC) and the Cynics.[1]

The philosopher Plato judged Diogenes of Sinope, the key founder of ancient Cynicism, a "Socrates gone mad." The Greek for "mad" is *mainomenos*, a word related to the English words "mania" and "maniac." Thus, his quip was not intended as a compliment. Rather, it was meant to undercut what Diogenes was doing. The man's crazy! insane! unhealthy! For Plato, Diogenes—and, therefore, Cynicism—was an extreme version of the far healthier, moderate, and *sane* Socrates.

If Diogenes was a Socrates *mainomenos*, then what was it that he and his wisdom and way of life took too far? Asked another way, What was Cynicism all about? The Cynics practiced the Socratic art of endurance—Socrates' self-control and indifference to suffering. They also emphasized Socrates' frank and open search for the meaning of reality and human life, and his free questioning of conventional terms used to describe the same. Then there was their habitual inattention to their own appearance, and their emphasis on frugality and living a simple life. All of these, and more, Diogenes of Sinope and the other Cynics took to a *mainomenos* extreme in imitation of Socrates.

The name itself—Cynic (*kunikos*) or Cynicism (*kunismos*)—comes from the Greek for dog (*kuōn*). Why the name? Because the Cynics behaved like dogs. More accurately, they discovered from dogs and other animals how to follow nature. So it was that they learned how to live life according to virtue since, for them, a virtuous life entailed a natural life. Doing so, they found out how to wag their tails no matter what was going on—which is to say they discovered how to be happy.

More than a theoretical philosophy, Cynicism was a way of life. Cynic practice consisted of two major aspects. One was concerned with becoming truly free or independent by means of ongoing training—the practice of endurance by reducing desires and cultivating self-control; the active embrace of hardship and suffering; the pursuit of a shameless, self-sufficient, and simple or frugal life centered on necessity alone. For this reason, Cynics wore a simple outfit consisting of, in addition to long hair and a beard, a worn garment, a staff, and a leather bag that held everything they required for their spare existence. The other aspect had to do with a mission to help others see through human vanity and the apparent value of many human conventions and cherished things in order to live a freer and more authentic and virtuous life according to nature. Frank truth-telling in the context of conversation or street preaching was the central way that Cynics reached others.

For nearly a millennium, then, from the late fifth century BC to the late fifth century AD, the average person would have encountered Cynicism through its representatives who lived and begged and taught in the open air. There they would be in the typical Cynic outfit, walking along the road, or standing in the marketplace, or sitting by a temple taking care of their own business, or talking with others, preaching even, criticizing society and challenging everyone to wake up in order to live freer, more authentic and self-sufficient lives— which is to say they wanted everyone to practice happiness.

IN THEIR OWN WORDS

We begin with the basic Cynic interest in happiness—that happiness is the goal of life. But what is happiness? Happiness is to live a life in step with nature. And doing so is to live a life according to virtue. So it is that the excellent or virtuous human is the happy human.

Julian (the Roman emperor) The main goal of the Cynics . . . was how they themselves might be happy.[2]

Julian (the Roman emperor) Now the aim and end of the Cynic philosophy, as with every philosophy, is to be happy — but to be happy in a life lived according to nature and not according to the opinions of the many.[3]

Diogenes Laertius (Diogenes of Sinope is speaking) "Rather than unprofitable, toilsome exercises, men should prefer those which follow nature in order to live happily."[4]

Diogenes Laertius The Cynics hold that the goal of life is to live according to virtue.[5]

Crates of Thebes We Cynics say that the good and excellent man, and no other man, is called happy.[6]

What must we do to be happy? We must take the steep and troublesome path to happiness. Doing so, we must endure much. Most significantly, rather than merely thinking and talking about it, happiness is a matter of practice.

Diogenes of Sinope I came, Father, to Athens, and learning that Socrates' associate was teaching about happiness, I went to him. And he happened to be speaking about the paths that lead to happiness. He declared that there are two and not many paths — and that one is a shortcut and the other is long. . . . The one is short, steep, and troublesome; the other is long, smooth, and easy. . . . While the others, who were struck with fear at the troublesome and steep nature of the one path, called on him to lead them along the long and smooth one, I, superior to the hardships, chose the steep and troublesome path — for the man speeding on to happiness must go on even if it is through fire and sword.[7]

Crates of Thebes One must go for happiness, as Diogenes used to say, even if the going is through fire.[8]

Crates of Thebes Long is the path that leads to happiness through words alone. But the path that leads to happiness through the practice of daily deeds is short.[9]

Julian (the Roman emperor) Diogenes *of Sinope* lived more happily than one who is counted the happiest of men. And he actually used to assert that he lived more happily than such a man. But if you do not believe me, try his way of life not by talking about it but by doing it. Then you'll get it.[10]

Dio Chrysostom When a man watching the Isthmian games at Corinth asked Diogenes of Sinope who his own competitors were, Diogenes responded as follows: "Hardships that are very severe and impossible to overcome for gluttonous and folly-stricken men who feast all day long and snore at night." . . .

Diogenes went on, saying, "The noble and excellent man believes that his hardships are his greatest opponents, and always wants to battle with them day and night—not to win a sprig of parsley, as so many goats might do, nor for a bit of wild olive, or of pine, but to win happiness and virtue throughout all the days of his life. . . . He is afraid of none of those opponents, nor does he pray to draw another, but he challenges them one after another, grappling with hunger and cold, withstanding thirst, and disclosing no weakness even though he must endure the lash or give his body to be cut or burned. Poverty, exile, loss of reputation, and the like have no terrors for him. No, he holds them as mere trifles, and while in their grip, the perfect man is often as sportive as boys with their dice and their colored balls."[11]

But where, for the Cynics, is happiness located? Is it out there or in here? The "where" of happiness is internal. True happiness is inside us—it is not something external. It is a mind or soul reality rather than a body reality or anything related to the body such as power, wealth, possessions, pleasure, experiences, imports, luxuries, and like things.

Julian (the Roman emperor) We must not be busy about happiness as if it were hidden away outside ourselves. . . . Is it not laughable when a man tries to find happiness somewhere outside himself, and thinks that wealth and birth and the influence of friends and, generally speaking, everything of that sort is of the utmost importance? . . . We must say that happiness resides in our minds, in the best and noblest part of us. . . . Diogenes *of Sinope* himself professed this belief.[12]

Epictetus the Stoic (writing as though a Cynic) Where are you hurrying? What are you doing, you miserable men? Like blind people you are wandering up and down. You are going by another road and have left the true road. You search for prosperity and happiness where they are not. . . . Why do you seek happiness outside yourself? In the body? It is not there. . . . It is not in possessions. . . . It is not in power.[13]

Crates of Thebes Take care of your soul—but your body only so far as what is necessary, and externals not even that much. I say this because happiness is not a pleasure that requires external things, nor does perfect virtue require these.[14]

Teles of Megara, the Cynic (from the discourse, "On Pleasure Not Being the Goal of Life") If the happy life must be measured by the yardstick of excessive pleasure, then no one, says Crates, will be judged happy. Rather, if anyone wishes to weigh every stage in the whole of life, he will discover that there is a far greater quantity of pain and suffering. . . . I do not see how someone will live a happy life if he really must measure it by an excess of pleasure.[15]

Lucian of Samosata (the Cynic is speaking to Lycinus in The Cynic, *a dialogue)* Now you . . . are like the greedy, unrestrained person who grabs everything. Local productions will not do for you—the world must be your storehouse. Your homeland and its seas are insufficient, so you purchase your pleasures from the ends of the earth, preferring the exotic to that which is home grown, the costly to the cheap, the rare to the common. In fact, you would rather have troubles and complications than avoid them.

Most of the precious instruments of happiness that you so pride yourselves on are won only with unhappiness and hardships. Give a moment's thought, if you will, to the gold you all pray for, to the silver, the costly houses, the elaborate clothing. And do not forget all the trouble and toil and danger they cost—the blood and death and ruin. Not only do large numbers of men perish at sea on their account, but many endure miseries in producing them. Moreover, they're very likely to be fought for—the desire for them makes friends plot against friends, children against parents, wives against husbands.

How pointless it all is! Embroidered clothes have no more warmth in them than others. Gilded houses do not do better in keeping out the rain. A drink is no sweeter out of a silver cup—or a gold one for that matter. An ivory bed makes sleep no softer; on the contrary, your fortunate man on his ivory bed between his delicate sheets constantly finds himself calling on sleep in vain. And as to the elaborate preparation of food, I hardly need to say that instead of aiding nutrition it injures the body and produces diseases in it.

And what is to be said about sex—about the many activities men do and suffer thanks to those things belonging to Aphrodite? This longing is easy to take care of unless a kind of licentious indulgence is the goal. And yet in this business, frenzied passion and moral corruption do not seem to be enough for these men. But these days, men pervert the use of everything they have, using it for unnatural purposes. Take the man who, rather than using a carriage, chooses to use a bed as though it were a carriage.[16]

Now that we've addressed the basic concern the Cynics had with being happy (that happiness is the goal of life), and we've presented their basic understanding of happiness (that happiness is a matter of living in step with nature, which is the same as living in accord with virtue), we continue with the three most significant Cynics in antiquity—Antisthenes of Athens, Diogenes of Sinope, and Crates of Thebes. Our questions: What did each believe about happiness? And how did each speak and act relative to the same?

We begin with Antisthenes of Athens (c. 445-365 BC). For him, to mention a few points, happiness is virtue, which is something one does rather than something one talks about. Happiness is not the enjoyment of pleasure;

rather, it is the ability to endure, to be indifferent to suffering. Happiness is having enough. As such, it coincides with self-sufficiency and a simple, frugal life.

Diogenes Laertius Making his home in the Piraeus, Antisthenes used to walk about five miles to Athens every day in order to hear Socrates. He learned the art of endurance from him, imitating his indifference to suffering. So it was that he began the Cynic philosophy and the Cynic way of life.[17]

Diogenes Laertius Antisthenes held that virtue is sufficient for happiness. Virtue requires nothing more than the strength of Socrates.[18]

Diogenes Laertius Antisthenes held that virtue is something you do—it is a matter of deeds. It doesn't require a stockpile of arguments or much learning.[19]

Diocles of Magnesia (reporting a saying of Antisthenes) Virtue is the same for a woman as it is for a man.[20]

Diogenes Laertius Antisthenes held that the wise man is self-sufficient since all the goods of others are his.[21]

Diocles of Magnesia (reporting a saying of Antisthenes) Practical wisdom is a sturdy wall that will neither fall down nor be betrayed.[22]

Diogenes Laertius Antisthenes said again and again, "I would rather go insane than enjoy myself with pleasure."[23]

Xenophon (Socrates is conversing with Antisthenes and others) Socrates said, "And you, Antisthenes, what do you pride yourself on?"

"I pride myself on wealth," he declared. . . .

"Okay, then," Socrates went on, "given the little wealth that you have, tell us how you pride yourself on wealth."

Antisthenes said, "I do because I believe that a man's wealth or lack of wealth is not a matter of household goods but of soul goods.

I notice many private citizens who think of themselves as poor even though they have a pile of money and possessions. For this reason, they give themselves over to any toil or danger in order to increase their wealth. And I know of brothers who have an equal share of their inheritance. One of them has plenty, more than enough to meet expenses, while the other is in utter want. And I've observed some tyrants who are so hungry for wealth that they are willing to do terrible things compared with those who are entirely poor. Because they lack things, some people snatch things, others break in and take things, and others follow the slave trade. But there are some tyrants who destroy whole families, kill men by the crowd, and oftentimes enslave even entire cities, all for the sake of money. I deeply pity these men for this oppressive disease. They are like the man who has plenty to eat but can't satisfy himself even though he keeps on eating.

"As for me, my possessions are so great that I can hardly find them myself. I have enough to eat so that I'm not hungry and enough to drink so that I'm not thirsty. And I have enough clothing so that when I'm outside, I'm no colder than Callias is, a man who is remarkably wealthy. And when I go into a house, I look on the walls as exceedingly warm tunics and the roofs as exceptionally thick mantles. And the bedding that I own is so satisfactory that it is actually a hard task to wake me up in the morning. If my body ever stands in need of satisfying the urges of Aphrodite, I am quite satisfied with whomever is nearby. And those I go to are quite fond of me since no one else is willing to be with them.

"All these things seem so pleasant to me that I would never pray for greater pleasure in engaging in any one of them. No, I'd rather pray for less. I would because I regard some of them as being more pleasurable than they are beneficial.

"But the most valuable part of my wealth I count as this, that even if someone robbed me of what I now possess, I see no occupation so humble that it would not furnish me with adequate provisions. For whenever I wish to enjoy myself, I do not purchase highly prized items in the marketplace since they are very expensive, but I withdraw wealth from my soul. And this makes a difference in producing enjoyment—whether I have something only when I truly want it, or when I have something extravagant, like this fine Thasian wine that fortune has presented to me, and I am drinking without the promptings of thirst.

"Yes—and it is natural that those whose eyes are set on frugality are more honest than those whose eyes are fixed on money-making. For those who are most contented with what they have are least likely to covet what belongs to others.

"And it is worth noting that wealth of this kind also makes people generous. My friend Socrates here and I are examples. For Socrates, from whom I acquired this wealth of mine, did not come to my relief limiting it by number and weight, but he gave me all that I could carry. And as for me, I am now stingy with no one; rather, I openly display my abundance to all my friends and share my soul wealth with anyone who desires it.

"But—most exquisite possession of all!—you observe that I always have leisure, with the result that I can go and see whatever is worth seeing, and hear whatever is worth hearing, and—what I prize the most—I pass the whole day, untroubled by business, in Socrates' company. Like me, he does not bestow his admiration on those who count the most gold, but he spends his time with those who are pleasing to him."[24]

Moving on from Antisthenes, the following selections and anecdotes offer some idea about Diogenes of Sinope's way of life and happiness—including how he thought about and practiced happiness. With him, we see the typical Cynic penchant for training, endurance, shamelessness, simplicity, frugality, self-sufficiency, independence, freedom, and frankness of speech.

Julian (the Roman emperor) In his happiness, Diogenes of Sinope was a king.[25]

Julian (the Roman emperor) Diogenes of Sinope freely submitted his body to toil and hardships so that he might make it stronger than it was by nature. He allowed himself to act only as the light of reason shows us that we ought to act. And the disturbances and confusions that attack the soul and are derived from the body—to which this envelope of ours often constrains us for its sake to pay too much attention—he did not take into account at all. Consequently, by means of this training the man made his body stronger, I believe, than that of any who have contended for the prize of a crown in the games. And his soul was so disposed that he was happy. And in this happiness he was a king no less—if not even more!—than the Great King, as the Greeks used to call him in those days, by which they meant the king of Persia.

Does Diogenes then seem to you of no importance, this man who was "without a city, homeless, a man without a country, owning not even a coin, neither an obol nor a drachma, and not a single slave,"—no, not even a barley-cake? . . . He lived more happily than one who is counted the happiest of men. And he actually used to assert that he lived more happily than such a man. But if you do not believe me, try his way of life not by talking about it but by doing it. Then you'll get it.[26]

Diogenes of Sinope (in a letter to the Cynic Monimus, Diogenes explains how he quickly came to the path to happiness) And coming to the place where happiness exists, I said, "Because of you, Happiness, and the greater good, I persisted in drinking water and eating cardamom and sleeping on the ground." Responding to me, Happiness said, "But rather than a hardship, I will make these things sweeter to you than the goods of wealth that human beings honor before me. But they do not understand that they are nourishing a tyrant for themselves." And from that point on, when I listened to Happiness talking about this, I no longer ate or drank these things as a matter of practice, but as a pleasure.[27]

Diogenes Laertius To the one who said, "I am unfit for doing philosophy," Diogenes replied, "Why then do you live if you do not care to live happily?"[28]

Diogenes Laertius Diogenes said that, rather than unprofitable, toilsome exercises, men should prefer those that follow nature in order to live happily. Men are unhappy because of a lack of understanding.[29]

Diogenes Laertius (Diogenes reports an inscription on a bronze statue of Diogenes of Sinope set up to honor the Cynic philosopher in his home town, Sinope) You alone revealed to mortal men the teaching that self-sufficient living is a way of life that is not burdensome.[30]

Diogenes Laertius His voice resounding, Diogenes often declared that the gods had given men an easy life. But the easy life had become obscure over time by their seeking honey-cakes and perfumes and like things.[31]

Diogenes Laertius Theophrastus declares in his work the *Megarian* that it was by watching a mouse — how it didn't long for a marriage bed, and how it didn't care about the dark, and how it didn't long for things that have a reputation for causing pleasure — that Diogenes discovered the means of adapting himself to circumstances.[32]

Diogenes Laertius One time Diogenes saw a child drinking out of his hands. Consequently, he pulled the cup from his leather bag and tossed it away, saying, "A child has outdone me in frugality." Another time, when he similarly observed a child who had broken his own spoon taking up lentil soup with a hollow crust of bread, he threw away his spoon.[33]

Diogenes Laertius Diogenes used any place for any purpose — eating, sleeping, or talking with others. And pointing at the colonnade of Zeus and the building that housed the sacred processional vessels, he would say that the people of Athens had furnished him with places to live.[34]

Diogenes Laertius Diogenes wrote a letter to someone asking him to provide a small house for him. He himself explains in his letters that, when the man delayed, he took for his abode a large wine-jar in the Temple of Cybele.[35]

Diogenes Laertius Diogenes used to teach the boys in his care to supply their own needs, and to be content with simple food and water to drink. He further accustomed them to cutting their hair close to the skin, and to shun fashionable adornments, and to go out with fewer clothes on and no shoes, and to walk along the way silently and without looking around.[36]

Diogenes Laertius Diogenes declared that there are two kinds of exercise—training of the soul and training of the body. And that the latter exercise gives rise to perceptions that facilitate virtuous deeds. Each practice is incomplete and ineffectual without the other. Good health and strength have to be present with whatever else is important, whether for the soul or for the body.

He offered positive proof for how easily we arrive at virtue by means of physical exercise. One can see that craftsmen acquire hand-speed with careful practice. And flute players and athletes excel by means of their own labor. And if these transferred the practices to the soul, then the exercises would not be without profit and incomplete.

Diogenes said that absolutely nothing in life is successful without training, which has the power to conquer anything.[37]

Diogenes Laertius In summertime, Diogenes used to roll in his wine-jar house over hot sand. And in wintertime, he used to hug statues of men covered with snow. He practiced endurance in every way.[38]

Diogenes Laertius According to Diogenes, contempt for pleasure is, if we get used to it, quite pleasant itself. And just as those who are accustomed to living with pleasure feel nauseous when they have to give this life up, so too do those who have practiced the opposite life feel pleasure when they look down on pleasure.[39]

Diogenes Laertius Diogenes said that bad men obey their desires as house slaves obey their masters. [40]

Diogenes Laertius Diogenes would continually say that for the conduct of life we need either reason or a bridle.[41]

Diogenes Laertius Diogenes would say that men strive in punching and kicking to outdo one another, but no one strives to become a good and noble man.[42]

Diogenes Laertius One day Alexander the Great stood by Diogenes and said, "I am Alexander, the great and mighty king." In response, Diogenes said, "And I am Diogenes, the dog."[43]

Diogenes Laertius One day, when he was sitting in the sun nearby the Craneum grove of Corinth, Alexander stood over him and said, "Ask me for anything you desire." Diogenes replied, "I would like you to stop blocking the light."[44]

Diogenes Laertius When someone asked him where he came from, Diogenes said, "I am a citizen of the world."[45]

Next is a story about Crates of Thebes from the Cynic Teles of Megara. Crates was a devoted follower of Diogenes of Sinope.

Teles of Megara In response to the man who asked, "What will it mean for me to do philosophy?" Crates said, "You will easily be able to open your bag and freely give from it rather than, as now, writhing and irresolute and shaking as men do with disabled hands. . . . If you notice that your bag is empty, you will not suffer distress. . . . You will live satisfied with what you have, neither desiring what is absent nor being displeased with whatever comes your way.[46]

We finish with a few points related to the Cynics, including why they were called Cynics and what sort of life they recommended.

The Cynics, or the Dogs, have their name for four reasons. First, it is for the detached carelessness of their way of life, for they emphasize a general indifference, and, like dogs, they eat and have sex in public spaces, and they go barefoot and sleep in wine-jars and tubs and along the way. . . . The second reason is that the dog is a shameless animal, and Cynics praise shamelessness as being superior to decorum and respectability. . . . The third reason is that the dog is good at keeping watch, and they guard the canons of their philosophy. The last reason is that the dog is a perceptive animal that can discriminate between its friends and enemies. . . . Accordingly, Cynics recognize those who are suited to philosophy as friends, and they welcome them kindly, while they bark like dogs at those who are ill-equipped for the pursuit of wisdom.[47]

Diogenes Laertius Cynics teach that men should live simply, procuring for themselves only necessary food and wearing only one piece of clothing, a worn garment. They think very little of wealth and reputation and noble birth. Some Cynics get by on herbs and vegetables and cold water. They live in any kind of shelter, or even large wine-jars, just as did Diogenes, who used to say that it was characteristic of the gods to need nothing, and that, consequently, when a man desires very little or nothing at all, he is like the gods.[48]

HAPPINESS FOR THE CYNICS

For the Cynics, happiness is fairly straightforward, if challenging. Generally speaking, happiness is living a life in step with nature. This natural life is itself a life in accord with virtue.

More specifically, happiness is not the enjoyment of pleasure. If anything, the desire for pleasure gets in the way of happiness. Rather, one must reduce one's desires and learn to put up with hardship and other forms of suffering. The Cynic practice of happiness, therefore, is identical to a program of training that will help one learn to endure and live with what is sufficient rather than always hunting for an abundance. The Cynic idea of happiness highlights self-sufficiency, simplicity, and frugality in living. As a result, the Cynic becomes independent from other people, no matter how powerful they are, and truly free. Part of the training for this independence is the Cynic practice of shamelessness, that is, intentionally doing what may be considered embarrassing—and even wrong—in public in order to get used to not wanting a good reputation. Finally, the Cynic's freedom allows him to speak his mind frankly to other men, including men as powerful as Alexander the Great.

NOTES

[1] Other significant Cynics were Antisthenes of Athens (c. 445-365 BC) and Crates of Thebes (c. 365-285 BC). Later significant Cynics were Crates' wife, Hipparchia of Maroneia, her brother Metrocles, Teles of Megara, Demetrius, Dio Chrysostom, and Demonax. The Cynics were known for their droll wit, their wry manner of speaking, and their radical way of life. That said, they were quite earnest in helping others in their own approach to happiness and excellence or virtue. For more, see the Cave's *The Best of the Cynics: The Lives, Writings & Teachings of the Ancient Cynics*.

[2] Julian (the Roman emperor), *Oration 6, To the Uneducated Cynics* 201.

[3] Ibid., 193.

[4] Diogenes Laertius, *Lives* 6.71.

[5] Ibid., 6.104.

[6] Crates of Thebes, *Letter 36, To Dinomachus*. The Cynic letters we possess—of Diogenes of Sinope and Crates of Thebes, among others—are not considered genuine by scholars. That said, they are clearly Cynic insofar as they remain faithful to Cynic goals and themes. The "good and excellent man" is the *spoudaios* man.

[7] Diogenes of Sinope, *Letter 30, To Hicetas*.

[8] Crates of Thebes, *Letter 6, To the Same, His Students*.

[9] Ibid., *Letter 21, To Metrocles the Cynic*.

[10] Julian (the Roman emperor), *Oration 6, To the Uneducated Cynics* 194.

[11] Dio Chrysostom, *Oration 8, Diogenes*, or *On Virtue* 13, 15-16.

[12] Julian (the Roman emperor), *Oration 6, To the Uneducated Cynics* 194.

[13] Epictetus, *Discourse* 3.22, 27.

[14] Crates of Thebes, *Letter 3, To the Same, His Students*.

[15] Teles of Megara, *Discourse* 5, "On Pleasure Not Being the Goal of Life" 49, 51.

[16] Lucian of Samosata, *The Cynic* 8-10.

[17] Diogenes Laertius, *Lives* 6.2.

[18] Ibid., 6.11.

[19] Ibid., 6.11.

[20] Ibid., 6.12.

[21] Ibid., 6.11.

[22] Ibid., 6.13.

[23] Ibid., 6.3.

[24] Xenophon, *Symposium* 3.8, 4.34-4.44.

[25] Julian (the Roman emperor), *Oration 6, To the Uneducated Cynics* 194.

26 Ibid., 194.

27 Diogenes of Sinope, *Letter 37, To Monimus.*

28 Diogenes Laertius, *Lives* 6.65.

29 Ibid., 6.71.

30 Ibid., 6.78.

31 Ibid., 6.44.

32 Ibid., 6.22.

33 Ibid., 6.37.

34 Ibid., 6.22.

35 Ibid., 6.23.

36 Ibid., 6.31. According to Diogenes Laertius, this incident happened when Diogenes of Sinope was enslaved by a man called Xeniades.

37 Ibid., 6.70-71.

38 Ibid., 6.23.

39 Ibid., 6.71.

40 Ibid., 6.66.

41 Ibid., 6.24.

42 Ibid., 6.27.

43 Ibid., 6.60.

44 Ibid., 6.38.

45 Ibid., 6.63.

46 Teles of Megara, *Discourse* 4a, "A Comparison of Poverty and Wealth" 38-39.

47 See *Scholia in Aristotelem* (Commentary on Aristotle), gathered by Christianus Augustus Brandis (Berolini, apud G. Reimerum, 1836), in Dudley, *A History of Cynicism*, 5.

48 Diogenes Laertius, *Lives* 6.104.

14

Zeno of Citium
& Early Stoicism

"Set before yourself what Socrates or Zeno would have done in this situation, and you will have no problem in doing what is suitable."

—Epictetus, the *Handbook*

Zeno of Citium (c. 335-263 BC) wanted to know "what he should do to live the best life," so he went and put the question to an oracle. In reply, the god of the oracle told him that he would have "to be in contact with the dead." What sort of contact? he wondered. After puzzling over the oracle's enigmatic response, he hit upon what the god meant. And so, as the story goes, Zeno began to read and "know the ancients"—those who had come before.[1]

Of the ancients, Zeno particularly came to admire Socrates, who had died just over six decades before he was born. The truth is we don't know when Zeno first read about Socrates, but we have a few reports. One recounts that his merchant father, Mnaseas, purchased scrolls related to Socrates in Athens and brought them home to Zeno when he was still a boy.

Home, by the way, was the city-state of Citium on the island of Cyprus in the eastern Mediterranean. Citium had long hosted a sizeable population of Greeks and Phoenicians.

Another story makes Zeno himself the merchant, one who dealt in "purple"—that is, purple dye and textiles. In this account, Zeno was shipwrecked near the Piraeus, Athens' port. Rather than going down with the ship, however, he swam ashore and made his way to the city. Diogenes Laertius tells us that he was then thirty years old. When in Athens, he went to the stall of a man who sold scrolls and sat down reading through the second book of Xenophon's *Memorabilia*, a work that features Socrates. "He was so delighted," Diogenes Laertius reports, "that he asked where he could find men like Socrates." Just as he was asking, the Cynic Crates of Thebes happened to be walking by, and so, pointing at him, the scroll vendor advised, "Closely follow that man." Zeno did. And in the end, he declared, "I made a good voyage when I was shipwrecked."[2]

Over the next ten years or so, Zeno practiced philosophy with Crates of Thebes—learning, among other points, "the shamelessness of the Cynics." He also studied and practiced with other philosophers. That said, given the ultimate similarity between the Cynics and the Stoic school of philosophy, the school Zeno founded, Crates was particularly important to Zeno's education. Indeed, Diogenes Laertius insists the Stoics were just like the Cynics in that they believed that virtue, or life-excellence, is the goal of life. He goes on to point out the "community between the two schools," and concludes that Zeno of Citium lived his life following the same Cynic pattern, which was "a shortcut upon the path of virtue," and so a shortcut to happiness.[3]

Why the "Stoics"?—that is, why did Zeno's school get *that* name instead of, say, the "Zenoists"? We are told that Zeno would walk back and forth lecturing in a covered colonnade located on the edge of Athens' *agora*—the city-state's central gathering and marketplace. In Greek, such a covered colonnade is called a *stoa*. This particular *stoa* had paintings in it by Panainos, Mikon, and Polygnotus depicting the battles of Marathon and of the Amazons, and the capture of Troy. As a result, it came to be called the *Stoa Poikilē*, the painted colonnade. Diogenes Laertius reports, "Here, then, *in the painted colonnade*, men came to hear Zeno. This is why his students are called men of the *stoa* or Stoics."[4]

In the end, the Athenians celebrated Zeno of Citium as one of their own, highly honoring him. According to Diogenes Laertius, they gave him keys to the city wall and honored him with a crown of gold and a bronze statue made to look like him.[5]

IN THEIR OWN WORDS

We begin with Zeno of Citium's widespread reputation for happiness and virtue, and his ability to instruct others in the life of virtue and, thus, in a happy way of life—a life like his own, a simple, moderate way of life.

Diogenes Laertius Zeno truly surpassed all mankind in blessedness.[6]

Letter from Antigonus to Zeno King Antigonus to Zeno the philosopher, greeting. I consider myself superior to you in glory and wealth. But in reason and education, and in the perfect happiness you have attained, I acknowledge that I am far behind you. . . . By all means, then, do your best to meet with me, understanding that you will not only be instructing me but all the Macedonians together. For he who teaches the Macedonian ruler and guides him along the path of virtue will also be training his subjects to be good men. For as the ruler is, so, for the most part, we may expect the subjects to become.[7]

Letter from Zeno to Antigonus Zeno to king Antigonus, greeting. I welcome your love of learning inasmuch as you hold to the truth that stretches out toward advantage . . . If anyone has longed for philosophy, turning away from well-known pleasure, . . . it is clear that he is inclined to nobility of life not only by nature but by deliberate choice. If any man with a nature such as yours receives a reasonable amount of training in terms of ungrudging instruction, he will easily reach perfect virtue. As for me, I am unable to join you due to old age and subsequent bodily weakness—I am eighty years old. But I send to you certain men who have studied with me. . . . If you join with these men, then you will lack nothing that is necessary for perfect happiness.[8]

An epitaph composed for Zeno of Citium by Antipater of Sidon (found in Diogenes Laertius) Here lies great Zeno, dear to Citium, who scaled high Olympus, even though he did not pile Pelion upon Ossa, nor did he toil at Heracles' labors—instead, this was the path he found to the stars: the way of moderation alone.[9]

Diogenes Laertius They say Zeno was fond of eating green figs and of basking in the sun.[10]

Diogenes Laertius The Athenians buried Zeno of Citium in the Ceramicus and honored him, . . . bearing witness to his virtue.[11]

Diogenes Laertius (the text of a decree that the people of Athens passed regarding Zeno) Whereas Zeno of Citium, the son of Mnaseas, has for many years been devoted to philosophy in the city and has continued to be a good man in all other respects, exhorting to virtue and moderation those of the youth who come to him to be taught, directing them to what is most excellent, offering to all in his own manner of living a pattern for imitation in perfect conformity with his teaching, it has seemed good to the people—and may it so happen—to bestow praise on Zeno of Citium, the son of Mnaseas, and to crown him with a golden crown according to the law for his virtue and moderation.[12]

Turning to the early Stoic views on happiness, the early Stoics teach that the happy life is "a good flow of life," which is to say it is a virtuous life. Virtue "is the only good," they say. Virtue guards "the lives of men and cities." In itself, virtue is enough for happiness.[13]

Sextus Empiricus Zeno and Cleanthes and Chrysippus have defined happiness as "a good flow of life."[14]

Diogenes Laertius The Stoics hold that virtue is sufficient in itself to ensure happiness.[15]

Diogenes Laertius Happiness consists in virtue, which is the state of the soul that tends to make the whole of life harmonious.[16]

Cicero (Varro is speaking) "Zeno declares that everything having to do with the happy life belongs to virtue alone."[17]

Cicero (Cato is speaking) "We Stoics understand that moral goodness alone is good, and that to live honorably, that is, virtuously, is to live happily."[18]

Plutarch According to Chrysippus, the gods do not differ from human beings in terms of happiness and virtue. . . . The Stoics say that if a human is not missing anything of virtue, then he will not be lacking anything of happiness.[19]

Diogenes Laertius Athenaeus the epigrammatist speaks of all the Stoics in common as follows: "You who are acquainted with the words of the Stoic Porch, you have committed to your divine books the best of teachings, that virtue of the soul is the only good. Her decrees alone protect the lives of men and cities. But those other men who declare that the goal of life is the enjoyment of the flesh are ruined by one of the Muses, the daughters of Memory."[20]

Diogenes Laertius In the second book of *On Life and Earning a Living*, while considering how a wise man should earn a living, Chrysippus says, "And yet why should he earn a living? After all, if it is for the sake of life, life is a thing indifferent. And if it is for pleasure, it is also indifferent. And if it is for virtue, it is sufficient in itself for happiness."[21]

In the next selections, we follow the general Stoic argument for why virtue is happiness.

The first point is that the "the end or goal of life is to live in agreement with nature, which is the same as living according to virtue."

Why is such a natural life virtuous and thus happy-making? It is because it is in harmony with Zeus or "the right reason that pervades all things."

What is the significance of Zeus—Zeus, who is reason or mind—pervading all things? In short, it is because Zeus through nature or as nature regulates all animals by means of impulse.

The first impulse of any animal is toward self-preservation rather than pleasure. For human beings, Zeus (again, reason or mind) gives reason in addition to impulse so that the latter may be shaped in a skillful manner. Such a reason-based formation of impulse results in a rational life. To live in such a way means that one is living in conformity with nature and so with virtue, a life which is sufficient in itself for happiness.

Diogenes Laertius In his treatise *On the Nature of Man*, Zeno . . . was the first to say that the end or goal of life is to live in agreement with nature, which is the same as living according to virtue since nature leads us toward virtue. Cleanthes says the same in his treatise *On Pleasure*, as do Posidonius and Hecaton in their works *On the Goal of Life*. Again, living according to virtue is equivalent to living according to the experience of nature as it actually happens—just as Chrysippus says in the first book of his *On the Goal of Life*. For our individual natures are portions of the whole of nature, which is to say the whole cosmos.[22]

Diogenes Laertius The goal of life is to live in conformity with nature—that is, with our own nature as well as with the nature of the whole cosmos. Accordingly, one holds back from every action forbidden by the law common to all things—that is to say, the right reason that pervades all things and is the same as Zeus, who leads the administration of every existing thing. This very thing is the virtue of the happy man and the good flow of life, when all actions promote the harmony of the divine power dwelling in each man with the will of the administrator of the whole cosmos.[23]

Cicero (Marcus Cato is speaking) "Inasmuch as the final good is to live in agreement and harmony with nature, it necessarily follows that all wise men at all times enjoy a happy, perfect, and fortunate life, free from all hindrance, interference, or want."[24]

Cicero (Balbus is speaking) "In gazing upon the stars, the rational soul comes to the knowledge of the gods. This knowledge is the source of piety, which is connected to justice and the other virtues. From these, emerge a happy life, one that resembles the life of the gods in everything but immortality—which, by the way, contributes nothing to living well."[25]

Diogenes Laertius The Stoics say that an animal's first impulse is to self-preservation since nature endears the animal to itself from the beginning, as Chrysippus affirms in the first part of his work *On the Goal of Life*. There he says that the dearest thing to every animal is its own constitution and the awareness of this. For it is not natural for any animal to be alienated from itself—or even to be brought into such a state so that it is indifferent to itself, being neither alienated from nor friendly to itself. We must assert that nature has made the animal so that it is near and dear to itself. As such, it pushes away all that is harmful and pulls near all that is suitable and fitting.

The Stoics declare false the assertion—made by some—that the first urge or impulse of animals is directed toward pleasure. By contrast they say that pleasure, if it is anything at all, is a byproduct that never comes until nature by itself has sought and taken those things suitable to the animal's constitution—a byproduct that is comparable to animals that have a cheerful expression and plants that are luxuriant or in full bloom.

The Stoics declare that nature originally made no difference between plants and animals. Nature regulates the life of plants without the use of impulse and sensation, just as certain plant-like processes go on in us. But for animals, impulse was added to this general rule of nature later on. Impulse makes animals pursue what is suitable. Nature's rule for animals is to follow the direction of impulse. Lastly, for those beings we call rational, the rational life correctly became the natural life when reason was given to them by means of a more perfect rule. Reason was added to shape impulse as a skilled craftsman. . . .

Accordingly, one holds back from every action forbidden by the law common to all things—that is to say, the right reason that pervades all things and is the same as Zeus, who leads the administration of every existing thing. This very thing is the virtue of the happy man and the good flow of life, when all actions promote the harmony of the divine power dwelling in each man with the will of the administrator • of the whole cosmos.[26]

But what is the nature of virtue? The following selections give some idea. Of significance is the notion that virtue is "the perfection of anything in general," and the belief in the unity or essential relation of virtue (that "the virtues involve one another"), as well as the primacy of some virtues (practical wisdom, courage, justice, and moderation). For the Stoics, skill in dialectic is virtue. Finally, "there is no middle ground between virtue and vice."

Diogenes Laertius Virtue is in one sense the perfection of anything in general, say of a statue. Virtue may be non-intellectual, such as health, or intellectual, such as practical wisdom.[27]

Diogenes Laertius Virtue is a harmonious disposition, choiceworthy for its own sake—not from hope or fear or any external motive.[28]

Diogenes Laertius (giving the view found in several ancient Stoic authors—Chrysippus, Apollodorus, and Hecaton) The Stoics hold that the virtues involve one another. The man who has one virtue has them all inasmuch as the virtues have common principles.[29]

Diogenes Laertius Among the virtues some are primary, and some are subordinate to these. The following are the primary virtues: practical wisdom, courage, justice, and moderation. . . . Similarly, among the vices, some are primary, and some are subordinate. Folly, cowardice, injustice, and immoderation are primary. The vices are ignorance of those things of which the virtues are the knowledge.[30]

Diogenes Laertius Stoics define practical wisdom as the knowledge of good and bad things and what is neither. And courage is the knowledge of what is choiceworthy and what one must be wary of and avoid, and what is neither.[31]

Diogenes Laertius Specific virtues are magnanimity, self-control, patient endurance, ready mindedness, and good counsel. . . . They define magnanimity as the knowledge or habit that makes one superior to whatever commonly happens to both base and excellent men. Self-control is an unbeatable disposition relative to those things that are in accord with right reason or a habit that is never conquered by pleasure. Patient endurance is the knowledge or habit that suggests what we must—and what we must not—abide by and endure, and what is neither. Ready mindedness is a habit that discovers the appropriate thing to be done at any moment. Good counsel is the knowledge by which we see what to do and how to do it if we are to act in a useful and profitable manner.[32]

Diogenes Laertius The Stoics hold that dialectic itself is necessary and a virtue, and that it encompasses the other kinds of virtues.[33]

Diogenes Laertius The Stoic belief is that there is no middle ground between virtue and vice, whereas the Peripatetics say that there is the middle ground of moral progress. The Stoics declare that just as a stick must be either straight or crooked, so a man must be either just or unjust. Neither are there degrees of justice and injustice. The same is the case for the other virtues.[34]

Diogenes Laertius [The Stoic] Herillus of Carthage declared that everything that is found between virtue and vice is indifferent.[35]

Diogenes Laertius The Stoics hold that all failures or sins are equal—this according to what Chrysippus says in the fourth book of his *Ethical Inquiries*, as well as Persaeus and Zeno. For if one truth is not truer than another truth, then neither is one falsehood more false than another falsehood. In the same way, one deception is not more deceptive than another deception, nor is one failure or sin more of a failure or more sinful than another failure or sin. For the man who is one hundred stadia from Canopus and the man who is only one stadium away are equally not in Canopus. In this way, the man who commits the greater and the one who commits the smaller sin are equally behaving incorrectly. Nevertheless, Heraclides of Tarsus, the follower of Antipater of Tarsus, and Athenodorus both assert that failures or sins are not equal.[36]

Next up are several selections that explore the nature of the good (or good things) and its relation to virtue and happiness. Relative to happiness, virtues are goods (beneficial, advantageous things) that can have either the nature of an end or a means to an end.

Diogenes Laertius Generally speaking, good is that from which there is some advantage or benefit. More specifically, it is either what is the same as or not different from what is useful or beneficial or advantageous.[37]

Diogenes Laertius "The fulfillment or perfection of a rational being *as* a rational being following nature" is another particular definition the Stoics give for the good.[38]

Diogenes Laertius Of good things, some are related to the soul and some to external things, while some are neither related to the soul nor to externals. The goods related to the soul are the virtues and acts done according to virtue. External goods are things such as having an excellent homeland and an excellent friend and the happiness that comes from these.[39]

Diogenes Laertius Some goods have the nature of ends or goals. Some have the nature of means. Some are both ends and means at the same time. . . . The virtues are goods that have both the nature of ends and means. Inasmuch as they produce happiness, they are means to good things. On the other hand, inasmuch as the virtues are the fulfillment of happiness, being a portion of happiness itself, they are ends.[40]

As the following selection demonstrates, the Stoics divide all things into three categories: good things, bad things, and things that are neutral, which is to say neither good nor bad. The virtues are good things; they are, as we have seen, sufficient for happiness. The Stoics term neutral things "indifferent," some of which are "preferred" and some of which are "rejected," depending on a thing's value. Indifferent things "contribute neither to happiness nor to unhappiness." It is possible to be happy apart from indifferent things such as wealth, reputation, health, and strength.

Diogenes Laertius Of things that are, the Stoics declare that some are good, some are bad, and some are neither.

Good things are the virtues, including practical wisdom, justice, courage, moderation, and the rest. Bad things are the opposite—

folly, injustice, and the rest. Things that are neither are those things that neither benefit nor harm—things such as life, health, pleasure, beauty, strength, wealth, good reputation, and noble birth, as well as their opposites, death, disease, pain, ugliness, weakness, poverty, bad reputation, low birth, and the like. . . .

These things are not good [or bad] things, but they are "things indifferent." . . . For just as being hot, rather than being cold, is the unique property of a hot thing, so too is being beneficial, rather than being harmful, the unique property of a good thing. But wealth and health do no more benefit than harm; therefore, neither wealth nor health is a good thing. Moreover, they say that what can be used well and badly is not a good thing. But wealth and health can be used well and badly; therefore, neither wealth nor health are good things. . . . To benefit is to move and maintain according to virtue, and to harm is to move and maintain according to vice.

The Stoics say that the term "indifferent" has two meanings. For one, it denotes those things that contribute neither to happiness nor to unhappiness—things such as wealth, reputation, health, strength, and similar things. It is possible to be happy apart from these things. It is the particular way that we employ these things that makes for happiness or unhappiness. Otherwise, something is indifferent if it does not excite impulse or disgust for a thing—as with the fact that the number of hairs on one's head is odd or even or whether you point or hold back your finger. By contrast, it was not in this latter sense that the former things mentioned above were called indifferent since those things do actually excite inclination or disgust for those things. That is why of those things having to do with the first kind of indifference, some are chosen, and some are not chosen, whereas of the other things having to do with the second kind, there is an equal reason for choosing or avoiding them.

Regarding indifferent things, they say that some are preferred, and some are rejected or not preferred. Those things that have worth or value are preferred, while those that do not have worth or value are rejected.

They define worth or value, firstly, as a contribution to a harmonious life. In this sense, every good has value. Secondly, value is some intermediary power or advantage that contributes toward living life according to nature. In other words, it is the assistance that wealth and health may offer in living life according to nature. . . .

Preferred things are those that have value. For example, among things of the soul, there are natural ability, skill, moral progress, and similar things. Among bodily things, there are life, health, bodily strength, vigor, wholeness, beauty, and so on. Among external things, there are wealth, reputation, noble birth, and similar things.

As for those things that are rejected, among things of the soul, there are a lack of natural ability, a lack of skill, and like things. Among bodily things, there are death, disease, weakness, lethargy, disability, ugliness, and like things. Among external things, there are poverty, bad reputation, low birth, and the like.

Those things that are in neither category are neither preferred nor rejected.

Yet again, of things preferred, some are preferred for their own sake, some for the sake of something else, and others are preferred both for their own sake and for the sake of something else. Those preferred for their own sake include natural ability, moral progress, and like things. Those preferred for the sake of something else include wealth, noble birth, and the like. Those preferred both for their own sake and for the sake of something else include strength, senses that work well, and wholeness.

Things are preferred for their own sake because they are in accord with nature. Things are preferred for the sake of something else because they produce more than a little of what is required or useful. The same may be said to hold for those things rejected—only the opposite.[41]

The next passage offers the early Stoic understanding of duty, that is, acting in such a way that is fitting or appropriate. "It is always fitting to live according to virtue." Consequently, to live a rational and virtuous life, one must carry out one's duty. Such a life is happy—or so it is implied.

Diogenes Laertius The Stoics say that duty or what is fitting or appropriate is that which, when done, may be supported by a reasonable account—for example, whatever is in conformity with living life. This is something that applies both to plant and animal life—for one may perceive, even with these, that which is fitting or appropriate.

Zeno was the first to use the word *kathēkon* for "what is fitting" or "what is appropriate." Etymologically, it is derived from *kata tinas hēkein*, that is, "belonging to something or someone." It is a fitting action or activity in relation to nature's arrangements.

Of actions done in relation to impulse, some are fitting, some are not fitting, and some are neither fitting nor not fitting. Those acts which are fitting are the ones that reason within us seizes upon and chooses to do, such as honoring one's parents, brothers, sisters, and homeland, and adapting oneself to and spending time with one's friends. Those acts which are not fitting are the ones that reason within us does not choose, such as neglecting one's parents, ignoring one's brothers and sisters, failing to be agreeable and available to one's friends, despising one's homeland, and like things. Those acts which are neither fitting nor not fitting are the ones that reason neither chooses to do nor forbids, such as picking up a twig, holding a writing utensil or a scraper, and like things.

Again, some things are duties or fitting activities regardless of the circumstances, while others depend on the circumstances. Those duties or fitting activities that do not depend on the circumstances include taking care of one's health and one's sense organs and the like. Those that depend on circumstances include, for example, maiming oneself and sacrificing or giving away one's property. The same holds analogously for those acts that are not fitting.

Once again, of those things which are fitting, some are always fitting, and some are not always fitting. It is always fitting to live according to virtue. But asking and answering questions and walking around and the like are not always fitting or appropriate. The same explanation goes for acts that are not fitting.[42]

The next selections present the early Stoic teaching regarding the soul and its parts; how error and the passions or emotions arise within the soul; what passion is (that passions are "contrary to reason and nature" and, so, we can conclude, they are contrary to virtue); and, finally, what may be considered the unhealthy or irrational versus the healthy or rational passions or emotions, which is to say those that tend toward unhappiness or happiness, respectively.

Diogenes Laertius The Stoics say the soul has eight parts. There are the five sense faculties, the vocal part, the intellectual part, which is the intellect itself, and the productive part.

From falsehood or error there arises a distortion or perversion, which extends throughout the intellect. And from this distortion grow many passions or emotions, which are responsible for much confusion and instability.

According to Zeno, a passion is itself a motion or excessive impulse of the soul that is contrary to reason and nature. . . .

The Stoics think that the passions or emotions are decisions or judgments—this according to what Chrysippus says in *On the Passions*. Avarice, for example, is the assumption that money is noble. It is similar with drunkenness and immoderation and the other passions.[43]

Diogenes Laertius According to Hecaton in the second book of his work *On the Passions*, and to Zeno in his own treatise *On the Passions*, there are four major kinds of passions or emotions: grief, fear, desire, and pleasure. . . .

Grief or pain is a contraction of the soul contrary to reason. . . .

Fear is the expectation of evil, or misfortune. . . .

Desire or longing is an appetite that is contrary to reason. . . . The state of want or lacking [which falls under the passion of desire] is the failure of desire, when desire does not reach its object but is nevertheless attracted to it in vain, stretching out to it. . . .

Pleasure is an elation that is contrary to reason that arises from getting and amassing what seems to be choiceworthy.[44]

Diogenes Laertius The Stoics say that there are three good passions or states of the soul: joy, caution, and willing. Joy, the opposite of pleasure, is sensible elation, that is, elation backed by good reason. Caution, that is, discretion or circumspection, is the opposite of fear.

It is avoidance backed by good reason, or the reasonable turning of one's course. Even though the wise man will never fear anything, he will nevertheless act with caution. And they say that willing is the opposite of desire insofar as willing is reasonable appetite, that is, appetite backed by good reason.[45]

We end with the Stoic conception of the nature of the wise man — what the wise man is, what he will do, and what he will not do. The following is a compilation of such statements. Though the equation is not explicitly made, for the Stoics, the wise man is by definition virtuous and thus happy.

Diogenes Laertius The wise man *is* . . . good and beautiful . . . without passion . . . free from vanity, for he is indifferent to good or evil report . . . austere or harsh since he neither has dealings with pleasure nor tolerates those who have such dealings . . . earnest for and attentive to his own improvement, employing a manner of life that banishes evil out of sight and makes what good there is in things appear . . . godlike, for he has something divine within himself (whereas the thoughtless man is godless) . . . a worshipper of god . . . holy and just in what concerns the gods . . . free, whereas bad men are slaves — where freedom is the power of independent action and slavery is the opposite . . . unharmed, for he does not harm others or himself . . . not pitiful and makes no allowance for anyone; he never relaxes the penalties fixed by the laws since indulgence and pity and even equitable consideration are signs of a weak soul that substitutes kindness for chastisement.[46]

Diogenes Laertius The wise man *will* . . . take part in politics . . . marry . . . offer prayers . . . do everything well in the same way that we say Ismenias plays everything well on the flute.[47]

Diogenes Laertius The wise man *will not* . . . live in solitude since he is naturally made for a community and action . . . form mere opinions — that is, he will never assent to anything that is false.[48]

Diogenes Laertius Ariston of Chios, the Bald, who was nicknamed "the Siren," declared that the goal of life was to live in a state of indifference to everything between virtue and vice. He did not recognize variation among things indifferent but treated them all alike. Accordingly, he said that the wise man is like a good actor, who, if called on to take the part of a Thersites or of an Agamemnon, will impersonate them in a suitable manner.[49]

HAPPINESS FOR ZENO OF CITIUM & EARLY STOICISM

For Zeno of Citium and the early Stoics, the happy life is a natural, rational, virtuous life.

Happiness is a life in conformity with nature. For human beings, this is a rational life, meaning a life that allows reason "to shape impulse in a skillful manner." Impulse itself is something provided by nature. It is that which causes animals, including human beings, to "pursue what is suitable." Human beings have a duty to do what is suitable or fitting. For humans, the rational life is the same as the virtuous life. To live virtuously is to live in harmony with "the right reason that pervades all things and is the same as Zeus." Virtue itself is, generally speaking, the perfection of a thing. Primary virtues are practical wisdom, courage, justice, and moderation.

Part of being rational is understanding what is good, what is bad, and what is neutral, neither good nor bad. Things such as the virtues are good in themselves since they harmoniously participate in "the right reason that pervades all things." Things such as the vices are bad since they do not. Neutral things are those things that may or may not contribute to a happy life. For instance, wealth may be used well (virtuously, in accord with reason and following nature) or badly (the opposite). Zeno and the early Stoics call neutral things "indifferent." Still, depending on their value, whether a thing does or does not contribute to a life in accord with nature, neutral things are either preferred or rejected (not preferred).

There are times when human beings judge falsely regarding things. These kinds of false judgments are errors that arise in the mind. They are what the Stoics call the passions or the emotions. For instance, if one experiences the passion of avarice, one incorrectly judges that money is good in itself rather than a neutral good. The four major kinds of passions are grief, fear, desire, and pleasure. In general, such passions judge contrary to reason and nature. As such, they are contrary to happiness. By contrast, three reason-backed passions are joy ("sensible elation"), caution ("avoidance backed by good reason"), and willing or wishing ("reasonable appetite").

NOTES

[1] Diogenes Laertius, *Lives* 7.2. The oracle's response was enigmatic given the meaning of "contact" that implied defilement since it advised skin-to-skin contact with the dead (*nekros*).

[2] Ibid., 7.2-4.

[3] Ibid., 6.104. "The Cynics hold that the goal of life is to live according to virtue . . . just like the Stoics. There is, after all, a certain community between the two schools. Therefore, some have said that Cynicism is a shortcut upon the path of virtue. Zeno of Citium passed his own life in this way."

[4] Ibid., 7.5. The referent for "here" —"in the painted colonnade" —comes a few lines before; I have thus put it in italics. For a second century AD description of Polygnotus' painting, see Pausanias, *Description of Greece* 10.25 ff.
Other significant early Stoics were Cleanthes of Assos (c. 331-232 BC) and Chrysippus of Soli (c. 280-207 BC), a prolific writer who significantly shaped and even reformulated Stoicism during his tenure as chief Stoic. For more, see the Cave's *The Best of the Early Stoics: The Lives, Writings & Teachings of the Early Stoics*.

[5] Diogenes Laertius, *Lives* 7.6.

[6] Ibid., 7.28.

[7] Ibid., 7.7.

[8] Ibid., 7.8-9.

[9] Ibid., 7.29.

[10] Ibid., 7.1.

[11] Ibid., 7.29.

[12] Ibid., 7.10-11.

[13] Still, there were some later Stoics (usually given as middle Stoics and thus not quite early or late Stoics) who believed that, in addition to virtue, other goods are required for happiness. For instance, Diogenes Laertius tells us that "Both Panaetius and Posidonius . . . deny that virtue is sufficient for happiness. Rather, they say that health is necessary, as well as some means of living, and strength" (ibid., 7.128). Panaetius of Rhodes lived from c. 185 to 109 BC. Posidonius of Apamea lived from c. 135 to c. 51 BC.

[14] Sextus Empiricus, *Against the Ethicists* 30.

[15] Diogenes Laertius, *Lives* 7.127. Diogenes Laertius further explains that this teaching is "according to what Zeno says, as well as Chrysippus in the first

book of his treatise *On Virtues*, and Hecaton in the second book of his treatise *On Goods*."

[16] Ibid., *Lives* 7.89.

[17] Cicero, *Academica* 1.35.

[18] Cicero, *On Ends* 3.29.

[19] Plutarch, *On Common Conceptions (Against the Stoics)* 1076a-b.

[20] Diogenes Laertius, *Lives* 7.30.

[21] Ibid., 7.188-189.

[22] Ibid., 7.87. Posidonius of Apamea (c. 135 to c. 51 BC) and Hecaton of Rhodes (first century BC) were both middle Stoics.

[23] Ibid., 7.88.

[24] Cicero, *On Ends* 3.26. To read more about what Cicero (through Marcus Cato) says about "the whole system of Zeno and the Stoics," including happiness and the points covered by Diogenes Laertius (life according to nature; the passions; and so on), see *On Ends* 3.20 ff., which may be found in the Cave's *The Best of the Early Stoics: The Lives, Writings & Teachings of the Early Stoics*.

[25] Cicero, *On the Nature of the Gods* 2.153.

[26] Diogenes Laertius, *Lives* 7.85-86, 88. The assertion "made by some" regarding the first "impulse of animals . . . toward pleasure" refers to either the Epicureans or the Cyrenaics.

[27] Ibid., 7.90.

[28] Ibid., 7.89.

[29] Ibid., 7.125.

[30] Ibid., 7.92, 93. "Primary virtues" are commonly called "cardinal virtues."

[31] Ibid., 7.92. Alas, we do not know how Diogenes Laertius gave the early Stoic definition of moderation or justice because there is a gap in the text. In his *Anthology* 2, Johannes Stobaeus (fifth century AD) gives the early Stoic definition of the two virtues this way: "Moderation is knowledge of what is to be chosen and what is to be avoided and what is neither. And justice is knowledge of the distribution of valuable things to each man." Regarding moderation and its opposite, Cicero, in the *Tusculan Disputations* 4.22, has one interlocutor, "M.," state: "The Stoics say that the fount of all disorders is immoderation or intemperance, which is a revolt from all guidance of the mind and right reason, so completely alien from the control of reason that the cravings of the soul cannot be guided or curbed. Therefore, just as moderation or temperance slays the cravings and causes them to obey right reason, and maintains the well-considered judgments of the mind, so its enemy immoderation or intemperance kindles, confounds, and agitates the whole condition of the soul, with the result that from it come distress and fear and all other disorders."

[32] Diogenes Laertius, *Lives* 7.92, 93.

[33] Ibid., 7.46. For the Stoic understanding of dialectic or skill in dialectic (*dialektikos*), see ibid., 7.42-44.

34 Ibid., 7.127. It would seem to follow that there is no middle ground between happiness and unhappiness. The Peripatetics were the inheritors of Aristotle's investigations and teachings.

35 Ibid., 7.165. Herillus of Carthage was a student of Zeno of Citium. Considered a heterodox Stoic, he declared that knowledge is the goal of life.

36 Ibid., 7.120-121. Persaeus of Citium lived from c. 306 to c. 243 BC. The latter three were early and middle Stoics who lived in the second and first centuries BC.

37 Ibid., 7.94.

38 Ibid., 7.94.

39 Ibid., 7.95.

40 Ibid., 7.96-97.

41 Ibid., 7.101-107. A third definition of value: "Thirdly, value is the price set by an appraiser, as determined by his experience with the facts, as when an appraiser says that wheat is worth so much barley with a mule thrown in to make up the difference."

42 Ibid., 7.107-109. "Maiming oneself" might sound like an odd example, but there are several instances from ancient history in which a man dutifully maims himself, for example, to infiltrate a city. For one, see Herodotus, *Histories* 3.153-160.

43 Ibid., 7.110-111.

44 Ibid., 7.110-114. Diogenes Laertius adds this: "Moreover, just as we say that there are certain bodily illnesses or infirmities, for example, gout and arthritic disorders, so also there are soul illnesses, such as love of reputation and love of pleasure, and the like. By illness or infirmity is meant a disease accompanied by weakness. By disease is meant an excessive notion about something that seems choiceworthy. And just as there is a tendency toward certain maladies in the body, such as the buildup of mucus and diarrhea, so with the soul there is a tendency to enviousness, pitifulness, quarrelsomeness, and the like" (ibid., 7.115).

45 Ibid., 7.116.

46 Ibid., 7.100, 117-123.

47 Ibid., 7.121, 124-125.

48 Ibid., 7.123, 121.

49 Ibid., 7.160. In Homer's *Iliad*, Thersites is a commoner who upbraids Agamemnon, the leading man of the Achaeans (see *Iliad* 2.210-267).

15

EPICURUS
& EPICUREANISM

"Regarding Epicurus, there is an abundance of witnesses who attest to his unsurpassed goodwill and kindness to all men. . . . His friends were so many in number that they could hardly be measured by whole cities. No one familiar with the siren charms of his teachings ever deserted him."
—Diogenes Laertius, *Lives and Opinions of Eminent Philosophers*

FOR WELL OVER half a millennium and beyond, Epicurus (c. 341-270 BC) greatly influenced the ancient world of Greece and Rome. His teachings provided the guiding light for a large number of human souls. For some, he was "the glory of the Greeks." For others, he was a "liberator" and "the very wisest of men."[1] The Roman statesman and philosopher Seneca counseled his friend Lucilius Junior, who was the emperor Nero's chief financial officer in Sicily, to "act as if Epicurus were always observing you." Seneca issued the advice well over three hundred years after Epicurus died. And even though he generally aligned himself with Stoicism—as many educated Romans did in the middle of the first century AD—Seneca nevertheless had a positive view of Epicurus and his philosophy, labeling Epicureanism "good and upright"—if, he cautioned, it was properly understood.[2]

Nearly four hundred years before Seneca, a young Epicurus was puzzled. Reading Hesiod's *Theogony*, he wondered what the ancient poet had meant by "Chaos."[3] Later, he posed the question about Hesiod's Chaos to his teachers. Apparently they could not answer him. And so, Diogenes Laertius reports, Epicurus "turned to philosophy" for answers, realizing that ancient myths or stories could not answer the questions he wanted to answer.[4]

Epicurus first learned from the Platonist Pamphilus. But he wasn't what the young man was looking for. Instead, the atomist philosopher Nausiphanes had a far stronger impact on his views and the later formation of his teachings. Nausiphanes adhered to the ideas of the Presocratic philosopher Democritus, who believed that all of reality was reducible to atoms (tiny, literally "uncuttable" or *atomos* bits of stuff) and the void or emptiness. In short, this "atomism" is what Epicurus also came to believe.

Born some seven years after Plato died, Epicurus grew up on the Greek island of Samos, just off the coast of modern Turkey. When he was eighteen, he sailed to Athens to register as an Athenian citizen and complete his military service. Over the next fifteen years or so, he taught and established his own following as a philosopher in several Greek cities before returning to Athens. There he bought some land and a house and established a school of philosophy in the house's garden around 306 BC. Given its location, his school was called "the Garden."

For the following nearly four decades, Epicurus taught and modeled his philosophy until his death. During those years, he inspired many to live well. He had found something—a simple practice of pleasure, a tranquility of mind, and a happiness of heart—that he wanted others to experience. He taught and wrote, therefore, in order to spread his wisdom and way of life. To offer one simple example: Whenever Epicurus wrote a letter, he replaced the usual greeting, which was "May you be glad" or "May you be delighted," with "May you do well" and "May you live earnestly."

It is to the content of this doing well and living earnestly—that is to say, the content of Epicurean happiness—that we now turn.[5]

Unless otherwise noted *in italics*, the following selections are all from Epicurus himself.

IN THEIR OWN WORDS

We begin with selections revealing what Epicurus and his school generally believed about the nature of happiness. In short, happiness is closely connected to pleasure—but pleasure rightly understood. The most important aspect of happiness is mental tranquility (ataraxia)—mental freedom from any kind of disturbance.

We say that pleasure is the beginning point and goal of living happily.[6]

Bodily health and mental tranquility . . . is the goal of a blessedly happy life.[7]

Mental tranquility means being released from all these troubles *(fear and mental disturbance resulting from the imagined activities of the divine heavenly bodies, thoughts about the nature of death, and "anticipation of some everlasting evil")* and keeping in mind the general and most important points *(of Epicurean philosophy)*.[8]

Practical troubles and anxieties and feelings of anger and the granting of favors do not accord with bliss but always imply weakness and fear and dependence upon one's neighbors.[9]

Diogenes Laertius (presenting Epicurus' distinction between katastematic and kinetic pleasures) In his work *On Choice*, Epicurus says, "Freedom from trouble and freedom from pain are katastematic pleasures—that is, they imply a state of rest. Joy and good cheer are viewed as kinetic and active."[10]

Diogenes Laertius (reporting the Epicurean position regarding the kinds of happiness) There are two kinds of happiness. There is the happiness of the god, the highest kind, which cannot be increased. The other kind may increase or decrease in terms of pleasures.[11]

It is not the young man that we consider most happy, but the old man who has lived well. Even though the young man is in his prime, he drifts, confused and many-minded thanks to the fortunes of happenstance, whereas the old man has passed into old age even as a ship sails into a harbor, secure in gratitude for the good things that earlier he did not even hope for.[12]

Diogenes Laertius In his letters Epicurus replaces the usual greeting, "May you be glad" or "May you be delighted," with "May you do well" and "May you live earnestly."[13]

We continue with a bit of cheerleading by Epicurus, and general advice, regarding how to move toward happiness. Significantly, we must act now—today—no matter where we are along life's trajectory. This acting centers on the study of philosophy and the practice of its conclusions. The big point: happiness is something actively done.

We must practice those things that produce happiness since if happiness is present, we possess everything, and if it is not, we do everything to acquire it.[14]

Do and practice those things that I have continually recommended to you, taking them to be the basic elements of living well.[15]

Let no one put off studying philosophy when he is young, nor become weary of it when he is old, for no age is too early or too late for the health of the soul. To suggest that the time for studying philosophy has not yet come or that it is long gone is like saying that it is too early or too late for happiness.[16]

We come into being only once and will not be born a second time. Rather, we necessarily will never exist again—forever. And though you have no power over tomorrow, you put off feeling joy today. Life is consumed by such indecision and procrastination! And so, each one of us is dying without engaging in life today.[17]

At one and the same time, we must laugh and do philosophy and manage our households and the rest of our private affairs, always proclaiming the sayings of the true philosophy.[18]

Take thought of and practice these matters and related precepts day and night, both by yourself and with others who are like-minded. If you do, then you will never be disturbed by confusion, whether you are awake or dreaming. Instead, you will live like a god among human beings. For the man who lives among immortal blessings loses every likeness to mortal beings.[19]

Next, Epicurus argues that we are free to choose and practice happiness. There is no Fate, he says, only necessity, chance, and human agency. In this way, he liberates the Greek mind from its long belief in the dominance of Fate and destiny. He also frees us to act apart from the approval or praise of others.

The man who has considered the natural goal of life and understands how easily the limit of good things can be reached and attained, and how the limit of bad things is either short in its duration or slight in its distress. He scorns the notion of destiny that some introduce as the master of all things, affirming rather that some things happen by necessity, others by chance, and others through our own agency. This is because he sees that necessity promotes irresponsibility and that chance or fortune is unstable, whereas our own actions are free, and it is to them that praise and blame are attached.[20]

The wise man does not hold chance (or luck or fortune) to be a god as the many do, assuming as he does that, with a god, nothing is done in a disorderly fashion. Nor does he hold that chance is even an unreliable cause, for he believes that chance delivers nothing good or bad to humans toward living happily—though, to be sure, chance furnishes the beginning point of the excessive goods of fortune and misfortune.[21]

Necessity is something bad, but there is no necessity to live by means of necessity.[22]

The approval of others is necessarily their own business. As for us, we must get on with our own healing.[23]

Moving on, Epicurus teaches that we must actively pursue the study of philosophy for the sake of happiness. For him, philosophy is divided into three parts: canonics (the means by which we may know things), physics or natural philosophy (the study of the nature of reality), and ethics (the pursuit of the good life). He stresses that the point of philosophy or knowledge is peace of mind, happiness—it is not merely to collect facts or build up a philosophical system. For Epicurus, knowledge without happiness is somewhat, if not wholly, pointless.

Let no one put off studying philosophy, . . . for no age is too early or too late for the health of the soul.[24]

We must hold that the function of the study of natural phenomena is to clearly understand the cause of the most important things. And we must hold that blessed happiness depends on this.[25]

We would have never needed to investigate natural phenomena if we had not been disturbed by worry about things that happen in the sky or by the misgiving that death means something to us or by our failure to understand the boundary markers of suffering and desire.[26]

Remember that, like everything else, knowledge of celestial phenomena—whether taken along with other things or in isolation—has no other purpose than tranquility of mind and resolute conviction and confidence.[27]

In the study of nature, we must not accept empty assumptions and arbitrary laws. Rather, we should follow the promptings of the phenomena, the facts themselves. We have come to the point where our life has no need for non-rational and empty opinion. Our one need is to live undisturbed, without trouble.[28]

The study of nature does not produce boastful men or bigmouths or those who show off the learning that the many argue about; rather, it produces fearless and self-sufficient men, who pride themselves on their own personal goods rather than on circumstances.[29]

Next up, in the context of "the basic elements of living well," Epicurus addresses how we can be happy relative to the gods, death, desire, and pleasure and pain, among other points.

First, the gods. Many in Epicurus' time were afraid of the gods, including the heavenly bodies (the sun, moon, and stars) that were revered as gods

*by many. To combat such fear, Epicurus teaches that it is unnecessary to
fear the gods since they are by nature happy and indestructible or immortal.*

You should acknowledge that the god is an indestructible and
blessed living being. This is the commonly held understanding of
the god, the common epithet in writing. Accordingly, do not attribute to him anything that is contrary to his indestructibility or incongruous with his blessed happiness. Instead, think about the god
whatever can defend and uphold his blessed happiness and his indestructibility.[30]

There is yet one more point to grasp—namely, that the greatest disturbance arises in the human soul thanks to the belief that the heavenly bodies are blessed and indestructible, while these same bodies
simultaneously wish and act and cause in ways that are incompat-
ible with these attributes.[31]

We should acknowledge that revolutions and solstices and eclipses
and risings and settings and the like take place without the administration or command, either now or in the future, of some being that
simultaneously enjoys perfect bliss as well as indestructibility. This
is so because practical troubles and anxieties and feelings of anger
and the granting of favors do not accord with bliss.[32]

A blessed and indestructible being is not bothered by troublesome
business, nor does this being trouble others. Therefore, such a being
is free from anger and the feeling that he is obliged to grant favors
since these feelings imply weakness.[33]

*Just as there is no need to fear the gods, so there is no need to fear death. "This
is so," Epicurus says, "because every good and every evil is connected to sensation. And death is the loss of all sensation." Not only that, but "when we
exist death is not present, and when death is present we do not exist."*

You should get used to the idea that death means nothing to us. This
is so because every good and every evil is connected to sensation.

And death is the loss of all sensation. It follows that a right under-standing of the fact that death means nothing to us makes the mortal nature of life beneficial to us—not by adding to life an unlimited amount of time, but by taking away the yearning for immortality.[34]

As long as the soul is in the body, it never loses sensation through the removal of some other part. The container may be dislocated in whole or in part, and portions of the soul may thereby be lost. Despite this, the soul will nevertheless retain sensation if it manages to survive. But as soon as those atoms that make up the nature of the soul have departed—however few—the rest of the human organism no longer has sensation, whether the whole of it survives or only a part. Moreover, when the whole of the human organism is broken up, the soul is scattered and no longer has the same powers as before, nor the same motions. Therefore, the soul no longer possesses sensation.[35]

There is no terror at all in living for the one who has thoroughly grasped that there is no terror at all in not living. Foolish, therefore, is the man who says that he fears death because it pains him to think about its eventual coming rather than actually paining him when it comes. Whatever causes no trouble when it is present causes only groundless pain in its mere anticipation. So then, death—that evil which most causes us to shudder—means nothing to us since when we exist, death is not present, and when death is present, we do not exist.[36]

As we've already noted, happiness for Epicurus is connected in some manner to pleasure. For this reason, it is tied to desire, which moves us toward pleasure. Since this is the case, these questions follow: what sort of pleasures should we desire? And what sort of desires should we seek to satisfy? In brief, Epicurus' answers are: not every pleasure and only some kinds of desire—in general, those that are natural and necessary. The pleasure that truly makes for happiness is easy to get and maintain.

A pleasant life is not produced by stringing together one drinking party after another, or by having sex with young boys or women, or by enjoying fish and other delicacies set on a luxurious table. Instead, it is produced by sober reasoning that examines what is responsible for every choice and avoidance, and expels those beliefs by which the greatest confusion lays hold of the soul.[37]

We must present the following questions to all our desires. What will happen to me if the desire I wish to satisfy is fulfilled? What will happen if it is not?[38]

Of the desires, some are natural and necessary, whereas some are natural but unnecessary. Others are neither natural nor necessary but arise thanks to groundless notions.[39]

We must consider that of the desires, some are natural, and some are groundless. Of the natural desires, some are necessary, and some are merely natural. And of the necessary desires, some are necessary for happiness, some for freeing the body from disturbance, and some for living itself.[40]

Unnecessary desires are those that lead to no pain if they remain unsatisfied. They involve an appetite that is easily relieved whenever its satisfaction is hard to procure or when it seems likely to cause harm.[41]

He who understands the limits of life knows how easy it is to procure what it takes to remove the pain of need and make the whole of life complete. Therefore, there is no need for things that can only be procured by means of struggle and troublesome business.[42]

The wise man is one who has considered the natural goal of life and understands how easily the limit of good things can be reached and attained.[43]

Natural wealth is both limited and easy to get. But wealth based on groundless opinion grows without limit.[44]

We desire pleasure, which, Epicurus declares, "is our first good." It is "the beginning point and goal of living happily." Exploring its nature, Epicurus observes that pleasure "is an appropriate feeling, natural," concluding that it is fundamentally "the absence of pain in the body and of trouble in the soul." This "absence," rather than some presence, is therefore the proper measure of pleasure. Any pleasure beyond this absence is simply variation.

We recognize that pleasure is our first good, present at birth.[45]

Diogenes Laertius (giving the Epicurean view of pleasure and pain) Epicureans say that there are two feelings in every living being. They are pleasure and pain. They further say that pleasure is an appropriate feeling, natural. By contrast, pain is strange, unnatural.[46]

We say that pleasure is the beginning point and goal of living happily. We recognize that pleasure is our first good.[47]

When we say that pleasure is the beginning point and goal of life, we do not mean the pleasures of decadent men or the pleasures of sensuality, as some ignorant persons believe, or those who do not agree with us, or those who have willfully misrepresented our position. Rather, by pleasure we mean the absence of pain in the body and of trouble in the soul.[48]

Diogenes Laertius (explaining the Epicurean position regarding soul pleasure and body pleasure) Epicurus recognizes both pleasure of the soul and of the body. . . . He believes that pleasures of the soul are greater than those of the body.[49]

Diogenes Laertius When it comes to the nature of pleasure, Epicurus and the Cyrenaics differ. The Cyrenaics only accept kinetic pleasure, that is, pleasure in motion; they do not accept static, or katastematic, pleasure. By contrast, Epicurus accepts both. . . . In his work *On Choice*, Epicurus says, "Freedom from trouble and freedom from pain are katastematic pleasures. Joy and good cheer are viewed as kinetic and active."[50]

The standard measure for the greatest amount of pleasure is the removal of every pain. Whenever pleasure is present, as long as it lasts, there is neither pain nor distress nor both together.[51]

Pleasure in the flesh will not increase after need-based pain is removed. After that, pleasure may only be varied. And the limit of pleasure in the mind is reached in thinking about these and like things that used to cause the greatest fears in the mind.[52]

Epicurus counsels us to choose those things that lead to happiness and avoid those that do not. This general advice once again brings up pleasure and pain — what they are and what our relation to them should be if we're shooting for happiness. The answer? We should choose pleasure but not every pleasure. Similarly, we should avoid pain but not every pain.

Diogenes Laertius It is by means of these two feelings (pleasure and pain) that animals either choose or avoid something.[53]

Pleasure is the beginning point of every choice and avoidance. We resort to pleasure when we use feeling as the measure for judging every good.[54]

Even though pleasure is our first and inborn good, we nevertheless do not choose every pleasure. Rather, we oftentimes forgo many pleasures when a greater annoyance will follow from choosing them. And oftentimes we acknowledge that many pains are better than many pleasures when an even greater pleasure follows from patiently enduring these pains for a long period of time. And so, even though every pleasure is naturally good and fitting, not every pleasure is to be chosen. In the same way, even though every pain is bad, not every pain is always to be avoided. To be sure, we may aptly judge every case by measuring one feeling in comparison with the other and taking a look at the advantages and disadvantages of both sides. Sometimes we treat a good thing as though it is bad. On the other hand, sometimes we treat a bad thing as though it is good.[55]

The same moment includes both the beginning of the greatest good and deliverance from what is bad.[56]

Epicurus suggests that a simple, frugal life is more likely to be a happy life compared with a life full of luxury. Such simplicity amounts to self-sufficiency and freedom.

Claudius Aelianus (Aelian) Croaking like a frog, Epicurus said that nothing is enough for the man who is not satisfied with just a little. He further said that he was prepared to contend with Zeus himself for happiness if only he had some barley bread and water.[57]

The flesh cries out, "No hunger! No thirst! No freezing cold!" Whoever confidently has what it takes to satisfy these desires may rival even Zeus for happiness.[58]

Simple food gives just as much pleasure as rich food does as soon as the hunger pains are gone. A barley cake and water offer the highest possible pleasure when they are given to a hungry man. Getting used to simple and inexpensive food, therefore, aids the health of a man and enables him to perform the necessary requirements of life with resolution. Not only that, but such a habit better disposes us for when we encounter extravagant fare now and again, and makes us fearless in the face of fortune.[59]

Diogenes Laertius Diocles, in the third book of his *Epitome*, speaks of the Epicureans as living a quite simple and frugal life. Anyway, they were, he says, content with a cup of poor wine. Otherwise, they were water drinkers.[60]

The greatest fruit of self-sufficiency is freedom.[61]

It is not possible for a man living a free life to amass a lot of money and possessions since this is no easy accomplishment without being servile to the masses or those in power. And yet such a free life has acquired everything in ongoing abundance.[62]

When measured by the goals of nature, poverty is great wealth. And wealth is great poverty if it is not limited.[63]

In the following selections, Epicurus explores the relationship between virtue, pleasure, and happiness.

Diogenes Laertius Epicurus declares that virtue is the only thing that is inseparable from pleasure.[64]

The virtues have become one with living pleasantly. Living pleasantly is inseparable from the virtues.[65]

Diogenes Laertius (reporting the Epicurean position on virtue and pleasure) We choose the virtues for the sake of pleasure and not on their own account, even as we take medicine for the sake of health.[66]

It is impossible to live pleasantly without living wisely, nobly, and justly—just as it is impossible to live wisely, nobly, and justly without living pleasantly. The person who fails to inaugurate a wise, noble, and just life is the person who does not have a pleasant life.[67]

Practical wisdom is the foundation of all of these things and the greatest good. For this reason, we value practical wisdom even more than philosophy. Every other virtue is produced from practical wisdom, teaching us that we cannot live pleasantly without living wisely, nobly, and justly—just as we cannot live wisely, nobly, and justly without living pleasantly.[68]

Finally, Epicurus suggests that we should cultivate friendship in order to "ensure blessed happiness."

Of all the means that are procured by wisdom to ensure blessed happiness throughout the whole of life, by far the most important is the acquisition of friendship.[69]

Friendship dances around the world of men calling out to all of us,

"Rise up to happiness!"[70]

Diogenes Laertius (reporting Epicurus' views regarding "the wise man" about friendship and how to be a friend) The wise man holds that friendship arises because we are in need. That said, friendship involves sacrifice, just as we have to cast seed into the earth. Friendship is maintained by a partnership in the enjoyment of life's pleasures. . . . The wise man never gives up a friend. . . . On occasion, the wise man will die for a friend.[71]

HAPPINESS FOR EPICURUS & EPICUREANISM

For Epicurus, happiness is fundamentally tied to the right sort of pleasure, which is the "absence of pain." As far as the soul or mind goes, this pleasure is mental tranquility. That said, there is also bodily pleasure, which is health. So it is that "bodily health and mental tranquility . . . is the goal of a blessedly happy life."

Rightly understood, happiness is something we freely choose and do, something we practice. Part of this practice is philosophy, which seeks to comprehend reality so that we may pacify some of the fears and anxieties we may have that have arisen from misunderstandings (that the gods are angry, for instance, or that death is something horrible). Philosophy also strives to understand the nature of desire so that we may practice the satisfaction of certain desires—those that are necessary to satisfy in order to quiet pain—and leave the rest alone. The best, happiest life is the simple, frugal life.

A final few points. Since happiness is a practice, it requires the excellence of the virtues. Consequently, the virtuous life is equivalent to the pleasurable life. Lastly, friendship is an essential aspect of the happy life.

NOTES

[1] For "the glory of the Greeks," "liberator," and "the very wisest of men," see Lucretius (*On the Nature of Things*), Lucian of Samosata (*Alexander the False Prophet*), and Cosma Riamondi (*Letter to Ambrogio Tignosi*), respectively.

[2] See Seneca, *Letter to Lucilius* 25.5 and *On the Happy Life* 13. "I myself believe, though my Stoic comrades would be unwilling to hear me say so, that the teaching of Epicurus was good and upright, and even, if you examine it narrowly, stern."

[3] This was the same Hesiod who, along with Homer, had given the Greeks their general understanding of the gods—this according to the ancient Greek historian Herodotus: "Hesiod and Homer . . . are the ones who made for the Greeks the genealogy of the gods, and gave the gods their names, and delineated their honors and abilities, and declared their outward forms" (see Herodotus, *Histories* 2.53.2). For an exploration of the nature of Chaos in Hesiod, see the "Introduction" to the Cave's *The Best of Hesiod's Theogony & Works and Days*, 34-35.

[4] Diogenes Laertius, *Lives* 10.2.

[5] For an extended introduction to Epicurus and his philosophy, and a collection of his own writings, see the Cave's *The Best of Epicurus: The Life, Writings & Teachings of Epicurus the Greek Philosopher*.

[6] Epicurus, *Letter to Menoeceus*, in Diogenes Laertius, *Lives* 10.128.

[7] Ibid., 10.128.

[8] Epicurus, *Letter to Herodotus*, in Diogenes Laertius, *Lives* 10.82.

[9] Ibid., 10.77. Although Epicurus makes the point relative to the gods (they are blissful and are, therefore, not full of worry and so on), it equally applies to human beings and human happiness.

[10] Diogenes Laertius, *Lives* 10.136.

[11] Ibid., 10.121. Though "the god" here is singular, Epicurus doubtlessly means all the gods since, apparently, he did not believe in one highest God.

[12] Epicurus, *Vatican Sayings* 17.

[13] Diogenes Laertius, *Lives* 10.14.

[14] Epicurus, *Letter to Menoeceus*, in Diogenes Laertius, *Lives* 10.122.

[15] Ibid., 10.123.

[16] Ibid., 10.122.

[17] Epicurus, *Vatican Sayings* 14.

[18] Ibid., 41.

[19] Epicurus, *Letter to Menoeceus*, in Diogenes Laertius, *Lives* 10.135.

[20] Ibid., 10.133.

[21] Ibid., 10.134.

[22] Epicurus, *Vatican Sayings* 9.

[23] Ibid., 64.

[24] Epicurus, *Letter to Menoeceus*, in Diogenes Laertius, *Lives* 10.122.

[25] Epicurus, *Letter to Herodotus*, in Diogenes Laertius, *Lives* 10.78.

[26] Epicurus, *Principal Teachings* 11, in Diogenes Laertius, *Lives* 10.142.

[27] Epicurus, *Letter to Pythocles*, in Diogenes Laertius, *Lives* 10.85.

[28] Ibid., 10.87.

[29] Epicurus, *Vatican Sayings* 45.

[30] Epicurus, *Letter to Menoeceus*, in Diogenes Laertius, *Lives* 10.123. By "common epithet in writing," Epicurus is referring to the typical way the gods are

described from Homer on. In particular, most ancient Greeks judged the gods to be immortal (or indestructible), ageless, and blessed.

[31] Epicurus, *Letter to Herodotus*, in Diogenes Laertius, *Lives* 10.81.

[32] Ibid., 10.76-77.

[33] Epicurus, *Principal Teachings* 1, in Diogenes Laertius, *Lives* 10.139.

[34] Epicurus, *Letter to Menoeceus*, in Diogenes Laertius, *Lives* 10.124.

[35] Epicurus, *Letter to Herodotus*, in Diogenes Laertius, *Lives* 10.65.

[36] Epicurus, *Letter to Menoeceus*, in Diogenes Laertius, *Lives* 10.125.

[37] Ibid., 10.132.

[38] Epicurus, *Vatican Sayings* 71.

[39] Epicurus, *Principal Teachings* 29, in Diogenes Laertius, *Lives* 10.149. Added commentary: "Epicurus regards as natural and necessary desires that bring relief from pain, such as drink when we are thirsty. And by desires that are natural and unnecessary he means those that merely vary the pleasure without removing the pain, such as costly food. And by desires that are neither natural nor necessary he means those for crowns and the erection of statues in one's honor."

[40] Epicurus, *Letter to Menoeceus*, in Diogenes Laertius, *Lives* 10.127.

[41] Epicurus, *Principal Teachings* 26, in Diogenes Laertius, *Lives* 10.148.

[42] Epicurus, *Principal Teachings* 21, in Diogenes Laertius, *Lives* 10.146.

[43] Epicurus, *Letter to Menoeceus*, in Diogenes Laertius, *Lives* 10.133.

[44] Epicurus, *Principal Teachings* 15, in Diogenes Laertius, *Lives* 10.144.

[45] Epicurus, *Letter to Menoeceus*, in Diogenes Laertius, *Lives* 10.129.

[46] Diogenes Laertius, *Lives* 10.34.

[47] Epicurus, *Letter to Menoeceus*, in Diogenes Laertius, *Lives* 10.128-129.

[48] Ibid., 10.131.

[49] Diogenes Laertius, *Lives* 10.136, 137.

[50] Ibid., 10.136. For discussions on the nature of and differences between kinetic and katastematic pleasure, see A.A. Long, *Hellenistic Philosophy: Stoics, Epicureans, Sceptics*, 2nd ed. (London: Duckworth, 1986), 64-65, and J.M. Rist, *Epicurus: An Introduction* (Cambridge: Cambridge University Press, 1972), 170-172. In short, kinetic pleasure is that which accompanies the ongoing act of satisfying some desire, whereas katastematic pleasure is that of being satisfied after the act. For example, when one is thirsty, one drinks water. The ongoing act of quenching thirst is satisfying—pleasing (a kinetic pleasure). When one stops drinking, one is satisfied (no longer thirsty), which is also pleasing (a katastematic pleasure). We might call the former "acting" (or "active") pleasure and the latter "standing" (or "static") pleasure.

[51] Epicurus, *Principal Teachings* 3, in Diogenes Laertius, *Lives* 10.139.

[52] Epicurus, *Principal Teachings* 18, in Diogenes Laertius, *Lives* 10.144.

[53] Diogenes Laertius, *Lives* 10.34.

[54] Epicurus, *Letter to Menoeceus*, in Diogenes Laertius, *Lives* 10.129.

[55] Ibid., 10.129-130.

[56] Epicurus, *Vatican Sayings* 42. The statement refers to the precise moment when pleasure appears and pain disappears.

[57] Aelian, *Various Histories* 4.13.

[58] Epicurus, *Vatican Sayings* 33.

[59] Epicurus, *Letter to Menoeceus*, in Diogenes Laertius, *Lives* 10.130-131.

[60] Diogenes Laertius, *Lives* 10.11. "Water drinkers" rather than wine drinkers. For more on the distinction, see Tim J. Young, *Drinking Wine with Homer & the Earliest Greeks: Cultivating, Serving & Delighting in Ancient Greek Wine.*

[61] Epicurus, *Vatican Sayings* 77.

[62] Ibid., 67.

[63] Ibid., 25.

[64] Diogenes Laertius, *Lives* 10.138.

[65] Epicurus, *Letter to Menoeceus*, in Diogenes Laertius, *Lives* 10.132.

[66] Diogenes Laertius, *Lives* 10.138.

[67] Epicurus, *Principal Teachings* 5, in Diogenes Laertius, *Lives* 10.140.

[68] Epicurus, *Letter to Menoeceus*, in Diogenes Laertius, *Lives* 10.132. "These things" refers to a truly pleasant life and the "sober reasoning" that leads us thereto—to the "practice [of] those things that produce happiness," which are "the basic elements of living well."

[69] Epicurus, *Principal Teachings* 27, in Diogenes Laertius, *Lives* 10.148.

[70] Epicurus, *Vatican Sayings* 52.

[71] Diogenes Laertius, *Lives* 10.120.

EPICTETUS, MARCUS AURELIUS, SENECA
& LATER STOICISM

"Epictetus says that God has given to every man the means of fulfilling all his obligations. Moreover, the means are always in our power. He further says that we must seek felicity through the things that are in our power since God has given them to us for this end. We must see what there is within us that is free."

—Blaise Pascal, *Conversation with M. de Saci on Epictetus and Montaigne*

TIME TRAVEL NEARLY four hundred years from the year when Zeno of Citium, the founder of Stoicism, was born in 335 BC to the middle of the first century AD and the beginning of Nero's frightening rule in Rome. Some nine hundred miles away—as the crow flies—from the imperial capital city, a baby boy was born in Hierapolis, the present-day western Turkish town of Pamukkale, a site known today for its white hot springs, which look like they belong to another world. The boy was eventually acquired by Epaphroditus, a former slave, who served as secretary to the emperors Nero and Domitian. The boy seems to have obtained his name, Epictetus, from this transaction—a name that means "acquired."[1]

Epictetus (c. 55-135 AD) grew up in Rome. From what we know, he worked there for his master in his master's villa. At some point, he also studied philosophy with the Stoic Musonius Rufus, whose teachings his own resemble. Epaphroditus eventually freed Epictetus sometime toward the end of the eighties AD. By then, Epictetus had already devoted himself to a life of philosophy. And with near missionary zeal, he wished to lead others into a more philosophical way of life, which is to say a life that would properly employ judgment to determine what is up to us and what is not.

When the emperor Domitian banished philosophers from Rome and Italy around 90 AD, Epictetus departed and made his way to the

Roman city of Nicopolis ("Victory City"), a city that commemorated Augustus' victory over Marc Antony at the naval battle of Actium in 31 BC. Here, in the Roman province of Epirus in what is now Greece, Epictetus set up a Stoic school of philosophy that catered to wealthier Roman families and students. For the many who attended the school, Stoicism was a practical way of life, one that taught them how to live well—that is, how to be happy.

Epictetus is known for his *Discourses* and *Handbook* (*Enchiridion*), which were recorded by his student Arrian (c. 90-160 AD).[2] Written in Greek, the *Discourses* and *Handbook* are the longest extant Stoic writings. Both works emphasize ethics.

Although we'll spend most of our time with Epictetus in this chapter, we'll also hear from two other later Stoics. One, the Roman emperor Marcus Aurelius (121-180 AD), wrote in Greek. Even though he himself was not Greek (he was born in Rome), his writing and thoughts nevertheless represent Greek thinking and practice. Trained in Stoicism, he is known for his journal of meditations, *To Himself* (often simply titled, *Meditations*).[3] Marcus Aurelius spent much of his time as emperor (161-80 AD) defending the Roman Empire against invasions in the east and west.

The other later Stoic, Seneca (the Younger) (c. between 4 BC and 1 AD-65 AD) was born in Spain.[4] He wrote in Latin, though channeling Greek philosophy. Living mostly in Rome, Seneca practiced Stoicism while engaged in various activities, including serving as an advisor to the Roman emperor Nero.[5] He also wrote tragedies, letters, and essays on many topics, including anger, the shortness of life, tranquility, and happiness. All these writings were flavored with Stoicism. We'll look at a few selections from his *On the Happy Life* to get an idea of what he and other Roman Stoics believed about happiness.

IN THEIR OWN WORDS

Epictetus

First, Epictetus states his general belief that God made all humans for happiness. Next, he suggests that the true Cynic should be able to imitate Socrates in his mission to call people to the care of their souls. By "true Cynic," we should understand the best sort of Stoic since Epictetus held that the latter was like a true Cynic. The essential points: happiness is something found within and not without; it is a soul possession not found in the body, possessions, or power.

God made every human being to be happy, to be steady and calm.[6]

It is the Cynic's responsibility, then, to be able with a loud voice, if the occasion arises, and appearing on the tragic stage, to say like Socrates: "Where are you hurrying? What are you doing, you miserable men? Like blind people you are wandering up and down. You are going by another road and have left the true road. You search for prosperity and happiness where they are not. And if another shows you where they are, you do not believe him."

Why do you seek happiness outside yourself? In the body? It is not there. If you doubt it, look at Myro. Look at Ophellius. It is not in possessions. But if you do not believe me, look at Croesus. Look at those who are now rich—with what lamentations their life is filled. It is not in power. If so, those must be happy who have been two and three times consuls. But they are not. Whom shall we believe in these matters? You who from without see their affairs and are dazzled by an appearance, or the men themselves? And what do they say? Hear them when they groan, when they grieve, when because of these very consulships and glory and splendor they think that they are more wretched and in greater danger. It is not in royal power. If it were, Nero would have been happy, and Sardanapalus. But neither was Agamemnon happy, even though he was a better man than Sardanapalus and Nero. And while the others are snoring, what is he doing? "He tore out his hair by the handfuls." And what is he saying to himself? "I'm perplexed and disturbed. I'm tossed back and forth, and my heart is leaping out from my chest." Wretched man, what is so wrong? Is it your possessions? No. Your body? No—you are rich in gold and copper. What, then, is the matter with you?[7]

Given the nature of happiness, we should focus on what is in our power rather than what is not. To do otherwise is to experience frustration and a kind of chosen enslavement. A sense of disturbance always results from a mistaken judgment about what is good and bad. We should bring a good disposition to all things and desire only those things that are in our power rather than those things that are not. Only in this way will we be happy. Finally, we must understand the price of tranquility or happiness; it is not free.

Examine yourself whether you wish to be rich or to be happy. If you wish to be rich, you should know that it is neither a good thing nor at all in your power. But if you wish to be happy, you should know that it is both a good thing and in your power, for the one is a temporary loan of fortune, whereas happiness comes from the will.[8]

If a man believes that his good and his interest are found only in those things that are free from hindrance and in his own power, he will be free, flowing well with a good life, happy, free from harm, magnanimous, pious, and thankful to God for all things. In no matter will he find fault with any of the things that have not been put in his power. Nor will he blame any of them. But if he believes that his good and his interest are found in externals and in things that are not in the power of his will, then he will necessarily be hindered, impeded, and a slave to those who have power over the things that he wonders at and fears. Furthermore, he will necessarily be impious since he believes that he is harmed by God.[9]

Of all the things that exist, God has put some of them in our power, that is, under our control, and some he has not.

He has placed in our own power that act which is the best and the most important—the act, indeed, by which he himself is happy—the use of presentations (that is, appearances or impressions). For when the use of presentations is rightly employed, there is freedom, good flow, cheerful contentment, and stable calm. There is also justice, law, moderation, and every virtue. But God has not placed all other things in our power. Therefore, we should unite in mind with God.

We should also make the following division of things: we should look after those things that are in our power and therefore under our control. As for those things that are not in our power, we should entrust them to the Cosmos, willingly giving up whatever the Cosmos requires—our children, our country, our body, or anything else.[10]

Of things that are, some things are up to us, but other things are not up to us.

Those things that are up to us are assumption, impulse, desire, aversion, and, in a word, whatever is our own doing. By contrast, those things that are not up to us include our body, property, reputation, official power, and, in a word, whatever is not our own doing.

Those things that are up to us are by nature free, unhindered, and unimpeded. By contrast, those things that are not up to us are weak, slavish, hindered, and not our own.

So then, remember that if you consider free those things that are by nature not free or slavish, and if you consider your own those things that belong to others, you will be fettered, grief-stricken, and troubled. And for this you will blame both gods and men. On the other hand, if you consider your things alone to be yours, and what belongs to another to belong to another, as it *actually* does, then no one will ever compel you or hinder you. You will not blame or prosecute anyone. You will do nothing against your will. You will have no enemies, and no one will harm you—for there is no harm that can touch you.

With goals as great as these, remember that you must urge yourself on with an extraordinary effort to achieve them. You will have to give up some things altogether. You will have to postpone others for the present moment.

But if your wish is to be powerful or wealthy in addition to these great things, then it may happen that you will not get even these latter things because you also aim at the former. And certainly you will fail to get the former, which alone bring freedom and happiness.

Right now, then, make it your practice to say to every rough or harsh presentation (appearance or impression) that "You are a presentation." And, "You are not at all what you appear to be."

After saying that, closely examine the presentation and test it by means of the rules or measures you have—and most importantly by the leading rule, which judges whether the presentation has to do with things that are up to us or with things that are not up to us. And if it has to do with something that is not up to us, then be ready with this explanation: "This thing is nothing to me."[11]

It is not the events themselves that trouble human beings; rather, it is our beliefs about the events.

For example, death in itself is nothing terrible. Otherwise, it would have seemed terrible to Socrates. But our belief about death that it is terrible—*this* is the terrible thing.

So then, whenever we are feeling blocked or troubled or upset, let us never say that some other thing besides ourselves is the cause. Rather, our own beliefs are the cause of our feelings.

It is the act of an inadequately formed person to blame other things when he fares poorly. The one who is just beginning his formation blames himself, whereas the one who is already formed blames neither other things nor himself.[12]

Don't go looking for things to happen as you wish them to happen. Instead, wish them to happen as they actually do happen, and things will go well for you.[13]

Someone asks, "Can I be benefited by these things [sickness, death, and other supposed negatives]?"

Yes, you can be benefited by all things. . . .

The problem? You don't know how to let humans benefit you.

Is my neighbor bad? Sure, he's bad to himself, but he's good to me in that he exercises my good disposition, my moderation. Is my father bad? Sure, he's bad to himself, but to me good.

This is the rod of Hermes. "Touch whatever you wish," as the saying goes, "and it will be made of gold." But I say, "Bring whatever you wish, and I will make it good." Bring disease, bring death, bring poverty, bring abuse, bring trial on capital charges—all these things will become beneficial through the rod of Hermes.

"But what will you do with death?"

What else?—it will honor you, or it will be the occasion by which you demonstrate what a man is like who follows the will of nature.

"What will you do with disease?"

I will show its nature. I will shine by being firm and serene. I will neither entreat the physician, nor will I wish to die.

"What else do you seek?"

Whatever I am given, I will make it blessed, happy, solemn, enviable.[14]

God made every human being to be happy, to be steady and calm. For this purpose, he gave them a starting point, giving each man some things that are his own, and other things that are not his own.

Some things are subject to hindrance and compulsion and deprivation. These things are not a man's own. Other things are not subject to hindrance. These are a man's own.

As for the essence of good and evil, God has made it our own. This was a fitting act for the one who takes care of us and protects us like a father.

"But," you say, "I have parted from a certain person, and he is grieved."

Why, I ask, did this person consider as his own that which belongs to another? Again I ask, why—when he was delighted to see you—did he not also consider that you are mortal, that it is natural for you to depart from him to a foreign country? Therefore, he suffers the consequences of his own folly.

And why are you complaining, crying for yourself? Is it because you also have not thought of these things? . . .

You enjoyed everything that gave you pleasure, as if you would always enjoy them—places and men send conversation. And now you sit and weep because you do not see the same people and do not live in the same places. . . .

Take Odysseus as an example. He knew that no man is an orphan. Instead, the father always takes care of all men—and will continuously. It was not merely by a report that he had heard that Zeus is the father of men. Odysseus thought that Zeus was his own father.

And so, he called him that, and he looked to him in whatever he did. Therefore, Odysseus was enabled to live happily in all places.

It is never possible for happiness and yearning for what is not present to come together. For the happy man must have all that he wishes to have. The happy man must resemble a full man, complete. He must not be thirsty or hungry.

"But," you say, "Odysseus yearned for his wife and wept as he sat on a rock."

Do you accept Homer and his stories in everything? Or, if Odysseus really wept, what was he other than an unhappy man? And what good man is unhappy?

Here's the truth. If Zeus does not take care of his own citizens so that they may be happy like he himself is, then the whole cosmos is managed badly. But these things are not right to think about.[15]

You can be undefeated if you do not enter a contest that is not within your power to win.

When you see that someone is honored above others or very powerful or distinguished in another way, make sure that you never pronounce him happy, seized and carried away by the appearance. For if the essence of the good equals those things that are within our power, then neither envy nor jealousy have a place. And you yourself will not want to be a general or chief magistrate or the highest official, but you will want to be free.

There is one way to move toward this goal. Look down on those things that are not in our power.[16]

If you intend to improve, throw away such thoughts as these: "If I neglect my affairs, I will not have the means of living." Or, "Unless I chastise my slave, he will be bad."

The truth is that it is better to die of hunger, and so, to be released from grief and fear, than to live in abundance with a troubled mind. And it is better for your slave to be bad than for you to be unhappy.

Begin, then, with little things. Is the oil spilled? Is a little wine stolen? When such things happen, say, "Such is the price of equanimity. Such is the price of tranquility. Nothing is free."[17]

Epictetus suggests that we should recognize and be elated by our kinship to God. Moreover, rather than associating happiness with the body, we should recognize its relation to the soul and reason, that part we share with the gods. Further, if we wish to be happy, we must play the role that God has given us to play in life. Finally, we must welcome God's lead in every circumstance, the lead of destiny and necessity.

If a man assents to this doctrine as he should—that we are all sprung from God, and that God is the father both of men and of gods—then I suppose that he will never have any ignoble or mean thoughts about himself. . . . As it stands, however, we are not elated by knowing we are sons of Zeus. Rather, since two things were mixed in the generation of mankind—the body in common with animals, and reason and intelligence in common with the gods—many incline to the kinship that is unfortunate and mortal, while a few favor that which is divine and blessed.[18]

Remember that you are an actor in a play—the kind of play the author and director wants to write and present. If it is short, then you are in a short play. If long, then long. If he wants you to play the part of a beggar, make sure that you play it skillfully. Or if he wants you to play someone who's physically disabled. Or a ruler. Or a private citizen. Your job is to play the assigned person well. But choosing the role belongs to another.[19]

In every circumstance we should keep in mind the following:

"Lead me, Zeus; lead me, Destiny. Lead me wherever you have fated me to go, for I am ready to follow without hesitation. But if I choose not to follow you, then not only will I make myself a base and miserable man, but I will also still have to follow."

"Whoever nobly yields to necessity—we hold that man wise and skilled in divine things."

And a third, "Crito, if it is pleasing to the gods, then let it happen. Anytus and Meletus can kill me, but they cannot harm me."[20]

▪ ▪ ▪

Marcus Aurelius, the Roman emperor

In line with typical Stoic themes, Marcus Aurelius counsels himself to be happy by doing well—that is, by living according to reason in light of what nature wills. The key is to have "set judgments" relative to what is good and bad.

You can always flow well if you fare well—if you take up and practice the way.[21]

Always remember this—that living happily depends on very few things.[22]

We should consider as enjoyment everything that is in our power to do according to our own nature.[23]

Remember that philosophy only wishes for what nature wants. By contrast, your wish was for something contrary to nature.

You say, "But it would have been so satisfying!"

True. But isn't this why pleasure messes us up? Anyway, look at the following and judge whether they are even more satisfying. Magnanimity. Independence. Simplicity. Kindness of heart. Piety. And what is more satisfying than practical wisdom itself?[24]

The *hēgemonikon*—or the leading part of the soul—never disturbs its own tranquility. For instance, it never gives itself over to lust. . . . In itself, the *hēgemonikon* lacks nothing—unless, that is, it makes up its own lacking. Accordingly, it is undisturbed and unimpeded unless it disturbs or impedes itself. Happiness is a good and noble *daemon*; happiness is a good and noble *hēgemonikon*.[25]

The following thought will help you get rid of the desire for an empty reputation—the realization that you are unable to live your whole life as a philosopher. . . . It is clear to you and others that you are far off from philosophy. . . . So, forget about what others think about you.

Be content if you live the rest of your life, however long it is, as nature wills you to live. Consider what nature wills, and let nothing draw you away from it.

Past experience reveals how much you have wandered without finding out how to live well. Happiness is neither found in syllogisms, nor in wealth, nor in reputation, nor in enjoyment.

Where, then, is happiness found? It is found in seeking after and doing what human nature requires.

How, then, will a human being do this? By putting set judgments in charge of your impulses and your actions.

What set judgments? The ones about the good and the bad—the judgment that there is nothing good for a human being except for that which makes him just, moderate, courageous, and independent. And that there is nothing bad except for that which makes him the opposite of these.[26]

Seneca

We finish with Seneca, who stresses the need to find the right way to happiness, a way that has nothing to do with the various ways of the majority. We need an experienced guide who knows the goal and thus the way forward to possessing a good soul. Happiness is a matter of being in harmony with nature, which means living an excellent or virtuous life, a stable life little affected by life events.

My brother Gallio, it is the wish of all to live happily. But we're in the dark when it comes to figuring out what makes for a happy life. . . .

As long as we wander aimlessly and without a guide, following the loud noise and confused shouting that beckons us to journey along different paths of happiness, life will be wasted following after one error or another. . . . Let us, therefore, determine the goal and the way. And let us find an experienced guide who has explored the region to which we are advancing.

I say this because the circumstances of this journey are different from most journeys. In most cases, some well-known road prevents you from going astray—that and talking to those who live in the area.

Not in this case. Here, the well-worn and most crowded ways to happiness are the most deceptive. . . . Nothing involves us in greater misfortune than when we connect ourselves with the talk of the many, supposing that "the best" is that which has received the greatest number of votes. . . . Let us separate ourselves from the crowd—then we will be healthy and whole. . . .

When discussing the happy life, it's no use answering me, as though we were counting the votes, "It seems *this* side has the majority." For that very reason, it is the inferior side. Humans, and things having to do with being human, are not so well ordered so that the many prefer that which is superior. . . . Let us, therefore, search for the best thing to do—not what is commonly done. Let us search for that which will constitute an enduring happiness—not what the many recommend. . . . Let the soul discover the good of the soul. . . .

I follow the direction of nature—a point about which all Stoics agree. Wisdom is this: when we do not stray from nature and we form ourselves according to her rule and pattern. The happy life, therefore, is a life in harmony with its own nature. . . .

The happy man is the one for whom there is no good and no evil other than a good soul and an evil soul. This man cultivates virtue and is content with excellence. He's not raised to the sky by chance events, nor is he dashed to the ground. Instead, the greatest good he knows is the good he can give to himself. For him, true pleasure is found in looking down on pleasure. . . . The happy life is a free soul, a liberated mind, upright, undaunted, and stable. It is a soul that is beyond the reach of fear and beyond the reach of desire. It counts virtue as the one good and baseness as the one evil. The rest—the great crowd of things—is of little value. . . .

The happy life is founded on correct and trustworthy judgment.[27]

HAPPINESS FOR EPICTETUS, MARCUS AURELIUS, SENECA & LATER STOICISM

According to Epictetus, Marcus Aurelius, Seneca, and later Stoicism, God has made all human beings to be happy. But to be happy, we must follow God's lead in every circumstance. In short, this means we must play the role we have been given in life.

But it is no easy task to discover the right path to follow or the lead of God. Nevertheless, if we ignore the so-called happiness of the many and follow a guide who knows where to go, it is possible to be happy by living oriented to reason, nature, and virtue.

Happiness is something found within and not without. It is a possession of the soul rather than the body or anything external. It is a matter of the will and those things that are within our power rather than happenstance or fortune or those things we have no control over. We will be happy when our desires correspond to what actually happens. Accordingly, we must be well-disposed to everything that happens in our lives. The price of happiness, of tranquility, is simply letting some things go.

NOTES

[1] The Greek is *Epiktētos*, which means "gained in addition; acquired."

[2] There is some controversy over whether Epictetus wrote the *Discourses* and the *Handbook*, or whether his student Arrian did. For a digest of the different positions, see Keith Seddon, *Epictetus' Handbook and the Tablet of Cebes: Guides to Stoic Living* (Abingdon: Routledge, 2005).

[3] Although Marcus Aurelius is typically identified as a Stoic, his *Meditations* betray more of an eclecticism, including Platonist and Epicurean philosophy. The *Meditations* were not published in Marcus Aurelius' lifetime—and apparently they were not meant to be. In fact, they seemed to have survived quite accidentally.

[4] To highlight what is perhaps already evident, we offer the three out of chronological order. Seneca came first, then Epictetus followed by Marcus Aurelius.

[5] Seneca's involvement with Nero did not end well. Implicated in the Pisonian conspiracy of 65 AD, he was forced to commit suicide.

[6] Epictetus, *Discourses* 3.24.2-3.

[7] Ibid., 3.22.26-28. As for those mentioned by Epictetus, Myro (Myron) and Ophellius were likely famous athletes or gladiators—but nothing is known about them. The Lydian ruler Croesus was fabulously wealthy—so much so that he supposed he was the happiest man in the world. See Herodotus, *Histories* 1.30. Nero was the Roman emperor. Sardanapalus was an Assyrian king who, according to legend, lived a phenomenally luxurious life. For Agamemnon, see Homer, *Iliad* 10.15, 91, 94-95.

[8] Fragments of Epictetus, see *Epictetus, The Discourses of Epictetus, with the Encheridion and Fragments*, trans. George Long (London: George Bell and Sons, 1890).

[9] Epictetus, *Discourses* 4.7.9-11.

[10] Epictetus, fragment 4, in Johannes Stobaeus, 2.8.30.

[11] Epictetus, *Handbook* 1.

[12] Ibid., 5.

[13] Ibid., 8.

[14] Epictetus, *Discourses* 3.20.9-15.

[15] Ibid., 3.24.2-6, 15-19.

[16] Epictetus, *Handbook* 19.

[17] Ibid., 12.

[18] Epictetus, *Discourses* 1.3.1-4. Zeus is regularly termed the father of gods and men in Homer's *Iliad* and *Odyssey*.

[19] Epictetus, *Handbook* 17.

[20] Ibid., 53. The third point quotes Socrates, who mentions those who had brought charges against him resulting in his death.

[21] Marcus Aurelius, *Meditations* 5.34. Note that "flow well" (*euroeō*) here, is the same as being well or being happy. "Fare well" (*euodeō*) means to journey well, that is, to travel along the good or favorable way or path (*eu* + *hodos*) of life. Happiness, then, is very much a *going* and a *doing*. We must "take up and practice" the good path. And it depends on us. Notice the "if you" ("*if you* fare well"; "*if you* take up and practice the way"). As for the "way" (*hodos*) itself, the specific "way" is not identified by Marcus Aurelius in this point. The implication, though, from the rest of 5.34 is that it is the way of "rational animals." It is the path of refusing to be impeded by others and of finding our "good in a disposition to and the practice of justice."

[22] Ibid., 7.67.

[23] Ibid., 10.33. For Marcus Aurelius, this enjoyment (*apolausis*) is the right kind of enjoyment since it has to do with "everything that is in our power to do according to our own nature." As the right kind of enjoyment, it is happiness.

[24] Ibid., 5.9.

[25] Ibid., 7.16-17. *Daemon*, here, means something like a guardian angel in the sense of a guide. But in this case, it is one's innermost self or spirit or even conscience. This understanding of *daemon* likely goes back to Socrates, who spoke of the *daemon* that led him, forbidding him to do one thing or another. That said, the phenomenon is present from the earliest Greek literature.

[26] Ibid., 8.1. "Enjoyment" (*apolausis*), here, in contrast to the enjoyment we encountered above (see 10.33), is a false kind of enjoyment—that of pleasure.

[27] Seneca, *On the Happy Life* 1-5 (parts).

17

Pyrrho of Elis, Sextus Empiricus
& Skepticism

"If any of the learned be inclined, from their natural temper, to haughtiness and obstinacy, a small tincture of Pyrrhonism might abate their pride by showing them that the few advantages which they may have attained over their fellows are but inconsiderable if compared with the universal perplexity and confusion which is inherent in human nature. . . . Another species of mitigated skepticism which may be of advantage to mankind, and which may be the natural result of the Pyrrhonian doubts and scruples, is the limitation of our enquiries to such subjects as are best adapted to the narrow capacity of human understanding." —David Hume, *Enquiry Concerning Human Understanding*

PYRRHO OF ELIS (c. 365-275 BC) began his adult life as a painter. Diogenes Laertius informs us that he was a "poor and unknown painter" of modest ability. He further reports that there are "still some okay looking torch-racers of his in the gymnasium at Elis."[1]

Whether Diogenes Laertius saw the paintings or not, we don't know. What is likely, though, is that Pyrrho was familiar with painters who had more talent than he ever had. If so, then Pyrrho probably saw the work of some very skilled Greek painters, ones who were able to fool the eye with their paintings in a tradition going back (at least) to the *trompe l'oiel* paintings of Zeuxis and Parrhasius. The story goes that they painted so realistically that the images in their works fooled both the human eye and that of animals. The point is significant because it is possible that the apparent realism of such paintings, and Pyrrho's own striving to realistically present three-dimensional reality in two dimensions, had a strong impact on Pyrrho's general thinking about the nature of things. *What you see is not always what you get*. Unfortunately, however, the possible impact is only conjecture, and we must leave it at that.

Pyrrho, in any case, seems to have eventually passed on from painting to philosophy. Diogenes Laertius tells us that he ultimately settled on what came to be called skepticism, "a most noble philosophy," Diogenes Laertius asserts, "that introduces the ideas of 'non-apprehension' or 'non-understanding' and 'suspension'"—in other words, a philosophy that refuses to say, "I understand," and so one that promotes a complete suspension of judgment relative to things. "The skeptics posit nothing definite—so much so that they even refute their own positing of nothing definite by saying, 'We posit nothing.'"[2]

The skeptics went by many names that indicate their basic mode of operation. They were called "zetetics," from the Greek verb *zēteō* (to seek, inquire), because "they were always seeking the truth." Similarly, they were called "skeptics," or those who thoughtfully reflect on or look at matters, from *skeptomai* (to look carefully; to examine), since "they were always examining things but never finding a conclusion." In such an inconclusive state, they were called "aporetics," those inclined to doubt, from *aporeō* (to be at a loss, doubtful, puzzled), because "they were at a loss" and, therefore, always doubtful about the matter at hand.[3]

But what was the point? Were the skeptics merely disagreeable? Were they the ancient equivalent of online trolls, arguing just to bother people? Did they simply want to tear everything down without building something up in its place? Not at all. Instead, as we'll see, the point of skepticism was the power to remain undisturbed by all things. In positive terms, the goal was tranquility, peace of mind—in a word, happiness.

Sextus Empiricus, who lived much later toward the end of the second century AD, expressed the point of skepticism this way: "The reason skepticism exists is the hope we have of attaining tranquility."[4] Although we know very little about him, except that he was a physician of the "Empiricist school of medicine," Sextus Empiricus is our major source for much of ancient skepticism. Through him we know the various "modes" that skeptics utilized to suspend judgment and thus be at peace or be happy.

In Their Own Words

We begin with a set of selections that offers insight into Pyrrho of Elis' training, beliefs, and way of life.

For him and the early skeptics, the goal of life is "impassibility" or "freedom from emotion," as well as "mildness or gentleness," a state of soul or mind that is brought about thanks to the suspension of judgment regarding what is good and what is evil.

Diogenes Laertius Pyrrho was Anaxarchus' pupil and traveled with him everywhere so that he even met up with the gymnosophists, the naked philosophers of India, and the Magi. Accordingly, he seems to have taken up a most noble philosophy—as Ascanius of Abdera related it—one that introduces the notions of "non-apprehension" or "non-understanding" and "suspension."

Pyrrho affirmed that there were neither honorable nor shameful things, just nor unjust things. Similarly, about all things, he said that no one thing truly or actually *is*. Instead, convention and custom accomplish all things for human beings since each thing is no more *this* than *that*.

Pyrrho led a life in keeping with this teaching, going out of his way for nothing and taking no precaution. Rather, he faced all risks as they came.[5]

Diogenes Laertius Some say that, according to the skeptics, the goal of life is impassibility—that is, freedom from emotion. Others say it is mildness or gentleness.[6]

Diogenes Laertius There is nothing good or evil by nature. The reason? If there is something good or evil by nature, then it must be good or evil for everyone, just as snow is cold for everyone. But there is no such thing that is good or evil for everyone. Therefore, there is no such thing that is good or evil by nature.[7]

Diogenes Laertius Now, we must not say that everything that is supposed good *is* good since the same thing is supposed good by one person and evil by another. Epicurus, for example, supposed that pleasure is good, whereas Antisthenes supposed that it is evil. If this were the case, then the same thing would be both good and evil.[8]

Diogenes Laertius There are differences between living beings relative to what gives them pleasure and pain, as well as what is harmful and helpful. By this fact, the Pyrrhonists infer that the same things do not always produce the same presentations (how things appear) in different living beings. Given this battle of presentations, it follows that one should suspend judgment.[9]

Diogenes Laertius Posidonius recounts the following story about Pyrrho. When some people who were sailing with him were looking gloomy and upset because of a storm, Pyrrho kept calm and strong-minded, pointing to a little pig in the ship that went on eating as though nothing were wrong. He told them that a wise man should similarly remain tranquil.[10]

The second set of selections presents the skepticism of Sextus Empiricus. Once again, we see that skeptics suspend judgment to attain tranquility (happiness). Contrary to what the so-called "dogmatists" say about what produces happiness, skeptics are at peace with the suspension of judgment.

Sextus Empiricus The reason skepticism exists is the hope we have of attaining tranquility.[11]

Sextus Empiricus Cyrenaicism differs from skepticism. It declares that pleasure and a certain smooth motion of the flesh is the goal for human beings, whereas we skeptics say that it is tranquility, which stands in opposition to their goal. This is so because, whether pleasure is nearby or not, troubles remain even for the one who confirms that pleasure is the goal.[12]

Sextus Empiricus The dogmatists [philosophers with defined judgments or beliefs—*dogmas*] all grant that the good is helpful and choiceworthy, . . . and that it produces happiness. But when they are asked about what it is, exactly, that possesses all these attributes, they implacably battle without end—some declaring the good to be virtue, others pleasure, others a state without pain, and others declare still other things to be the good. . . . These dogmatists similarly differ about what is evil. . . . It is clear, therefore, that they have not actually helped us understand any of these things. But this is nothing unreasonable. They are tripping over things that are probably non-existent.[13]

Sextus Empiricus Skepticism is a skill that opposes appearances to judgments, examining both in every possible way. The result is that, given the equipollence of the objects and the rational considerations thus opposed, we skeptics come first to a suspension of judgment, and after to tranquility. . . . "Suspension of judgment" is the condition of our thoughts and understanding in which we neither choose nor posit things. Tranquility is freedom from disturbance and calmness of soul.[14]

Sextus Empiricus When skeptics suspend judgment, tranquility happens to follow even as a shadow follows a body.[15]

Sextus Empiricus The skeptic's goal is tranquility relative to those things having to do with opinion, and measured emotion relative to those things having to do with necessity.

For skeptics first did philosophy in order to pass judgment on presentations (how things appear) so that they could grasp which ones were true and which ones were false—and all this for tranquility. But falling into equipollent contradictions, they were unable to pass judgment, and so they suspended judgment. It just so happened that, when they suspended judgment relative to those things having to do with opinion, tranquility followed.

By contrast, those who suppose that anything is good or evil by nature are always disturbed. Therefore, when they don't have the things that they suppose are good, they believe they are tormented by things that are evil by nature. And so they go after things that are good—or so they imagine. Yet when they get these, there's even greater disturbance thanks to all the irrational and immoderate elation they experience. And then, fearing change, they do everything so that they won't lose those things that seem good to them.

In contrast to these men are those who refuse to determine what is naturally good or evil. The latter men neither eagerly flee from nor eagerly pursue things. Consequently, they experience tranquility.

There's a story about what happened to the painter Apelles. Well, the same thing happened to the first skeptics. Once, they say, when Apelles was painting a horse, he wanted to portray the foam coming from the horse's mouth in the painting. He was so unsuccessful, however, that he gave up the attempt. And taking the sponge he used to clean the paint from his brush, he flung it at the painting. This—the mark of the sponge—produced a copy of the foam coming from the horse's mouth. Similarly, the skeptics hoped to achieve tranquility by making judgments about the inconsistencies that show up relative to things of sense and things of thought. Being unable to do this, however, they suspended judgment. But when the skeptics suspended judgment, tranquility happened to follow even as a shadow follows a body.

That said, we do not believe the skeptic is wholly undisturbed. Rather, we say he is disturbed relative to those things having to do with necessity. . . . Therefore, we say that, relative to those things having to do with opinion, the skeptic's goal is tranquility, and relative to those things having to do with necessity, it is measured emotion.[16]

HAPPINESS FOR THE SKEPTICS

For the skeptics, including Pyrrho of Elis and the much later Sextus Empiricus, happiness is tranquility, which is a kind of impassibility or freedom from emotion. Tranquility is the goal of life.

How to reach this goal? The path to follow is the suspension of judgment relative to whether something is good or evil, beneficial or harmful, and so on. In doing so, tranquility naturally follows—yet not tranquility relative to all things but only to those things having to do with opinion or judgment. Relative to those things having to do with necessity, things that do not rely on judgment, the goal is measured emotion.

One final point. According to what "some say," anyway, the skeptic's life of tranquility and measured emotion leads to a mild or gentle disposition.

NOTES

[1] Diogenes Laertius, *Lives* 9.62.

[2] Ibid., 9.61, 74. Of interest, perhaps, is the fact that Diogenes Laertius ties Pyrrho's skepticism to his travels with the Greek philosopher Anaxarchus and their time with the naked philosophers (gymnosophists) of India and the Magi of Persia. Among other topics of study, Thomas McEvilley explores the relation between skepticism and Pyrrhonism and various Indian schools of philosophy in *The Shape of Ancient Thought: Comparative Studies in Greek and Indian Philosophies* (2002). See, for instance, Chapter Thirteen, "Skepticism, Empiricism, and Naturalism," and Chapter Seventeen, "Pyrrhonism and Mādhyamika."

[3] Ibid., 9.69-70. Diogenes Laertius also calls them "Pyrrhoneans" "from [the name of their] teacher" and "Ephectics" from the Greek *ephektikos*, which refers to the feeling or condition (*pathos*) skeptics experience in conjunction with the process of seeking—that is, *epochē* or the suspension the judgment.

[4] Sextus Empiricus, *Outlines of Pyrrhonism* 1.12.

[5] Diogenes Laertius, *Lives* 9.61. According to Diogenes Laertius, Anaxarchus of Abdera (mid to late fourth century BC) studied with Diogenes of Smyrna, who studied with Metrodorus of Chios, who studied with Nessas of Chios or Democritus of Abdera. Metrodorus, Diogenes Laertius reports, "Used to say that he knew nothing—not even the fact that he knew nothing." As for Anaxarchus, he was "called the Happy Man" or "the one who promotes happiness" thanks to his "tranquility and contentment of life" (ibid., 9.60).

By "suspension" (*epochē*), Diogenes Laertius means "suspension of judgment"—the refusal to judge whether something is or is not.

[6] Ibid., 9.108. "Impassibility" or "freedom from emotion" is *apatheia*. Mildness or gentleness is *praotēs*. *Apatheia* is often given as "insensible." The idea is that the impassible or insensible person cannot be affected in any significant way by pain or suffering—that is, by any negative passion or emotion, including any negative thoughts or judgments that may lead to negative emotions.

[7] Ibid., 9.101.

[8] Ibid., 9.101. For Epicurus on pleasure as good, see ibid., 10.128-129, "We say that pleasure is the beginning point and goal of living happily. We recognize that pleasure is our first good ." For Antisthenes the Cynic on pleasure as evil, see ibid., 6.3, "Again and again [Antisthenes] said, 'I would rather go insane

than enjoy myself with pleasure.'" And ibid., 6.8, "When someone extolled a luxurious life, [Antisthenes] said, 'May the sons of your enemies have a luxurious life'" —that is, a life filled with ease and pleasure.

9 Ibid., 9.79. "Presentation" is *phantasia*, sometimes given as "impression."

10 Ibid., 9.68. "Calm" is *galēnos*. "Tranquil" is *ataraxia*.

11 Sextus Empiricus, *Outlines of Pyrrhonism* 1.12. "Tranquility" may also be given as "non-disturbance."

12 Ibid., 1.215. "Trouble" is *tarachē* whereas the Skeptic goal is to be *without tarachē* or *a-tarachē* (*ataraxia*).

13 Ibid., 3.175-176, 178.

14 Ibid., 1.8, 10. "Freedom from disturbance" is *aochlēsia*. "Calmness" is *galēnotēs*.

15 Ibid., 1.29.

16 Ibid., 1.25-30.

18

Plotinus
& Neoplatonism

"Now, Plotinus, you have set aside the body, the tomb that held your soul. You have entered the assembly of divine beings, where delightful breezes blow, . . . and where Minos and Rhadamanthus dwell, the brothers of the golden race of mighty Zeus, and where just Aeacus and Plato dwell, . . . and noble Pythagoras, and the others who form the choir of immortal love, who share a family in common with the happiest of divine beings. There, O blessed one, your heart is always warmed with abundance and good cheer!"

—Porphyry, Life of Plotinus

PLOTINUS (c. 205-270 AD) WAS ENAMORED with ideas. That's the clear report that Porphyry of Tyre (c. 235-305 AD), his student and literary executor, makes in the short biography he wrote about him and appended to the *Enneads*, Plotinus' philosophical essays. Ideas were Plotinus' life. He wanted to capture reality with ideas. Most significantly, he desired to understand the nature of reality up to the absolutely transcendent, ineffable One, from which emanates the rest—Thought or Mind; Soul; and individual souls plunged into the material world of matter and bodies.

Why the desire to grasp reality, to capture it in the form of ideas? It was for life and living. Plotinus wanted to understand reality so that he would know how best to live, to *be*—and that in order to be mystically joined with the One. In short, Plotinus was "carried along by an urge for philosophy." Thinking about and living by these ideas drove Plotinus from the time he was twenty-seven years old to the end of his life nearly forty years later.

After a decade of studying with the Alexandrian philosopher Ammonius Sacca,[1] Plotinus departed from his native Egypt for an adventure abroad. He traveled with the Roman emperor Gordian to Mesopotamia on his campaign against the Persian ruler Shapur.

Porphyry explains that Plotinus' goal was to investigate Persian and Indian philosophy. The plan didn't work out, however, since Gordian was violently supplanted by the praetorian prefect Philip the Arab. Consequently, Plotinus and the other Romans fled. So it was that Plotinus journeyed to Rome when he was forty.

In Rome, Plotinus set up a school and began to attract students to his "conferences" or "talks." According to Porphyry, he had a large following that included both men and women. The latter—Porphyry names three (Gemina; her daughter, who was also called Gemina; and Amphiclea)—"were very devoted to philosophy." As for the men, they practiced a range of occupations, including politics, medicine, poetry, oratory, and literary criticism, to give those Porphyry mentions. There were a number of senators (Marcellus Orontius, Sabinillus, and Rogatianus among them) and several doctors (Paulinus of Scythopolis, Eustochius of Alexandria, and Zethos the Arab). The latter names indicate the far-flung constituency of Plotinus' school. If we include Porphyry of Tyre, they came from present-day Lebanon, Israel, Jordan or Saudi Arabia (depending on where, exactly, Zethos the Arab was from), Egypt, and Italy. And doubtlessly there were other followers from other places.

Plotinus encouraged his students to ask questions during these conferences. In other words, these talks were not merely the philosopher pontificating about one topic or another. He and his students also read aloud philosophical papers by other philosophers—though mostly by Platonists. The choice to read Platonist philosophers made sense considering that Plotinus judged himself a Platonist—and this nearly 600 years after Plato had died.

Following his own teacher, Ammonius Sacca, Plotinus was a "new Platonist," what historians now call a "Neoplatonist." Even so, he was influenced in one way or another by much of the philosophy that had been developed in contemplation and practiced in word and deed over the long centuries before he lived: Aristotelianism, Stoicism, Epicureanism, Skepticism, Pythagoreanism, and the many moods of Platonism.

Whatever his precise philosophical outlook, one thing is certain. Plotinus agreed with all prior Greeks—most, anyway—that happiness is the goal of life. And if we can trust Porphyry (see the above epigram), we can assume that Plotinus was happy in life and even happier after he died, when he "entered the assembly of divine beings, where delightful breezes blow."[2]

But what, exactly, did Plotinus think about the good life and happiness? In what follows, mostly from his treatise *On Happiness* (found in *Enneads* 1.4), we'll find out. All other selections are also from Plotinus' *Enneads*.

In Their Own Words

Plotinus begins by examining the scope of happiness (the sort of things or beings that can be happy—whether plants, non-human animals, or humans) and the basis of happiness (for instance, the fulfillment of being, impulse, pleasure, tranquility, sense perception, or reason).

What? Are we to make happiness the same thing as living well, or well-being, and, therefore, within the reach of other living beings—including plants and all animals, as well as ourselves?[3]

Even if we make happiness some goal pursued by inborn tendency, even then we must allow animals to be happy from the moment they reach this ultimate.[4]

If pleasure is the goal, that is, if pleasure is the same as living well, then it would be impossible to deny living well to any other kind of living being (apart from human beings). If the goal is tranquility, it would likewise be impossible to deny it. The same goes for the equation of living well with living life in accord with nature.[5]

Those men who deny living well, or well-being, to the whole range of plants, and those who make living well consist in some kind of sense perception, are actually seeking a grander sort of well-being. . . . They categorize the better—that is, the grander sort of well-being—with a more complete life, one that is somehow clearer and more distinct.

Perhaps, then, those are right who base happiness not on mere existence and living, or even on sense perception, but on the life of reason. If so, then they must explain why happiness should be restricted in this way, and why happiness is only found in the life of reason or the rational life.[6]

But, Plotinus says, there are also problems with this approach—that is, identifying happiness with the life of reason. He goes on to argue that happiness is fullness of life—a fullness relative to each living thing or being. Such happiness consists in what may be termed an intrinsic fullness rather than one extrinsic, imported from the outside. The happy man is "self-sufficient in terms of happiness and good things." So it is that "adverse fortune does not diminish his happiness." This is so because all fortune is extrinsic to the intrinsic fullness of life the happy man lives. "He himself is the good by what he is and by what he possesses."

What, then, is happiness? Let us try basing it on life itself.

Now, if we draw no distinction as to kinds of life, then every living thing will be capable of happiness, and those living beings will be effectively happy that possess the one common gift of which every living thing is by nature receptive. We could not deny happiness to non-rational beings while allowing it to rational beings. If happiness were intrinsic to bare being-alive, then the common ground in which the cause of happiness could always take root would be life itself—simply life.

Those philosophers, then, who place happiness not in life itself, or bare living, but in the life of reason, seem to overlook the fact that they are not really making it depend on life at all. They admit that this reasoning faculty upon which they base happiness is a property rather than the subject of a property. To them, the subject of the property must be life-that-reasons or the reasoning-life. . . . Consequently, they are basing happiness not on life but on a particular kind of life.

Now, in many ways this term "life" embraces many meanings and forms with varying degrees—first, second, and so on, all included under the common term "life." There is plant life and animal life, each kind of life more or less complete. Quite plainly, the same is analogously the case for living well. If one living thing is the image of another living thing, then manifestly one kind of living well will once again be an image of another kind living well.

If mere being, or mere living itself, is insufficient for living well—that is, if happiness demands fullness of life, and if happiness exists where nothing of the best life is lacking—, then happiness can exist only in a being that lives fully. And such a being will possess not merely the good but the supreme good—if, that is, in the realm of existents, the supreme good can be none other than the authentically living, none other than life itself in its greatest fullness, life in which the good is present as something essential and not as something imported, a life requiring no foreign substance called in from a foreign realm to establish it in good. After all, what could be added to the fullest life to make it the best life?[7]

If, therefore, the fullest life is within human reach, then the man who possesses this life is happy. If this is not the case, then we must cede happiness to the gods, for the perfect life is for them alone. But since we say that happiness is also available for human beings, we must consider what this *full life* is.

We may consider it this way. It has been shown elsewhere that a man possesses fullness of life, or the fullest life, when he possesses not only the life of sense perception but also a life of reason and a mind in harmony with truth.

But are we to picture this kind of life as something foreign, something imported into its nature? No. There exists no single human being who does not either potentially or actually possess this thing that we hold to constitute happiness.

Are we, then, to think of man as including this kind of life, the full and perfect life, as if it were a portion of him? The answer is twofold depending on the man. On the one hand, it is present in some men as a mere portion of their whole being. This is the case for those men who possess it potentially. On the other hand, there is the man who is already truly happy. This man has passed over into actually possessing it. Everything else is now mere clothing upon the happy man.

We do not call all of this part of the man since, unsought, it is upon him—he never actively wished for it or willed it.

What is the good to the man in this state? He himself is the good by what he is and by what he possesses. And the cause of what he is and has is the supreme good in itself. The proof that this state has been achieved is that this man seeks nothing else. What else, after all, could he possibly seek? Certainly none of the less worthy things. Rather, he is always linked with the best. The man who lives life in this manner is self-sufficient.

Once the man is a sage, that is, an excellent man,[8] he is self-sufficient in terms of happiness and good things. He lacks nothing good. Whatever else he seeks, he seeks as a necessity—not for himself but as for a subordinate, for the body bound to him. Since the body has life, the sage must furnish the needs of life—not the needs, however, of the true man. This man knows that he himself stands above all such needs, and what he gives to the lower, he gives in order to leave his true life undiminished.

Adverse fortune does not diminish this man's happiness. Rather, the happy life remains. Suppose death strikes his household or his friends. The sage knows what death is. Those who die also know what it is if they are wise. And if the death of family members and friends does cause grief, the sorrow will not reach the innermost part of his being. Instead, it is the non-rational part of him that suffers.[9]

But what about sorrow, illnesses, and everything else that hinders the activity? . . .

Now, if happiness does in fact require freedom from pain, sickness, misfortune, or disaster, then it will be utterly denied to anyone who is confronted by such trials. But if happiness is the possession of the true good, then why turn away from this true good to seek mere accessories? Why imagine that, to be happy, a man needs a variety of things—none of which is part of the essence of happiness? If, in fact, happiness consists in heaping together all that is at once desirable and necessary, then we must also seek to attain these. But if the goal is one and not many—otherwise a man would be seeking not one goal but many goals—, then we must seek the ultimate and most valued goal, that which the soul must conceive within.[10]

Plotinus contrasts happiness, the goal itself, with things that may be called necessities, things like health and freedom from pain and suffering.

We generally avoid what is bad. But such an avoidance is not what we would have willed. Rather, we would rather not need to avoid the bad. This is what happens, for example, when one possesses health and is free from pain and suffering. Which of these is alluring in itself? We attach very little value to these states as long as we are healthy and do not suffer. But that which, when present is not alluring in itself and adds nothing to happiness, and when absent is sought because of the suffering that arises from the presence of its opposite—*that* may reasonably be called a necessity but not the good. Such things can never be counted as part of the goal. Instead, even though things like health and freedom from pain and suffering are absent and their opposites are present, our goal is nevertheless the same.[11]

Though the wise and happy man has good will to all men, his own happiness remains whether or not they are happy.

The sage prefers that all men do well and do not experience misfortune. Still, even if it happens otherwise, he is happy.[12]

Plotinus explores the pleasure of the wise and happy man. It is a stable and ongoing pleasure.

The pleasures demanded for the sage's life are not found in the enjoyments of the licentious or in any gratifications of the body since there is no place for these, and they stifle happiness. Nor are they found in any violent emotions. After all, what could move the sage in this way? Instead, the sage's pleasure is the same as that which is the good's pleasure—pleasure that does not result from movement or from some process. For all that is good is immediately present to the sage, and the sage is present to himself. His pleasure, his contentment, stands immovable. Therefore, the sage is always cheerful and content; the state of his life is always still and quiet. Nothing evil can upset his life since he is a sage.[13]

Though happiness is fullness of life or "living well," for the human being it has nothing directly to do with the body; rather, happiness has everything to do with the soul, with "the man behind the appearances." Happiness "is an act of the soul." More specifically, it is an act of the highest part of the soul. Therefore, the wise and happy man will "desire nothing of this world, whether pleasant or painful." As Plato taught, the happy man "draws his good from the supreme good." As for the body, he will relate to it and care for it as a musician cares for his lyre.

Man is not the couplement (the coupling) of soul and body. This is particularly true for the sage. The proof of this is that man can be disengaged from the body and disdain its so-called goods. It would be absurd to think that happiness begins and ends with the living body. No, happiness is living well. It is associated, therefore, with the soul. It is an act of the soul. It is not an act of the whole soul, however. This is so because it is not characteristic of the vegetative or plant-like soul, the soul of mere growth. If it were, then that would connect happiness with the body. . . . No, the body must be reduced so that the true man might show up, the man behind the appearances.[14]

The sage will desire nothing of this world, whether pleasant or painful. His one desire will be to know nothing of the body. If he encounters pain, then he will pit against it the powers he possesses to meet it. But pleasure and health and ease of life will not amount to any increase of happiness for him, nor will their contraries destroy or lessen his happiness.[15]

Someone might say, "Suppose there are two wise men. And suppose one of them has every so-called good, and the other has nothing. Are they equally happy?" The answer: "Yes, they are equally happy if they are equally wise."[16]

The life of true happiness is not a thing of mixture. And Plato rightly taught that the man who is wise and possesses happiness draws his good from the supreme good, fixing his gaze on it, becoming like it, and living by that supreme good.[17]

The sage will relate to the body as a musician relates to and cares for his lyre. He will tend to its needs as long as it can serve him just as a musician will care for the lyre as long as it can serve him. When the lyre fails him, he will exchange his lyre for another one. Or he will give it up, along with playing the lyre. He'll do this as though he is now practicing a new art, one which does not require a lyre. And then he will let it sit there at his side, not looking at it, while he sings without an instrument. Nevertheless, the instrument was not originally given without a point. Until the moment he set it aside, he found it useful on many occasions.[18]

Happiness itself is not caused, augmented, or lessened by anything else that is not part of its essence. The happy man, thanks to his virtue, is unshakeable in his happiness. He remains happy in all situations, whether or not he senses or is aware of his happiness. This is due to his essential tie to wisdom itself, which is the "authentic existence" in act.

If the happy man encounters some turn of fortune that he would not have chosen, there is nevertheless not even the slightest decrease in his happiness. If there were, then his happiness would be shifting and lessening from day to day. The death of a child would bring him down or the loss of some trivial possession. No—a thousand mischances and disappointments may befall him without disturbing the good he has achieved.[19]

We must remember that the sage sees things very differently from the average man. Neither ordinary experiences nor pains and sorrows—whether touching him or others—pierce his inner self. To allow this would be weakness of soul.[20]

We cannot be negligent or indolent. This is an arena for the powerful combatant holding his ground against the blows of fortune. And knowing that, as painful as they are to some natures, these blows of fortune are hardly painful to the sage's nature. They are nothing dreadful. They are no more than nursery terrors. . . . When they come, they come up against the virtue that gives the sage his passionless, unshakeable soul.[21]

Some may say, "Sure, let him remain a sage. Still, having no sensation and not expressing his virtue in act, how can be happy?"

The answer: a man who does not sense his own health may nonetheless be healthy. Or again: a man may not sense his own attractiveness, but he may be handsome. Or he may not sense his own wisdom, but he may be wise.

Perhaps it may be urged that sensation is essential to wisdom and that happiness is only wisdom brought to act. Now, this argument might have weight if understanding and wisdom were something externally obtained. But this is not the case. Wisdom itself, in its essence, is some being in itself, some authentic existence. More: wisdom is being itself, *the* authentic existence. And this being, this existence, does not vanish when a man is asleep. Nor does it vanish for the man who is not aware of it. The act of this existent being is continuous within him. It is a sleepless activity. The sage, therefore, even when unaware, is still a sage in act.[22]

Plotinus explores why it is that the "continuous activity" of happiness, that is, wisdom's ongoing activity, might remain unperceived. He compares it to the intellective act, of which we are often unaware, even though we are in the middle of the act.

Perhaps the reason this continuous activity remains unperceived is that it has no connection with things of sense. Doubtlessly action upon material things, or action dictated by them, must proceed through the sensitive faculty that exists for that use. But why shouldn't there be an immediate activity of the intellect and of the soul that attends it, the soul that is prior to sensation or any perception? For if understanding and authentic existence (existent being itself) are identical, this prior-to-perception must be a thing in act.

Let us explore the conditions under which we become conscious of this intellective act. When the intellect is in upward orientation, that (lower part of it) which contains (or corresponds to) the life of the soul, is, so to speak, flung down again and becomes like the reflection resting on the smooth and shining surface of a mirror. In this illustration, when the mirror is in place, the image appears. Nevertheless, even when the mirror is gone or poorly disposed, all that would have acted and produced an image still exists. The same is the case for the soul. When there is peace and calm in that within us that is capable of reflecting the images of ratiocination and the intellect, these images appear. Then, side by side with the primal knowledge of the activity of the intellect and ratiocination, we also have, as it were, a sense perception of their operation. When, on the contrary, the mirror within is shattered through some disturbance of the harmony of the body, ratiocination and the intellect act without being imaged. In that case, the act of understanding has no corresponding mirror image.

In summary, we may safely gather that while the intellective act may be attended by the image, it is not to be confused with it. And even in our waking life we can point to many noble activities, whether oriented to thinking or acting, which at the time in no way compel our consciousness or awareness. A reader will often be quite unaware when he is most intent upon reading. Or, to take another example, in an act of courage there may be no awareness either of the brave action or of the fact that all that is done conforms to the rules of courage. And so on in cases beyond number. Moreover, it seems that awareness tends to actually blunt the activities upon which it is exercised, and that in the degree to which these activities pass unobserved, they are purer and have more effect, more vitality. Consequently, the sage who has arrived at this state has the truer fullness of life—life not blunted by sensation but gathered closely within itself.[23]

One last point. Final happiness—that is, complete union with the One—is never quite complete in this life. It requires the ongoing effort of virtue, an effort that reorients the individual toward the highest manifestations of reality and toward the One itself. It is the movement away from "non-being" to the soul's "very self"—a flight away from "this realm" in order to "become like god." Plotinus compares it to Odysseus' journey home in Homer's Odyssey—*and so we see that Plotinus is a kind of recapitulation or reinterpretation of the whole of Greek thinking on happiness.*

The man formed by this mingling with the Supreme must, if only he will remember, carry its image impressed upon him. He is to become the One, nothing within him or without inducing any diversity—no movement now, no passion, no outward-looking yearning, once this ascent is achieved. . . .

Moving in the opposite direction of non-being, the soul comes not to something other than itself but to its very self. . . .

When the self is lifted in this manner, we are in the likeness of the Supreme. If from that heightened self we pass still further, from image to archetype, we have won the goal of all our journeying.

Yet fallen back again from the vision, we awaken again the virtue within until we know ourselves to be wholly ordered again. Once more, then, we are released from the burden and move by means of virtue toward the intellect by means of wisdom to the self.

This is the life of the gods and of divine and happy human beings—release from other things here, a life beyond pleasure, a flight of the alone to the alone.[24]

Since evils are here in this realm, and since these evils "prowl about this realm by necessity," and since the soul wishes to flee these evils, then "we must flee from this realm."

But what is the nature of this flight we must take? Plato says that it is in becoming like god—like the divinity. And this, he says, is found if one "is becoming just and holy, and in one who is beginning to live by means of practical wisdom"—which is to say the whole of virtue.[25]

"Let us flee, then, to the beloved homeland." This is unerring counsel. But what is this flight? And how do we flee? It seems to me that

Odysseus is a hint or parable for us when he talks about his flight from the sorceress Circe or from Calypso. He is not satisfied to remain even given all the pleasure presented to his eyes and all the sensual beauty he experienced. The "homeland" for us is where we have come from. And there in that place is the father. What, then, is our journey? And what is the nature of the flight? We should not go by means of our feet, . . . or by horse, or by some ship belonging to the sea. We should let go of these and not think of them. Rather, we should close our eyes, exchanging this way of seeing for another, waking up. Everyone possesses this way, but few use it.[26]

HAPPINESS FOR PLOTINUS

For Plotinus, happiness is fullness of life; it is living well. In its ultimate sense, happiness is full union with the One—not merely with one of the highest manifestations of reality but with the highest reality, that reality which is itself manifested.[27]

The problem is this life is far from that supreme, highest reality, in that we have fallen, as it were, into a far lower reality, one associated with the body and other material realities. During this life, therefore, the wise and virtuous person will act to orient—or reorient—him or herself toward the Supreme. In this sense, then, happiness is the ongoing act of the highest part of the soul toward the supreme good. This good is the soul's own good, its true fullness.

Seen in this way, happiness is an intrinsic rather than an extrinsic good. In the final analysis, anything else such as health or pleasure is extrinsic to the wise and happy man's happiness.

NOTES

[1] Many credit Ammonius Sacca with the inspiration of Neoplatonism. His philosophy was, according to Plotinus' own declaration, the philosophy that Plotinus "had been seeking all along."

[2] It is a place that sounds like Homer's Elysian plain. See Homer, *Odyssey* 4.561-565: "As for you, god-nourished Menelaus, it is not decreed for you to die and meet your destined doom in horse-grazing Argos. Rather, the immortals will escort you to the Elysian plain and to the limits of the earth where yellow-

haired Rhadamanthus is. Here, life is the easiest for men. There's no falling snow or much of winter or thunderstorms. But a clear West Wind always blows—sent up by Ocean to cool and refresh the men there."

[3] Plotinus, *Enneads* 1.4.1. The translation presented in this chapter is a modified version of that of Stephen Mackenna.

[4] Ibid., 1.4.1.

[5] Ibid., 1.4.1.

[6] Ibid., 1.4.2.

[7] Ibid., 1.4.2-3.

[8] "Sage," here and elsewhere, is the good, excellent, serious (*spoudaios*) man.

[9] Ibid., 1.4.4.

[10] Ibid., 1.4.5, 1.4.6.

[11] Ibid., 1.4.6.

[12] Ibid., 1.4.11.

[13] Ibid., 1.4.12.

[14] Ibid., 1.4.14.

[15] Ibid., 1.4.14.

[16] Ibid., 1.4.15.

[17] Ibid., 1.4.16.

[18] Ibid., 1.4.16.

[19] Ibid., 1.4.7.

[20] Ibid., 1.4.8.

[21] Ibid., 1.4.8.

[22] Ibid., 1.4.9.

[23] Ibid., 1.4.10. Modern psychologists call this, when we act and are not immediately aware, or something very like this, "flow." In sports, it is called "being in the zone." See Mihaly Csikszentmihalyi, *Flow: The Psychology of Optimal Experience* (New York: Harper Perennial, 1990).

[24] Plotinus, *Enneads* 6.9.11. For Plotinus' view of virtue (*aretē*), see Chapter 14, "Plotinus," in the Cave's *Aretē: Excellence or Virtue—What the Ancient Greeks Thought and Said about Aretē.*

[25] Plotinus, *Enneads* 1.2.1.

[26] Plotinus, *Enneads* 1.6.8. The "father" may be understood as the intelligible world—that is, the spiritual world of Forms or Ideas, which is itself an emanation of the One, the Absolute or God.

[27] For an excellent collection of passages exploring Plotinus' understanding of the nature of reality, see *The Essential Plotinus*, trans. Elmer O'Brien (Indianapolis: Hackett Publishing Company, 1964).

CONCLUSION
WHAT THE ANCIENT GREEKS
THOUGHT & SAID ABOUT HAPPINESS

"I endeavored always to conquer myself rather than fortune, to change my desires rather than the order of the world. In general, I was persuaded that there is absolutely nothing in our power except our own thoughts. . . . I believe that in this chiefly consisted the secret of the power of such philosophers as in former times were enabled to rise superior to the influence of fortune, and, amid suffering and poverty, enjoy a happiness that their gods might have envied." —René Descartes, *Discourse on the Method*

"The philosophical schools that propose a happiness delivered by the enjoyment of the body or the enjoyment of the mind must give way to the school that proposes the enjoyment of God." —St. Augustine, *City of God*

HAPPINESS IS THE goal of life. Among all points gleaned from reading what the ancient Greeks thought and said about happiness, this point stands out as the most evident and clearest. Whatever it is, we humans long for and direct ourselves to happiness.

As for what happiness is, the simplest and perhaps most pervasive answer shows up in Homer, who represents the earliest Greek thinking and speaking we have. Happiness is the satisfaction of desire for a variety of things. These things fall on a spectrum of desiderata ranging from basic life and what supports life (food, drink, sex, sleep, comfort, pleasure, a household, family, friends, and allies) to a life of abundance enabled by wealth, power, and recognition in the form of honor and glory. The latter empowerment often involves violent conflict and so a need for strength—the power and force required to take and control whatever and, yes, whomever is desired.

As time went on, even though many Greeks continued with the Homeric tradition, other Greeks modified the basic formula—that happiness is the satisfaction of desire for a variety of things (by means of power). The truth is such modifications even show up in Homer. But moving beyond him, Hesiod and others focused on a happiness centered on hard work and justice—"the right kind of strife," as Hesiod expresses it—rather than, let's say, might makes right, where the power to satisfy desire is the ultimate thing that counts. Accordingly, we witness the daily toil of the heroic farmer beneath the sun versus the hard work of war, that of the warrior or "hero" beneath the walls of Troy or Thebes. Still, there was much that was the same. There was, for instance, an ongoing reliance on Fate and the gods for happiness, and an emphasis on our relationship to others.

All satisfaction, from Homer to Hesiod and on, relied on knowledge or practical wisdom to determine how best to satisfy desire. We see this with Nestor's counsel in the *Iliad* (that Agamemnon should "appease *Achilles* with presents and gentle and soothing words"); Tiresias' admonition in the *Odyssey* (that Odysseus and his men will get home—that is, attain happiness—if and only if they will restrain their desires); Hesiod's recognition of the significance of knowledge in his formulation of happiness (that the happy man will "know all these things" and act accordingly); and the many times choruses and others praise and acknowledge the role of wisdom in the tragedies of Aeschylus, Sophocles, and Euripides (particularly the wisdom that comes from suffering).

Aristippus, Epicurus, and others resorted to knowledge and wisdom to determine whether and how, exactly, pleasure is happiness. For Aristippus and Epicurus, happiness *is* pleasure. But as we've seen, it is not any and every pleasure but only some pleasure. For Aristippus, it is pleasure that is relatively easy to get, that is, pleasure that does not involve a great deal of trouble or pain in its attainment and experience. For Epicurus, it is simple pleasure signified by the absence of pain. To briefly mention others such as Isocrates, Plato, and Aristotle, happy pleasure is, respectively, honorable pleasure; pleasure experienced at the right time and place; the sort of pleasure that completes choiceworthy, morally good activity.

Strictly speaking, pleasure was not happiness for Plato and Aristotle. Rather, as indicated by Aristotle, pleasure is only the accompaniment of morally good or virtuous activity (on which, more in a moment). For others such as the Cynics, pleasure is the very opposite of happiness insofar as pleasure inflames desire, weakening us and taking us captive, rather than reducing desire and so increasing satisfaction. For the Stoics, pleasure may be a preferred indifferent, but in itself it is not something good. Rather, the only good and, therefore, the only actual happiness is virtue.

In a way, all Greeks held that happiness is virtue or excellence (*aretē*)—if, that is, we take excellence in its broadest sense (the manliness and courage of a warrior and leader of men, for instance, along with the ability to command and take what is desired). But Greeks beginning with Socrates (if not before, with some of the Presocratics), viewed excellence or virtue differently. Now it was the fulfilment of human *being* or human nature—that being or nature given by God, the creator. To give Plato's influential definition: "Virtue is the means by which a thing performs its function well," where the function of a thing is "that which it alone can do, or what it does better, than anything else." To live well, then, according to one's natural function (physical, psychological, spiritual, relational, political, social, economic, and like functions), was happiness.

And with that, happiness shifted from an external to an internal happiness, from things that are often out of our control or not up to us to things within our control or up to us, as the Stoics expressed the point. But to better see how this shift occurred, and to grasp its nature, let's explore what we might call the geography of Greek happiness.

The Geography of Greek Happiness

If the Elysian fields or the Elysian plain of Plotinus' afterlife (see Porphyry's description in Chapter 18) differed from Homer's portrayal of the same in the *Odyssey* (see Chapter 6), so too did the Greek conception of happiness change over the thousand years from when Homer's epic poems were first written down around 700 BC to when Plotinus' mortal frame perished in 270 AD and his soul was taken up to the "choir of immortal love." The question is this: How did the Greek conception of happiness change? What, exactly, was the shift? The answer comes with what we may term the geography of Greek happiness, a geography charted by different Greeks and Romans over time.

One influential happiness cartographer—if we may call him such—was the Roman statesman, orator, and philosopher Cicero. In February of the year 45 BC, Cicero was grief-stricken when his daughter Tullia suddenly died. Alone and barred from the political life he adored thanks to the power of Julius Caesar and his legions, Cicero retired to one of his country villas outside Rome in order to reflect on the best and happiest way to live life.

In Book 5 of his *Tusculan Disputations*, an imaginary dialogue between Cicero and Brutus, one of Julius Caesar's eventual assassins, Cicero declares that we have a choice. On the one hand, we can turn outward and entrust ourselves to the vicissitudes of fate and fortune, relying on the up and down world of externals—of wealth and glory and other desired goods and pleasures. On the other hand, we can turn inward and intentionally choose to live a life of greater freedom and independence of external fate and fortune by seeking moral virtue and excellence.

Broadly speaking, this choice—from external to internal goods, from dependence to independence, from hope to habit, from unpredictable accident to predictable purpose—maps the basic geography of Greek happiness from Homer to Plotinus, and its ongoing course beyond.

Cicero goes on to expound a short history of philosophy, "the captain of our lives," he says, "she who searches for all that is excellent in us and who drives out all that is not."[1] In doing so, he captures the historic, tectonic shift. After beginning with the wisdom of Odysseus and Nestor of Homeric fame and advancing up to the seven wise men of Greece, some of whom, like Thales, studied the origins of the cosmos and the nature of the stars (read externals), Cicero asserts that Socrates radically changed everything. Socrates "was the first to beckon philosophy down from the heavens of the sky," he declares, down into human lives, into human homes and cities, to the very heart of the matter, to ask what humans truly desire. "He summoned philosophy to explore how a man should live and conduct himself, and to query the nature of good things and evil things."[2] For Cicero, this is philosophy's job. Thanks to Socrates, philosophy searches for the best way to live, with the ultimate "hope of living happily."[3]

It is possible that Cicero discovered this shift while reading Plato's *Phaedo*. There, Socrates describes the evolution of his own thinking and concern away from external nature and causation to a belief in various absolutes—in "Beauty itself and the Good and Magnitude,"—and to an emphasis on human participation in these absolutes, that we humans most of all should be concerned with the care of our souls. "We should keep in mind that, if the soul is immortal, we must pay attention to it and care for it." Socrates goes on to say that the only way to save the soul from evil is to become "as excellent and as wise as possible."[4] To do so is to live well. And, as Cicero likely would have known from Plato's *Republic*, to live well is to be "blessed and happy."[5]

A few pages from his paean to philosophy and Socrates' revolutionary shift, Cicero provides us with an example illustrating the choice. In terms of external goods, the Persian ruler Xerxes had everything a man could possibly desire thanks to fortune, Cicero explains. He was "loaded with all the privileges and gifts that fortune bestows." Yet this "everything" wasn't enough. Rather, Xerxes "set out a prize for anyone who could discover a pleasure and satisfaction that was new." Cicero's point is that even when fortune doesn't fail, desire itself does, and consequently satisfaction. We get bored—what modern psychologists call hedonic adaptation. Xerxes no longer desired what he had. He no longer gained satisfaction from possessing *everything* (including "boundless stores of gold") and having every power (cavalry, infantry, a "host of ships"). Cicero's conclusion: "Yet, even if such a pleasure had ever been discovered, he still would not have been satisfied since such desire can never be satisfied." Why? Because "desire will never come upon a limit."[6]

Cicero doesn't stop there, however. Rather, in contrast to Xerxes, he says he would like to hold his own contest and offer a prize to the man who could clearly demonstrate that "virtue brings about a happy life"—that is, an internal happiness based on chosen excellence.[7] This happiness is the promise of living a philosophical life. "Philosophy," Cicero announces, promises that whoever "submits to her principles and precepts will always be armed against the vicissitudes of fortune. He will always possess within himself every aid and support that will help him live well and happily so that he will forever by happy."[8]

Yet this isn't even the end of the matter. If so far we have the shift from happiness as external goods delivered by mostly extrinsic means to happiness as internal goods supplied by independent, internal means, then Cicero's friend in the discussion brings up a third option—namely, a combination of the two in one way or another. This third option is the same as when Aristotle conceded that, "Being a human being, one will also need external goods and advantages since our nature is not self-sufficient for the purpose of contemplation [the highest happiness]. Instead, our body must also be healthy. Further, it must have food and other attention."[9]

And there we have it. These are the three basic regions the Greeks (and Greek-influenced Romans) charted on the map of human happiness—the land of external goods dependent on some external power; the land of internal goods independent of external power and things; and the borderland between the two, that is, a combination of the external and the internal.

A few centuries after Cicero, Diogenes Laertius confirmed Socrates' role in the revolutionary shift away from the more traditional good and noble life based on externals to one based on internals. In his synopsis of Socrates' life, he notes a movement away from "natural philosophy," that is, the study of things external to human beings, to ethical questions having to do with the good life. "Judging that speculation about nature had nothing to do with us, Socrates began to investigate ethical matters both in his workshop and in the marketplace."[10] Summarizing this move, Diogenes Laertius relates that Socrates "was the first who conversed about human life"—that is, how we humans can live well and be happy.[11]

For both Cicero and Diogenes Laertius, Socrates' move was the key revolutionary shift in Greek ethics—the great continental divide, as it were. Depending on how we look at things and live, the world and life can suddenly appear in an entirely different manner from how it has appeared before. Whereas before we relied on un-reliable externals and were thus often unhappy, at least somewhat unhappy, now we shift to rely on "up to us" internals, and so we experience a far more reliable "up to us" happiness. To reference another geographical divide, the experience is similar, perhaps, to the one that one has in summertime in driving through the tunnel that passes beneath the Pyrenees that separate Spain and France. One side is dry and brown; the other is wet and green.

St. Augustine, the late fourth and early fifth century AD bishop of Hippo in Roman Africa, and one of Christianity's most significant theologians, baptized the great divide, expressing it in Christian terms, while retaining its essential meaning. In the *City of God*, a lengthy work that explores the true nature of happiness, Augustine describes two basic cities. First, there's the City of Man, the earthly city of lust that "seeks to dominate . . . but is itself dominated by its own passion to dominate others."[12] Misfortune punishes its citizens, and, paradoxically, what passes for good fortune—wealth and the like—corrupts them. Consequently, there's no experience of true happiness. By way of contrast, Augustine presents the City of God, the city of love. Full of divine humility and meekness, its citizens lose nothing when they lose the use of their earthly riches. Citing St. Paul, he asserts that even though some may be "outwardly poor," they are nevertheless "inwardly rich."[13] Augustine argues that the good man, even if he is in fact a slave to some other man, is free, while the wicked man with his many vices is enslaved to many masters.[14] We've encountered the general idea before.

Later on, Augustine gives the same history of philosophy that we've encountered in both Cicero and Diogenes Laertius.[15] From "natural science," philosophy moved to a study of happiness. "Given the fame of his life and death," says Augustine, "Socrates left behind many adherents to his philosophy." Eventually their conversations led to the question of "the highest good, that which is able to make a human being happy."[16] Augustine goes on to acknowledge the geog-raphy of happiness' three basic regions, which he describes in terms of a happiness that depends on the body, the soul-mind, or both—which is to say it depends on externals, internals, or a combination of the two. This, he observes, follows from basic anthropology, that humans are made up of a body and a soul. In addition to the usual three, perhaps, Augustine delineates a fourth region, "the enjoyment of God."[17]

In the *Confessions*, the work he's most famous for, Augustine expresses the shift in a more personal way. Describing how he sought various external things that did not ultimately satisfy him, and how he gave himself over to different ideas and fanciful cosmologies, he explains that he ended up finding God, or true happiness, within. Speaking of all humans, Augustine begins the *Confessions* by declaring, "Humans desire to praise you, O God—humans who are only a tiny part of your creation. You have roused us to take delight in praising you, for you have made us for yourself, and our hearts are restless until they rest in you, O God."[18] The resting is inward; the resting in God is happiness itself.

Boethius, a statesman and philosopher like Cicero and a theologian like Augustine, professed much the same at the end of the classical age in the West, though in more classical terms. After the Germanic king Theodoric wrongly threw him into prison for political intrigue, Boethius bemoaned the fact that Lady Fortune had betrayed him. In *The Consolation of Philosophy*, he complains how fickle Lady Fortune gave him everything before suddenly taking it away. In her defense, Lady Fortune explains that inconstancy is her very nature. Lucky for Boethius, however, Lady Philosophy comes along and wakes him up from his slumbering in Lady Fortune's bed. The conclusion? It's the same as we've seen with the others. True happiness is not wealth or power granted by the likes of Lady Fortune; rather, it is an intentionally chosen, morally good life, capped with knowing God. Anything else is simply a roll of the dice.

Ongoing Greek Happiness

So it was that, just about the time the alpha male Theodoric and his alpha goons bludgeoned Boethius to death in Pavia in Italy in order to secure the blessings of Lady Fortune, the classical age died as well and transitioned into the Middle Ages. It was the classical age—beginning with the Greeks and completed by the Romans—that demarcated the basic zones of happiness. But later times explored the same regions, following along in well-worn tracks that had been mapped for centuries.[19]

The majority of men and women continued to seek happiness in externals. Others turned inward or Godward. Taking their cues from Greek and Roman philosophy, many Jewish, Christian, and Muslim thinkers trekked along the heights of the Greek approach to happiness, whether Platonist, Aristotelian, Cynic, Stoic, Plotinian, or a combination thereof.[20] To name a few, there were the Jewish thinkers Philo of Alexandria, who was eclectic in his approach, and the much later medieval great, Moses Maimonides, who, in his "Eight Chapters" took a very Aristotelian approach to the good life. Among Christians, there were the early theologians St. Basil the Great, the bishop of Caesarea; St. Ambrose, the bishop of Milan; and his protégé, one we've already encountered, the very Platonist St. Augustine of Hippo. Later, the medieval philosopher and theologian St. Thomas Aquinas followed Aristotle's program for happiness in his *Summa Theologica*, where he frequently cites "the Philosopher" (Aristotle) and his *Nicomachean Ethics*. Among medieval Islamic thinkers, there were al-Kindi and his Epictetus-inspired *On the Art of Dispelling Sorrows*; Ibn Sina, known as Avicenna in the Latin west; and the Sufi Muhammad al-Ghazali, who wrote *The Alchemy of Happiness*.

All these thinkers, whether Jewish, Christian, or Muslim, harmonized the ancient Greek and Roman path with the beliefs and requirements of their own religion. They translated what Plato had to say, for instance—or Aristotle, Diogenes of Sinope, Zeno of Citium, or Plotinus—into their own language, their own worldview. Other less religious individuals, or religious in different ways, were influenced by Epicurus or the Skeptics.

Greek (and Roman) influence didn't end with the Middle Ages. On the contrary, we can track through history whatever ancient Greek path we choose all the way to the present moment. Take, for example, the revival of Socratic-inspired virtue ethics; or the ongoing attraction of Epicurean-like, if not inspired, utilitarianism and certain recent formations of a more overt hedonist philosophy; or the hugely popular Stoic-inspired Rational-Emotive Behavior Therapy of Albert Ellis in the realm of counseling and thus living well and happiness.

Greek thinking about happiness has inspired every age of western history, from the classical period through the Middle Ages, Renaissance, early modern era and the Enlightenment, up to now. It would be a tragedy, therefore, if we forgot the original trailblazers—and the eventual mapmakers.

Let's not. Let's keep in mind what the Greeks from Homer to Plotinus had to say about happiness. And more. Let's look into what they said about other matters, too.[21]

Beyond this, let's practice what they've said about happiness. For as the Cynic philosopher Crates of Thebes said, "Long is the path that leads to happiness through words alone. But the path that leads to happiness through the practice of daily deeds is short."

On that note, if you'd like to get a start on your happiness practice, turn to "Ways of Practice toward Happiness" on page 293. Or find additional ways to practice in the Cave's Gymnasium (go to www.theclassicscave.com). See you there!

NOTES

[1] Cicero, *Tusculan Disputations* 5.5. For Cicero, philosophy is the means by which we may lead "a good and happy life" so that we will "always be happy" (see ibid., 5.19). On another note, if not named for this passage, the name of the honorary academic university society Phi Beta Kappa nevertheless means the same: *Philosophia Biou Kubernētēs* or "philosophy captain of life" (*kubernētēs* can also mean steersman, guide, or governor). Cicero's Latin for the same is, "*O vitae philosophia dux.*"

[2] Ibid., 5.10. Prior to Socrates, Cicero declares that "philosophy dealt with numbers and movements, with the problem of the origin of all things and the 'where' of their return, and zealously inquired into the size of the stars, the space in between them, their courses, and all celestial phenomena" (ibid., 5.10).

[3] Ibid., 5.2. "Happily" here is derived from the Latin *beatus* (happy, prosperous, blessed, fortunate).

[4] Plato, *Phaedo* 100d, 107c-d.

[5] Plato, *Republic* 1.354a.

[6] Cicero, *Tusculan Disputations* 5.20. "Desire" here in the last line (*libido*) may also be given as lust. It is the kind of desire the Buddha refers to in the Four Noble Truths that is the cause of so much suffering. As long as there is fuel, desire—like fire—is never satisfied.

[7] Ibid., 5.21. The English "virtue" hails from the Latin *virtus*, a word that originally meant "manliness" (related to the Latin word for man, *vir*) but came to mean, among other things, courage, goodness, and moral excellence.

[8] Ibid., 5.19.

[9] Aristotle, *Nicomachean Ethics* 10.8.9 (1178b-1179a). Still, Aristotle goes on: "Nevertheless, we must not imagine that the happy man will require many or great things."

[10] Diogenes Laertius, *Lives* 2.21.

[11] Ibid., 2.20.

[12] Augustine, *City of God* 1, preface.

[13] Augustine, *City of God* 1.10. Augustine quotes Paul (1 Timothy 6.6-10), who, from all appearances, has also internalized this basic geography of happiness. A little later, Paul says, "Command those who are rich in this present world not to be arrogant nor to put their hope in wealth, which is so uncertain, but to put their hope in God, who richly provides us with everything for our enjoyment" (1 Timothy 6.17). Note that "enjoyment" here is the same right kind of enjoyment (*apolausis*) referred to by Marcus Aurelius (see Chapter 16).

[14] Augustine, *City of God* 4.3.

[15] See ibid., 8.2 forward—but particularly 8.3 on Socrates. Behind Cicero, Diogenes Laertius, and Augustine, of course, is likely Plato's *Phaedo* mentioned above.

[16] Ibid., 8.3.

[17] Ibid., 8.8. I say "perhaps" because one could make the argument that what we may call the God region is actually just another portion of the land of internal goods. After all, "the kingdom of God is within" (Luke 17.21). Augustine nevertheless seems to have judged it a separate land.

[18] Augustine, *Confessions* 1.1.

[19] Though the Greeks, and Greek-influenced Romans, were the trailblazers, we must not forget that the Greeks themselves were influenced by ancient Indian thinking about happiness and the good life—not to mention others. To get some idea of this influence or exchange between cultures, see Thomas McEvilley, *The Shape of Ancient Thought: Comparative Studies in Greek and Indian Philosophies* (2002).

[20] Most eschewed Cyrenaic or Epicurean happiness as focusing on pleasure, or, as they judged it, hedonism or immoderate pleasure. Only later on during the Renaissance in Europe would Epicurus and Epicureanism be rehabilitated. For more, see the introduction in the Cave's *The Best of Epicurus: The Life, Writings & Teachings of Epicurus the Greek Philosopher*.

[21] To see what the Greeks had to say about other matters such as *aretē* (excellence or virtue), and to read the best of ancient Greek literature (Homer, Hesiod, the Cynics, the early Stoics, Epicurus, Basil the Great), visit the Cave (go to www.theclassicscave.com). Or you may wish to sign up for The BAGL (Best of Ancient Greek Literature) newsletter. Among other content, we'll send you short readings and reflections every week, as well as ways to practice what you've read.

PART 3

Points of Wisdom & Ways of Practice

including

- A Plan of Life Aimed at Happiness

- Points of Wisdom Related to Happiness

- Ways of Practice toward Happiness

- My Own Happiness Practice

- Quiz for Happiness

A Plan of Life
Aimed at Happiness

The following presents a plan of life aimed at happiness—a plan represent-ing ancient Greek wisdom and practice from the course of a thousand years.

1. **Be happy. Follow the happiness imperative.** Be convinced that happiness is the goal of life, what we humans shoot for in every-thing we feel, think, say, and do. Seek happiness, the goal of life. Knowing the goal, take care to look for happiness in the right place.

2. **Understand happiness.** Realize what happiness is and why and how we are happy. Recognize that happiness can be different for dif-ferent people and yet, on a deeper level, similar or the same for eve-ryone. Try to summarize what happiness is. Know the formula(s) for happiness. Identify your own happiness formula—what happiness is for you, a more subjective formula. Try to live by it. At the same time, identify a more objective happiness formula—what happiness is for all people. Again, try to live by it.

3. **Desire well. Grasp that happiness is the satisfaction of desire.** Seek a deeper understanding of desire—what it is and why it is, its different kinds and how it operates. Identify what you truly desire— deep down, from yourself rather than desires externally imposed by others, by convention, social pressure, marketing, and the like. Try to satisfy desire at the right time and place and in the right way. Follow natural and necessary desires.

4. **Experience delight. Seek the true pleasure that is happiness.** Explore the relationship between happiness and pleasure. Realize that happiness both is and is not connected to pleasure (at least every pleasure). Distinguish between true pleasure, a sustaining tranquility and simple joy, versus pleasure that is sporadic, intense, and (possibly) disruptive, often ending in pain and dissatisfaction or a craving for more. Let go of some pleasures.

5. Seek happiness that is stable (at least more stable). Recognize the—at times—up and down nature of the pursuit of happiness. Be aware of the instability of certain kinds of happiness and the greater stability of other kinds. Since human life is often unstable, our pursuit of happiness will likely also be unstable. Internal happiness that is "up to us" is more stable than external forms of happiness that are not always up to us. Seek the former over the latter.

6. Be virtuous. Be convinced that happiness is a life lived in conformity with virtue, which is a life lived in accord with nature. Happiness is goodness. As such, happiness is an act—the ongoing act of living well.

7. Grasp how happiness is tied to virtue. If virtue is, as Plato says, "the means by which a thing performs its function well," then happiness is the excellent performance of our natural human functions given by the creator—or, if you prefer, by nature. These functions are physical, psychological, spiritual, relational, and the like in dimension—who and what we are meant to be as human beings (in general) and as specific human beings (you, me, us).

8. Practice happiness. Do happiness. As said, happiness is an act. Know that happiness often requires effort and hard work. We must train to be happy. Just as we lift weights again and again to build muscle, so we must do that which leads to excellence or virtue again and again to be happy. As Crates of Thebes puts it, "The path that leads to happiness through the practice of daily deeds is short."

9. Be a friend. Do happiness with others in friendship. Though it is possible to experience a certain level of happiness without friends, friendship is an essential dimension of a fuller happiness. Reach out to others. Be a friend.

10. Explore the transcendent dimension of happiness. For some, happiness is a participation in divine mysteries. Happiness is a journey into divinity. Happiness, therefore, is a profound transformation of human into divine being—what some term *theōsis*.

Points of Wisdom
Related to Happiness

The following points of wisdom related to happiness, from a variety of ancient Greeks, are organized according to the points given in bold.

Seek the goal of life—happiness.

Aristotle Happiness is the goal of human life. . . . It is evident all men shoot to live well and to be happy.

Epictetus God made every human being to be happy.

Julian (the Roman emperor) Every living thing naturally yearns and stretches out for happiness. . . .The aim and end of . . . every philosophy is to be happy.

Happiness is different for different people.

Homer (Odysseus is speaking) "Different men delight in different things."

Archilochus of Paros There is no single kind of human nature, but different things warm different people's hearts.

Aristotle The crowd of men and the few who are educated and refined call the highest good that action can achieve happiness, and they assume that "living well" and "doing well" is the same thing as "being happy." But they argue about what happiness is. The account given by the many is not the same as that given by the wise.

Be aware of the instability of human happiness.

Simonides of Ceos You are a man—so don't ever say what will happen tomorrow. Or when you see a happy man, don't ever predict how long he'll be happy. The long-winged housefly doesn't even buzz off so fast.

Euripides (the chorus leader is speaking) "Happy is the mortal man who can manage life with gladness and without suffering misfortune."

Realize that happiness equals the satisfaction of desire. Therefore, know what you truly desire. Furthermore, know what is best to desire. Look for happiness in the right place and activity.

Homer (the hero Odysseus is praying for his son, Telemachus) "Lord Zeus, may Telemachus be happy among men, and may everything happen as he desires in his heart."

Dionysus Chalcus (the Bronze) From beginning to end, what is better than that which a man longs for most?

Epictetus People want things that produce happiness, but they search for them in the wrong place.

Isocrates Happiness is not merely the ability to do whatever you want. . . . Freedom is not the same as licentiousness.

Diogenes Laertius Menedemus heard someone say that the greatest good for a man would be to get what he longs for. . . . Hearing this, he said, "It is a much greater good to long for what is proper."

Happiness is Earth-provided abundance.

Happy is the man who you—Earth, the mother of all—readily honor in your spirit! He has an abundance of everything.

Friendship is key to happiness.

Epicurus Of all the means that are procured by wisdom to ensure blessed happiness throughout the whole of life, by far the most important is the acquisition of friendship.

Epicurus Friendship dances around the world of men calling out to all of us, "Rise up to happiness!"

For some, happiness is a participation in divine mysteries.

Pindar Happy is the man who beholds the mysteries at Eleusis before going beneath the earth. He knows the end of life and its god-given beginning.

Happiness is the satisfaction of certain desires for certain pleasures.

Plato (the Athenian is speaking) "Pleasure and pain are two streams released by nature to flow. Whoever draws the right amount from them, at the right place and time, is happy."

Isocrates Hunt after pleasures that enjoy a good reputation. For enjoyment with honor is the best thing—but without it, enjoyment is absolutely worthless.

Diogenes Laertius (stating the Cyrenaic philosopher Aristippus' position) Happiness as a whole is made up of particular pleasures.

Epicurus We must consider that of the desires, some are natural, and some are groundless. Of the natural desires, some are necessary, and some are merely natural. And of the necessary desires, some are necessary for happiness, some for freeing the body from disturbance, and some for living itself.

Epicurus We say that pleasure is the beginning point and goal of living happily. We recognize that pleasure is our first good. . . . When we say that pleasure is the beginning point and goal of life, we do not mean the pleasures of decadent men or the pleasures of sensuality, as some ignorant persons believe. . . . Rather, by pleasure we mean the absence of pain in the body and of trouble in the soul.

Happiness is *not* about luxury or pleasure.

Xenophon (Socrates is speaking) "My dear Antiphon, you appear to imagine that happiness is living luxuriously with extravagance. As for me, I hold that standing in need of nothing is divine."

Teles the Cynic I do not see how someone will live a happy life if he really must measure it by an excess of pleasure.

Happiness is something internal rather than something external.

Julian (the Roman emperor) We must not be busy about happiness as if it were hidden away outside ourselves. . . . Is it not laughable when a man tries to find happiness somewhere outside himself, and thinks that wealth and birth and the influence of friends, and, generally speaking, everything of that sort is of the utmost importance? . . . We must say that happiness resides in our minds, in the best and noblest part of us. . . . Diogenes *of Sinope* himself professed this belief.

Crates of Thebes Take care of your soul—but your body only so far as what is necessary, and externals not even that much. I say this because happiness is not a pleasure that requires external things, nor does perfect virtue require these.

Epictetus If a man believes that his good and his interest is found only in those things that are free from hindrance and in his own power, he will be free, flowing well with a good life, happy. . . . But if he believes that his good and his interest are found in externals and in things that are not in the power of his will, then he will necessarily be hindered, impeded, and a slave to those who have power over the things that he wonders at and fears.

Plato (the Athenian is speaking) "I would never agree that a wealthy man is truly happy if he is not also a good man."

Happiness is a good soul and mind; it is living well;
it is a life in conformity with virtue.

Aeschylus (the chorus is speaking) "Happiness comes from a healthy mind and heart."

Pythagoras The most important thing in human life is persuading the soul to be good or evil. Happy are those men who acquire a good soul.

Plato Socrates: In whatever he does, the good man does well and nobly. And he who does well is blessed and happy.

Plato The Athenian: One kind of life is sweeter than the other . . . In comparison with a vicious life, the virtuous life in body and soul is not only more pleasant, but it also rises above the other in terms of beauty, correctness, excellence, and good reputation. Consequently, if a man lives with virtue, he will live with complete happiness.

Plato Socrates: Virtue is the means by which a thing performs its function well. . . . The function of a thing is that which it alone can do, or what it does better, than anything else. *The most important virtues are wisdom, courage, moderation, and justice.*

Xenophon (Virtue personified is speaking to the hero Heracles) "I associate with the gods and with good men, and no fine action, whether the deed of a god or of a man, is done without me. . . . So, Heracles, . . . if you toil hard along the path that I, Virtue, have mapped, you can acquire the most blessed happiness."

Aristotle Happiness is an activity of the soul that accords with perfect virtue.

Crates of Thebes We Cynics say that the good and excellent man, and no other man, is called happy.

Zeno of Citium (the Stoic) Happiness consists in virtue, which is the state of the soul that tends to make the whole of life harmonious.

Diogenes Laertius (giving the position of the early Stoics) The virtues are goods that have both the nature of ends and means. Inasmuch as they produce happiness, they are means to good things. On the other hand, inasmuch as they are the fulfillment of happiness, being a portion of happiness itself, they are ends.

Practice happiness—happiness is something we do. Happiness requires education and training.

Xenophon Socrates judged that education and training would make men not only happy for themselves, . . . but it would also help them make other men happy, and to even make their cities happy.

Epicurus We must practice those things that produce happiness since if happiness is present, we possess everything, and if it is not, we do everything to acquire it.

Crates of Thebes Long is the path that leads to happiness through words alone. But the path that leads to happiness through the practice of daily deeds is short.

Xenophon (Socrates is speaking) "Do you not know, Antiphon, that by training, practice, and exercise, those who are by nature weak in the body grow mightier than the very strongest man who doesn't train, practice, and exercise? And that the training itself becomes easy and bearable? Since, then, I am always training my body to bear patiently whatever happens, don't you think that I am more able to bear everything with ease than you are without training?"

Happiness is serious business.

Aristotle The happy life is a serious life spent in effort rather than a less serious life engaged in various amusements.

Aristotle Amusement is a kind of rest or relaxation. We need rest because we cannot work continuously. Rest itself, then, is not an end or goal; rather, we rest for the sake of further activity. . . . In this way, Anacharsis' maxim seems right: "Play and amuse yourself in order to be serious and busy."

Ways of Practice
toward Happiness

The following Ways of Practice are offered with the goal of practice in mind, the application of ancient wisdom to our contemporary ways and lives. We hope they will serve, in some small measure, as a source of inspiration and motivation. Use them to contemplate your life—where you are now, where you are going, and how you can better get there. Then act.

One last note. You will likely find that the space given for responses is not enough. If so, jot your thoughts and practices down in a separate place.

Practice 1: Acting-Doing-Practicing Happiness

Contrary to its etymology, happiness is not something that merely happens to us. It is not chance, good luck, or fortune as the Old Norse word *happ* implies—not the happiness of most ancient Greek philosophers, anyway. Rather, as Aristotle says, "happiness is an activity"; it is something we do. As such, it is something we can practice. Indeed, according to Epicurus, we *must* practice happiness. In his words—

> We must practice those things that produce happiness since if happiness is present, we possess everything, and if it is not, we do everything to acquire it. Do and practice those things that I have continually recommended to you, taking them to be the basic elements of living well.

How should we practice? According to the Cynic philosopher Crates of Thebes, we should practice daily, moving along "the path that leads to happiness" one step at a time.

> Long is the path that leads to happiness through words alone. But the path that leads to happiness through the practice of daily deeds is short.

The question, then, is what should the nature of our happiness practice be? If we follow Epicurus and Crates, there will be three features of our practice. First, "we must practice those *things* that produce happiness." Such "things" will be "basic" things—the "basic elements of living well." Our practice need not be complex.

Instead, we ought to choose specific things that are simple and straightforward. These things should be unambiguous, specific, concrete things that directly correspond to happiness. Second, our practice should be "daily." We must do our happiness "things" day in and day out. Finally, we should keep in mind that happiness is a "doing" thing and not merely a "saying" thing. Sure, we might read, think, and talk about happiness. But remember: "Long is the path that leads to happiness through words alone." So, let's get going. Let's act-do-practice happiness.

Brainstorm ▪ Identify and briefly describe three basic, specific, concrete, active things you can practice daily to be happy (or happier).

Thing 1: ____

____

Thing 2: ____

____

Thing 3: ____

____

Practice one thing and evaluate ▪ Now, from the three, choose one thing (only one) to practice daily over the next three weeks, faithfully doing it day after day. At the end of three weeks, evaluate how your happiness practice is going. Should you keep on doing what you've been doing? Should you modify it somewhat? Finally, once this one happiness practice becomes a habit for you, something you regularly do (it'll take some time—many weeks or longer), add another practice. Remember, keep it basic, simple, specific, concrete.

Evaluation: ____

____

____

"Education and training make men happy." —Xenophon

PRACTICE 2: WRITING A RECIPE FOR HAPPINESS

The big question is what, exactly, adds up to happiness. We know that practice is essential. But what else?

In thinking about our answer to this question, we would do well to keep in mind a few points. The first comes from the Stoic philosopher Epictetus: "People want things that produce happiness, but they search for them in the wrong place." Stated positively, we must look for the ingredients of happiness in the right place. The second point is from the poet Dionysus Chalcus (the Bronze), reminding us there is nothing "better, . . . from beginning to end, . . . than that which a man longs for most" (to reformulate his point). Yet we must keep in mind Isocrates' response to this basic truth that "happiness equals the satisfaction of desire." For Isocrates, "happiness is not merely the ability to do whatever we want." Rather, as Menedemus puts it, "It is a much greater good to long for what is proper."

With these points in mind, what ingredients make for happiness? In answering the question, first consider general ingredients for all or most human beings. Then identify more specific "you" ingredients for *you*. Finally, combine the ingredients for a recipe for happiness.

General "all or most people" ingredients for happiness • Name and describe three things or activities (things most people can do and practice) that will generally make most people happy (or happier). These are your three general "all or most people" ingredients.

Ingredient 1: ____

____

Ingredient 2: ____

____

Ingredient 3: ____

____

Specific "you" ingredients for happiness • Name three things or activities (things you can do and practice) that will make you happy (or happier). These are your three specific "you" ingredients.

Ingredient 1: ____

____

Ingredient 2: ____

____

Ingredient 3: ____

____

Recipe for happiness ▪ Now, add the general "all or most people" ingredients to the specific "you" ingredients to get a recipe for happiness. Write them here (try to use one or two words for each).

1. _______________________   4. _______________________

2. _______________________   5. _______________________

3. _______________________   6. _______________________

Add, stir, cook ▪ Finally, as always, practice—that is, *do* the ingredients. Remember: our job is not finished with merely *knowing* the ingredients. We must *do* something with them. "Happiness is an activity." So, add, stir, and cook them to get something beneficial.

Evaluate the recipe ▪ As always, evaluate how things are going. Ask yourself if you are happier after you've enacted your happiness recipe for some time. Focus on how you are doing (acting) instead of how you are feeling. It is the *doing* that is happiness. What is going well? What requires modification? What do you need to add or subtract?

____

____

____

"Happy the man who . . ." —Stesichorus

PRACTICE 3: PRACTICING THE VIRTUES (EXCELLENCES)

"Happiness is an activity of the soul that accords with perfect excellence or virtue (*aretē*)." So says Aristotle. In one form or another, it is the common view of most ancient Greek philosophers. Crates of Thebes, for instance, declares, "We Cynics say that the good and excellent man, and no other man, is called happy." Plato says that "if a man lives with virtue, he will live with complete happiness." And for the Stoic Zeno of Citium, "Happiness consists in virtue." Even Epicurus, who declares "pleasure" to be "the goal of life," holds that "we cannot live pleasantly without living wisely, nobly, and justly"—which is to say without living virtuously.

The big question for us, then, is this: What is virtue? And how can we practice the virtue that aims at happiness or is the same as happiness?

Reflection ▪ Generally speaking, what is excellence or virtue (*aretē*)? More specifically, what is excellence or virtue (*aretē*) for you? Give an example for each.

General *aretē* ____

____

Example: ____

____

Aretē for me ____

____

Example: ____

____

Virtue and the Four Cardinal Virtues

For Plato, excellence or virtue (*aretē*) is "the means by which a thing performs its function well," where "the function of a thing is that which it alone can do, or what it does better, than anything else." Things get their "function" from their maker. For instance, a craftsman makes a knife to cut (its function). The knife's excellence or virtue (*aretē*) is sharpness, the means by which it cuts well.

For Aristotle, the *aretē* of a thing is a mean that falls between two extremes—between deficiency (dullness for a knife leading to the inability to cut) or an excess (over sharpness leading to brittleness).

For both Plato and Aristotle and other ancient Greek philosophers, there are four cardinal virtues: wisdom, courage, moderation, and justice. Look back to pages 118-121 for Plato's description of each cardinal virtue. For Aristotle, see pages 153-154; 156.

Practicing the cardinal virtues ▪ Describe your own understanding of each of the cardinal virtues. Identify one thing you can regularly do to practice each. Remember, be specific and concrete.

Wisdom ____

____

Wisdom practice: ______________________________________

____

Courage ____

____

Courage practice: _____________________________________

____

Moderation ____

____

Moderation practice: __________________________________

____

Justice ____

____

Justice practice: ______________________________________

____

> "Virtue is something you do. . . . It doesn't require
> a stockpile of arguments." —Antisthenes

MY OWN HAPPINESS PRACTICE

Now that the Cave has offered three ways to practice happiness, it is your turn to come up with one happiness practice from all the Greek wisdom you've encountered. The following are suggestions to assist you in coming up with your own practice.

First, glance through each chapter to discover and be inspired by something—some point or practice—that is worthy of a happiness practice. For example, you might train yourself in Cynic simplicity in the form of desire reduction. Or maybe you'll practice Cyrenaic pleasure. Or you'll regulate the amusement you seek, realizing with Aristotle that amusement is only meant to be a break from serious activity. Or you'll concentrate on the joy of friendship that was so important to Epicurus. Or with most of the philosophers, you'll focus on some other aspect of excellence or virtue (*aretē*). Or you'll seek the transcendent happiness of Plotinus, orienting yourself to the highest of realities. Whatever you do, know that there are many ways to practice happiness.

Second, try to feature a quote or two related to your happiness practice. Third, include an opportunity to brainstorm or reflect. Finally, devise one or two specific, concrete happiness practices.

When you've finished, share your practice with us at the Cave (as a PDF).* Send the Cave an email with your formatted, ready-to-share happiness practice (again, as a PDF) to **contact@theclassicscave.com** (with a subject line of "My Happiness Practice").

When you do, we very well might share your happiness practice with the Cave community in the Cave Gymnasium. Thanks!

MY OWN HAPPINESS PRACTICE

Quotation:
Brainstorm or reflection:
Practice:
Other:

*You'll likely want to use other space to make and write your practice.

QUIZ FOR HAPPINESS

What to do: Choose the best answer for each question.

1. _____ The following philosopher(s) believe(s) virtue is essential for happiness.
    A. Plato
    B. Aristotle
    C. Diogenes of Sinope (the Cynic)
    D. Zeno of Citium (the Stoic)
    E. All of the above

2. _____ Pleasure is central to _________________ happiness.
    A. Stoic
    B. Cyrenaic
    C. Aristotelian
    D. Cynic
    E. Homeric

3. _____ For _______________, happiness is the satisfaction of desire.
    A. Plotinus
    B. Sophocles
    C. Homer
    D. Aristotle
    E. Zeno of Citium (the Stoic)

4. _____ Who said that "he who lives well is blessed and happy," and that "virtue is the means by which a thing performs its function well"?
    A. Julian (the Roman emperor)
    B. Zeno of Citium (the Stoic)
    C. Hesiod
    D. Plato
    E. Sappho of Lesbos

5. _____ For Aristotle, _______________ is/are the highest level of happiness.
    A. Necessary, external goods such as wealth and honor
    B. Pleasure
    C. Life lived according to practical wisdom
    D. Amusement
    E. Contemplation

Answers: 1. E, 2. B, 3. C, 4. D, 5. E

OTHER MATTERS OF INTEREST

Related to Happiness

HAPPINESS
IN BRIEF

The following briefs present ancient Greek happiness in summary form spanning the thousand years from Homer to Plotinus.

HOMER · Happiness is the satisfaction of desire. What is desired? Life (simply being alive). Food. Drink. Love and sex. Sweet sleep. Comfort, pleasure, delight. Security. A household. Loyal family members, friends, and allies. Freedom. Wealth. Power. Status and reputation. Shame avoidance. And most of all, honor and glory. All to secure the rest (life, food, *etc.*). Happiness, therefore, is the ability to satisfy desire that comes from wealth, power, and recognition (honor and glory).

OTHER EARLY GREEKS · It is challenging to present briefs of happiness for other Greeks. For Hesiod (from his *Works and Days*), happiness is a matter of toil (farming) and proper behavior before the gods. It is knowing when to do what—according to the days given by the gods. It is relating well to others. Finally, rather than participating in the harmful strife of violence that takes what is desired from another by means of power (where might makes right), happiness is engaging in the beneficial strife of hard work and fair competition. As such, happiness is justice. For other Greeks, happiness is, we might say, a mixture of Homer and Hesiod. Happiness continues to be the satisfaction of desire for all those desired things witnessed in chapters 2 and 3— and this by means of Fate and the gods, wisdom, and various forms of excellence or virtue (*aretē*). Yet there's more. There is the search for deep wisdom seeking permanence rather than a more surface wisdom that only deals with the flux of life, however successfully or not. The deep transformation of Oedipus in Sophocles' *Oedipus the King* and *Oedipus at Colonus* is representative.

ISOCRATES · Happiness is not the satisfaction of any and every desire; it is not doing whatever we want. Rather, happiness is a kind of restraint that looks to what is best—to the best humans who stive for virtue and what is honorable. Happiness is a sober life lived with practical wisdom and self-control, faithful to family, friends, and the gods (God), enjoying only honorable pleasures.

XENOPHON (SOCRATES) • Happiness is the satisfaction that comes from reduced desires. Happiness, therefore, is desire reduction by means of training in self-control and endurance. As our desires (wants, needs) decrease, our satisfaction and thus happiness increases. In the end, then, happiness is the satisfaction of reduced desire.

PLATO (SOCRATES) • As for Isocrates and Xenophon, happiness is not the satisfaction of any and every desire. Rather, it is desiring well and thus the beneficial satisfaction that corresponds to desiring well. More specifically, happiness is living well, which is the result of desiring well. Living well is the fulfillment of God-given human nature, including the various functions of the body and the soul (with its three parts). Fulfillment itself is excellence or virtue (*aretē*); it is flourishing. Virtue is the means by which a thing performs its function well, where a thing's function is that which it alone can do, or what it does better, than anything else. Relative to the human soul (the rational, spirited, and desiring parts of the soul, as well as the soul acting as a whole), the four cardinal virtues are, respectively, wisdom, courage, moderation, and justice. Wisdom directs desire, encouraging us to desire well according to moderation. Courage enables us to satisfy desire according to wisdom and moderation. Justice is the harmony that comes from such as satisfaction, which is happiness.[1]

ARISTOTLE • Happiness is the goal of life. It is something we do. Happiness is an ongoing activity of the soul in accord with reason (man's proper function) and, therefore, a life in conformity with virtue. Virtue is a mean between two extremes (an excess and a defect). There are three levels of happiness. Contemplation is the highest; it is a life lived with theoretical wisdom. Life lived according to practical wisdom is the next. The happiness of necessary, external goods is third. Finally, happiness "is a serious life spent in effort rather than a less serious life engaged in various amusements." We seek amusement not to be happy, but to get back to the serious work of happiness.

THE CYRENAICS (ARISTIPPUS OF CYRENE) • Happiness is found in pleasure. Pleasure is the goal of life. More precisely, each specific, individual pleasure—*this* pleasure, *that* pleasure—is the goal of life. Though we seek the happiness of pleasure, we should not hunt for any and every pleasure since the attainment of some pleasures is troublesome or painful, the very opposite of pleasure.

THE CYNICS (CYNICISM) • Happiness is living a life in step with nature, which is a life in accord with virtue. Said another way, happiness is a natural life, which is a virtuous life. The natural happiness of a dog and other animals, and children before they are corrupted by society's desires and goals (wealth, luxury, power, reputation, and the like), is true happiness. Happiness is not the satisfaction of pleasure; rather, it is desire reduction. As such, it is a self-sufficient, simple life. Happiness embraces rejection. It is the practice of endurance and shamelessness. It is a life free from convention, the artificial stamp of society. Most importantly, happiness is a matter of daily deeds rather than what we merely think or talk about.

THE STOICS • Happiness is a life centered on "what is up to us" versus what is not up to us. The following details what is up to us. Happiness is a life lived according to nature, which is the product of a rational, divine mind. Happiness, therefore, is the harmonious participation in "the right reason that pervades all things." For human beings, this means that happiness is a rational life, where natural impulse is skillfully shaped and guided by reason to seek and do what is suitable. What is suitable is virtue, the perfection of a thing. Virtue is the only true good; vice is the only true evil. Consequently, happiness is a life lived according to virtue. In addition to virtue, humans may otherwise seek preferred indifferents, things such as skill, health, and wealth. But only virtue is essential to happiness.

EPICURUS (EPICUREANISM) • Happiness is the satisfaction of natural and necessary desires toward the end of simple pleasure, which is an absence rather than a presence—the absence of pain. Happiness is a simple, frugal life with friends. Friendship is an important ingredient of happiness. Body happiness is health. Mind happiness is mental tranquility. Bodily health and mental tranquility are the twin goals of a happy life. Happiness requires philosophy—not for the sake of argument or to grasp needless points about the nature of things, but to understand reality enough so that we may seek health and be at peace. Happiness relies on practice for its perfection. Happiness is the practice of the virtues since a virtuous life is the same as a pleasurable life.

THE SKEPTICS (PYRRHO OF ELIS & SEXTUS EMPIRICUS) • Happiness is tranquility, which is a kind of impassibility or freedom from emotion. Relative to judgment or opinion, happiness comes by means of skepticism or the suspension of judgment (*epochē*) about whether something is good or evil, beneficial or harmful, and so on. Relative to necessary things, things that do not rely on judgment (things that simply exist or *are*), happiness is measured emotion.

PLOTINUS (NEOPLATONISM) • Happiness is fullness of life; it is living well. Seen in the fullest light, happiness is full union with the One, the highest, truest reality (God or the Supreme). Happiness, therefore, is the internal, active orientation of the wise and virtuous person toward the Supreme. For now, it is an on-the-way virtuous life, and so an on-the-way happiness. It is living well, being a good human being. In its fullness, however, happiness is complete assimilation to the divine. As such, it is the completion of our journey insofar as it is a return to our origin, our true homeland.[2]

NOTES

[1] The four cardinal virtues are the same for most ancient Greeks.

[2] Interestingly, Plotinus' transcendent happiness also shows up in Homer (with the desire for the divine blessedness of immortality and agelessness), in Plato (where true, immortal happiness is the satisfaction of our desire for the One, for God, for the Good, the True, the Beautiful), and in other ancient Greeks, not to mention the ancient Christian goal of *theōsis* (deification).

GLOSSARY

OF ENGLISH WORDS AND GREEK EQUIVALENTS
RELATED TO HAPPINESS

Abundance, plenty; good cheer; festivities (pl.): *thalia* (θαλία).

According to nature, following nature: *kata phusis* or *kata physis* (κατά φύσις).

Advantage; that which brings profit or help; a means of strengthening, refreshment (thus, food): *oneiar* (ὄνειαρ).

Ageless; not decaying: *agēraos* (ἀγήραος).

Anger, wrath; natural impulse: *orgē* (ὀργή). **Wrath**: *mēnis* (μῆνις).

Anxiety, worry: *phrontis* (φροντίς).

Appetite, desire: *orexis* (ὄρεξις).

Bad, evil; bad fortune, misfortune; worthless; cowardly; a bad man or thing: *kakos* (κακός). **Failure**; badness, baseness, vice, cowardice, harm, misery: *kakotēs* (κακότης).

Beautiful, fair; noble: *kalos* (καλός).

Benefit, utility, profit, advantage: *ōpheleia* (ὠφέλεια).

Bliss, happiness: *makariotēs* (μακαριότης).

Blessed, happy: *makar* (μάκαρ) or *makarios* (μακάριος).

Bloom, flourish; to bloom, abound, be luxuriant: *thallō* (θάλλω).

Body: *sōma* (σῶμα).

Calm: *galēnos* (γαληνός). **Calmness**: *galēnotēs* (γαληνότης). **Calming** (of the mind): *galēnismos* (γαληνισμός). **Spend life calmly**: *engalēnizō* (ἐγγαληνίζω).

Capacity, power, faculty: *dunamis* or *dynamis* (δύναμις).

Cheerful: *euthumos* (εὔθυμος). **Cheerful**, merry: *euphrōn* (εὔφρων).

Courage; manliness: *andreia* (ἀνδρεία). Also: *tharsos* (θάρσος).

To **delight**, enjoy, take pleasure in: *terpō* (τέρπω).

Desire; love: *erōs* (ἔρως). **Longing**, yearning, desire; lust: *epithumia* (ἐπιθυμία). **Yearning**, longing, fond desire: *pothos* (πόθος).

Disturbance, annoyance, distress: *ochlēsis* (ὄχλησις). **Freedom from disturbance**: *aochlēsia* (ἀοχλησία).

To **do well**: *eu prassō* or *eu prattein* (εὐ πράσσω or εὐ πράττειν).

Easy to get: *euporistos* (εὐπόριστος). **Hard to get**: *dusporistos* or *dysporistos* (δυσπόριστος).

Elysian fields or plain: *Ēlusion* or *Ēlysion pedion* (Ἡλύσιον πεδίον).

Endurance, patience; patient endurance; the art of endurance; the ability to endure: *karterikos* (καρτερικός).

Enjoyment, delight: *terpsis* (τέρψις).

To **enjoy oneself**, take delight, take one's pleasure: *hēdomai* (ἥδομαι).

Envy, ill-will, jealousy: *phthonos* (φθόνος).

Ethics; that which pertains to the ethical: *ēthikos* (ἠθικός).

Excellent, good; serious (man), earnest: *spoudaios* (σπουδαῖος).

Falsehood, untruth, lie: *pseudos* (ψεῦδος).

Fate (personified); fate, portion: *Moira; moira* (μοῖρα).

Fear, terror: *phobos* (φόβος).

Flowing well; a life that flows well: *eurrous* (εὔρρους).

Fortune, chance, luck: *tuchē* or *tychē* (τύχη).

Frankness, outspokenness; freedom of speech: *parrhēsia* (παρρησία).

Freedom, liberty: *eleutheria* (ἐλευθερία).

Freedom from pain: *aponia* (ἀπονία).

Friend: *philos* (φίλος).

Function, work: *ergon* (ἔργον).

Gain, profit, advantage; shrewd counsel: *kerdos* (κέρδος).

Glory, fame, report: *kleos* (κλέος). **Glory**: *kudos* (κῦδος).

Goal, end, target, purpose: *telos* (τέλος).

God, a god: *theos* (θεός). A **goddess**: *thea* (θεά). **Gods**: *theoi* (θεοί).

Good, noble: *agathos* (ἀγαθός).

Good cheer, joy, merriment: *euphrosunē* (εὐφροσύνη).

Gratitude, thankfulness; the sense of favor received: *charis* (χάρις). **Gratitude**: *eucharistia* (εὐχαριστία).

Grief, pain of mind; pain of body: *lupē* (λύπη).

Habit; disposition, ongoing state; possession: *hexis* (ἕξις). **Good habit**; good condition; good habit of body or health: *euexia* (εὐεξία).

Happiness, prosperity: *eudaimonia* (εὐδαιμονία). **Happy**, prosperous; blessed with a good *daimōn* or spirit: *eudaimōn* (εὐδαίμων). **Happiness**, fortune, riches: *olbos* (ὄλβος). **Happy**, blessed: *olbios* (ὄλβιος). **Happy**, prosperous, fortunate, lucky: *eutuchēs* or *eutychēs* (εὐτυχής). See also blessed (*makarios, makar*).

Health, soundness: *hugieia* or *hygieia* (ὑγίεια).

Honor: *timē* (τιμή).

Ill-fated; having bad fortune: *dusmoros* or *dysmoros* (δύσμορος).

Immortal, undying: *athanatos* (ἀθάνατος).

Impassability; freedom from emotion: *apatheia* (ἀπάθεια).

Impulse: *hormē* (ὁρμή).

Indifferent; things neither good nor bad: *adiaphoros* (ἀδιάφορος).

Indifference to suffering; freedom from suffering or emotion; un-affected: *apathēs* (ἀπαθής).

Insatiate desire, greediness: *aplēstia* (ἀπληστία).

Islands of the Blessed: *makarōn nēsoi* (μακάρων νῆσοι).

Joy, delight: *chara* (χαρά).

Justice, righteousness: *dikaiosunē* (δικαιοσύνη). **Justice**; custom; right as dependent on custom: *dikē* (δίκη). **Just**: *dikaios* (δίκαιος).

Life; livelihood, means of life, what it takes to live: *bios* (βίος).

Live well: live (*zaō*) (ζάω) well or beautifully (adj. of *kalos*) (καλός).

Moderation: *sōphrosunē* (σωφροσύνη). Moderate: *sōphrōn* (σώφρων).

Mortal, liable to death: *thnētos* (θνητός).

Nature: *phusis* or *physis* (φύσις). **Natural**: *phusikos* or *physikos* (φυσικός).

Necessity, force, constraint: *anankē* (ἀνάγκη).

Noble, good: *esthlos* (ἐσθλός).

Olympus: home of the blessed gods: *Olumpos* or *Olympos* (Ὄλυμπος).

Pain, suffering; grief: *algēdōn* (ἀλγηδών).

Passion, feeling, emotion: *pathos* (πάθος).

Philosopher, lover of wisdom: *philosophos* (φιλόσοφος).

Pleasure, delight, enjoyment: *hēdonē* (ἡδονή). **Pleasant**: *hēdus* (ἡδύς). To **please**, delight, gratify: *handanō* (ἀνδάνω).

Practical wisdom, prudence: *phronēsis* (φρόνησις).

To **rejoice**: *gētheō* (γηθέω).

Self-control, self-restraint: *enkrateia* (ἐγκράτεια). **Lack of self-control**: *akrateia* (ἀκράτεια).

Self-sufficient, self-supporting, self-reliant; having enough; inde-pendent (of others): *autarkēs* (αὐτάρκης).

The **shame** done one; disgrace, dishonor; ugly: *aischros* (αἰσχρός).

Simple, frugal, thrifty; easily paid for: *euteles* (εὐτελής). **Simplicity**, frugality, thrift: *euteleia* (εὐτέλεια).

Soul; life: *psuchē* or *psychē* (ψυχή). The **soul's three parts** (from Plato): the **rational** part: *logistikos* (or *logistikon*) (λογιστικός); the **spirited**

part: *thumos* or *thumoeidēs* (θυμός or θυμοειδής); the **desiring** (or appetitive) part: *epithumētikos* (or *epithumētikon*) (ἐπιθυμητικός).

Stability, tranquility: *eustatheia* (εὐστάθεια).

Still, quiet: *hēsuchos* (ἥσυχος).

Suffering, misery, calamity, woe: *pēma* (πῆμα).

The **suspension** of judgment: *epochē* (ἐποχή).

Sweet: *glukeros* or *glykeros* (γλυκερός).

Toil, hard work; suffering: *ponos* (πόνος). Love of toil: *philoponia* (φιλοπονία).

Tranquility, tranquility of mind; calmness: *ataraxia* (ἀταραξία). **Not disturbed**, without confusion; tranquil; calm: *ataraktos* (ἀτάρακτος). **Trouble**, confusion, disorder, disturbance; anxiety: *tarachos* (τάραχος) or *tarachē* (ταραχή) (thus, *ataraxia* and *ataraktos* is the negation of *tarachos*).

Truth, reality: *alētheia* (ἀλήθεια).

Unhappiness, misfortune: *kakodaimonia* (κακοδαιμονία). **Unhappy**, miserable: *kakodaimōn* (κακοδαίμων). **Unhappy**, miserable, wretched: *dustēnos* or *dystēnos* (δύστηνος).

Untroubled, without trouble; unperturbed: *athorubos* (ἀθόρυβος).

Vanity, conceit; delusion; smoke, vapor: *tuphos* or *typhos* (τῦφος).

Vice; badness, wickedness: *kakia* (κακία). Also: *ponēria* (πονηρία).

Virtue; goodness, excellence; success; merit; manliness; valor: *aretē* (ἀρετή).

To **warm** (psychologically), cheer: *iainō* (ἰαίνω).

Wealth, riches: *ploutos* (πλοῦτος).

Well-ordered; habit of good management: *euthēmosunē* (εὐθημοσύνη).

Wine: *oinos* (οἶνος).

Wisdom; theoretical wisdom: *sophia* (σοφία). **Wise man**: *sophos* (σοφός). **Love of wisdom**, philosophy: *philosophia* (φιλοσοφία).

Without care, without sorrow: *akēdēs* (ἀκηδής).

Woeful, pitiable, miserable: *oizuros* (ὀιζυρός).

Word; reason, discourse, account: *logos* (λόγος).

Wretched, miserable; pitiable: *athlios* (ἄθλιος). **Wretched**, unhappy: *deilos* (δειλός).

FURTHER READING

Adkins, A.W.H. *Merit and Responsibility: A Study in Greek Values.* Chicago: The University of Chicago Press, 1975.

Anderson, Øivind. "Happiness in Homer." *Symbolae Osloenses* 85, no. 1: 2-16.

Boardman, John, Jasper Griffin, and Oswyn Murray. *The Oxford History of Greece and the Hellenistic World.* Oxford: Oxford University Press, 2001.

Bourke, Vernon J. *History of Ethics: Volume 1 Graeco-Roman to Early Modern Ethics.* Mount Jackson: Axios Press, 1968.

Charry, Ellen T. *God and the Art of Happiness.* Grand Rapids: William B. Eerdmans Publishing Co., 2010.

Copleston, Frederick. *Greece and Rome: From the Pre-Socratics to Plotinus.* Vol. 1 of *A History of Philosophy.* Westminster: Newman Press, 1946.

De Heer, Cornelis. *ΜΑΚΑΡ–ΕΥΔΑΙΜΩΝ–ΟΛΒΙΟΣ–ΕΥΤΥΧΗΣ: A Study of the Semantic Field Denoting Happiness in Ancient Greek to the End of the 5ᵗʰ Century B.C.* Amsterdam: Adolf M. Hakkert, 1969.

Delumeau, Jean. *History of Paradise: The Garden of Eden in Myth & Tradition.* Translated by Matthew O'Connell. Urbana: University of Illinois Press, 1995.

Dover, K.J. *Greek Popular Morality in the Time of Plato and Aristotle.* Indianapolis: Hackett Publishing Co., 1974.

Gottlieb, Anthony. *The Dream of Reason: A History of Western Philosophy from the Greeks to the Renaissance.* New York: W.W. Norton & Company, 2016.

Greene, William Chase. *Moira: Fate, Good, and Evil in Greek Thought.* New York: Harper Torchbooks, 1963. First published 1944 by Harvard University Press.

Hadot, Pierre. *What Is Ancient Philosophy?* Translated by Michael Chase. Cambridge: Harvard University Press, 2002.

———. *Philosophy as a Way of Life*. Translated by Michael Chase. Malden: Blackwell Publishing, 1995.

Hall, Jonathan M. *A History of the Archaic Greek World ca. 1200-479 BCE*. Malden: Blackwell Publishing, 2007.

Kenny, Anthony. *Ancient Philosophy*. Vol. 1 of *A New History of Western Philosophy*. Oxford: Oxford University Press, 2004.

Jaeger, Werner. *Paideia: the Ideals of Greek Culture*. Translated by Gilbert Highet. 2nd ed. 3 vols. New York: Oxford University Press, 1945.

———. *Early Christianity and Greek Paideia*. Cambridge: Harvard University Press, 1961.

Lesky, Albin. *A History of Greek Literature*. Translated by Cornelis de Heer and James Willes. Indianapolis: Hackett Publishing Company, 1996.

Martin, Thomas R. *Ancient Greece: From Prehistoric to Hellenistic Times*. New Haven: Yale University Press, 1996.

McMahon, Darrin M. *Happiness: A History*. New York: Grove Press, 2006.

Myer, Susan Sauvé. *Ancient Ethics: A Critical Introduction*. New York: Routledge, 2008.

Pearson, Lionel. *Popular Ethics in Ancient Greece*. Stanford: Stanford University Press, 1962.

Rosen, Jeffrey. *The Pursuit of Happiness: How Classical Writers on Virtue Inspired the Lives of the Founders and Defined America*. New York: Simon & Schuster, 2024.

Young, Tim J. *A Hero's Wish: What Homer Believed about Happiness and the Good Life*. Sugar Land: EuZōn Media, 2015.

You may also wish to read the Cave's *Aretē: Excellence or Virtue — What the Ancient Greeks Thought and Said about Aretē.*

Note: Some Cave translations in this book (*Happiness*) are from public domain versions of ancient Greek literature. If so, most are modified.

Will you help the Cave? Here's how . . .

- **Buy** a book. **Join** a club. **Sponsor** the Cave. **Give** a donation.
  • **Talk** to friends and family about Cave books and the free online Cave content at the Cave (www.theclassicscave.com).
- Leave a **positive review** online—if possible, **five stars** with a **brief remark** about what you liked. This truly helps!
- **Write us** at contact@theclassicscave.com to let us know how you've benefited from our work. This inspires us to do more!

THE CLASSICS CAVE is a small, shoestring operation, on fire to spread the wisdom and ways of ancient Greek literature. We **rely on you**, the friend of the Cave, to let people know how you liked and benefited from what we're doing. We also **depend on you** to **improve our books**. Did you see something that requires editing? Something we got wrong? Something we need to add? Despite our great effort and care to get everything right, it happens. So please **let us know** by emailing us at contact@theclassicscave.com. Otherwise, **visit** the Cave to benefit from our ever-growing collection of free online content at www.theclassicscave.com. And don't forget to **support our mission** to spread the wisdom and ways of ancient Greek literature by **buying** and **reading** Cave Books, **enjoying** Cave Gear, **joining** The BAGL Club or AAGS, or by **sponsoring** or **giving** to the Cave. **Thanks!**

Read and enjoy more from **the Cave!**

If you benefited from reading *Happiness*, you may wish to pick up another Cave book presenting the ancient Greeks. There are many now available or in the works.

Visit the Cave at . . .

www.theclassicscave.com

www.theclassicscave.com

Looking for the **best books** ever?
And new ways to read and benefit from them?

Hunting for **wisdom** and **ways** that
are time-tested and people-approved?

READ A CAVE BOOK

VISIT THE CAVE ONLINE
www.theclassicscave.com

When you read a Cave book, an ancient classic,
you'll have a better idea about where you're
going in life and how to get there.

You'll feel smarter. Be wiser.
And if you practice what you've encountered,
you'll live a better life. Be a little happier.

Enjoy the Cave's **free online content**. Or **choose a book** from one
of **our series**. The Cave Best of Series. The Cave Wisdom & Way
Series. The Cave Workbook & Journal Series. And more!
You'll be glad you did!

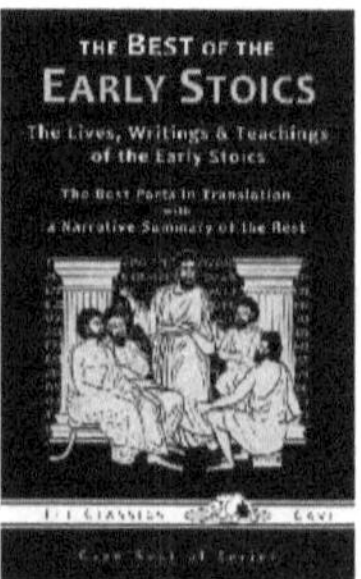

www.theclassicscave.com

Pick up a **CAVE** book . . .

from HOMER . . .

from the CYNICS . . .

From EPICURUS . . .